Making a [illegible]eory

Making a Difference in Theory brings together original work from an international group of authors on the roles of theory in educational research and practice. The book discusses the different roles theory plays, can play and should play, both from a historical perspective and in light of contemporary discussions and developments.

Particular attention is paid to the question of whether there are or should be distinctively educational forms of theory and theorizing. The double engagement with the theory question in education and the education question in theory and theorizing provides original insights into what theory does, might do or should do in educational research and practice.

With contributions from internationally-renowned authors in the field of educational theory, research and practice, the book will be of value to academics, researchers and postgraduate students in education.

Gert Biesta is Professor of Educational Theory and Policy at the University of Luxembourg, Luxembourg, and editor-in-chief of *Studies in Philosophy and Education*.

Julie Allan is Professor of Equity and Inclusion at the University of Birmingham, UK, and Visiting Professor of Education at the University of Borås, Sweden.

Richard Edwards is Professor of Education at the School of Education, University of Stirling, Scotland, UK.

Theorizing Education Series

Series Editors
Gert Biesta, *University of Luxembourg, Luxembourg*
Julie Allan, *University of Birmingham, UK*
Richard Edwards, *University of Stirling, UK*

Theorizing Education brings together innovative work from a wide range of contexts and traditions which explicitly focuses on the roles of theory in educational research and educational practice. The series includes contextual and socio-historical analyses of existing traditions of theory and theorizing, exemplary use of theory, and empirical work where theory has been used in innovative ways. The distinctive focus for the series is the engagement with educational questions, articulating what explicitly educational function the work of particular forms of theorizing supports.

Books in this series:

Making a Difference in Theory
The theory question in education and the education question in theory
Edited by Gert Biesta, Julie Allan and Richard Edwards

Making a Difference in Theory

The theory question in education and the education question in theory

Edited by
Gert Biesta, Julie Allan and Richard Edwards

LONDON AND NEW YORK

First published 2014
by Routledge
2 Park Square, Milton Park, Abingdon, Oxfordshire OX14 4RN

Simultaneously published in the USA and Canada
by Routledge
711 Third Avenue, New York, NY 10017

First issued in paperback 2014

Routledge is an imprint of the Taylor and Francis Group, an informa business

British Library Cataloguing in Publication Data
A catalogue record for this book is available from the British Library

Library of Congress Cataloging in Publication Data
A catalog record for this book has been requested

ISBN 978-0-415-65694-8 (hbk)
ISBN 978-1-138-90790-4 (pbk)
ISBN 978-0-203-07743-6 (ebk)

Typeset in Bembo
by Saxon Graphics Ltd, Derby

Contents

SECTION II
The practice of doing theory 83

SECTION III
Refractions on and agendas for theory 135

List of contributors

Julie Allan is Professor of Equity and Inclusion at the University of Birmingham, UK and Visiting Professor at the University of Borås, Sweden. Her research interests are in disability, inclusion and children's rights and she has undertaken both theoretical and empirical work in these areas. She has worked with the Council of Europe on research on diversity and as an expert adviser for meetings of European Government Ministers. Her most recent books are *Rethinking inclusive education: The philosophers of difference in practice* (2008, Springer); *Doing inclusive education research* (2008, with Roger Slee, Sense) *Social capital, children and young people: Implications for practice policy and research* (2012, with Ralph Catts, Policy Press) and *Social capital, professionalism and diversity* (2009, with Jenny Ozga and Geri Smyth, Sense).

Anna Anderson is an early career researcher having been awarded her PhD (Social Science) in 2011. Her areas of research interest include the education discourse, policy and practice of student or youth participation, contemporary techniques and rationalities of power, the history of the social sciences, approaches to critique, and the public policy impacts of social science research. She is currently teaching on a sessional basis in the sociology programs of Swinburne University and the Australian Catholic University in Melbourne, Australia, and is writing a number of chapters and articles for publication.

Johannes Bellman is Professor and Chair of 'Allgemeine Erziehungswissenschaft' (Foundations of Education, Philosophy of Education) at the University of Münster (Germany) since 2009. His doctoral thesis is on the construction of economics in twentieth century educational theory and his second book, *Habilitation*, is on John Dewey's naturalization of educational theory. His main areas of research are: frameworks and concepts of educational theory, particularly social-theoretical foundations of educational theory; history of educational theory and its methodology, particularly the history of pragmatism and its reception in educational theory as well as the history of quality management in education; and educational policies, particularly standards-based reforms and choice policies, and the analysis of their theoretical premises and empirical consequences. At the moment Professor Bellman is conducting an empirical research project, funded by the German Ministry of Education and Research, on the unintended consequences of recently introduced standards-based reforms and choice policies in four German federal-states.

Gert Biesta (www.gertbiesta.com) is Professor of Educational Theory and Policy at the University of Luxembourg. He previously worked at universities in Scotland, England and the Netherlands. His research focuses on the theory and philosophy of education and educational research. He has a particular interest in relationships between education, citizenship and democracy. Recent books include *Beyond learning: Democratic education for a human future* (2006); *Good education in an age of measurement* (2010); *The beautiful risk of education* (2013) (all with Paradigm Publishers); and *Making sense of Education: Fifteen contemporary educational theorists in their own words* (2012, Springer).

Richard Edwards is Professor of Education at the University of Stirling, Scotland, UK. He is a member of the TheoryLab, based in the School of Education. He has researched and published extensively in the area of educational theory, in particular in relation to adult education and lifelong learning. He has sought to conceptualize educational issues in relation to theories drawing upon poststructuralism, postmodernism, spatiality, and actor-network theory. His most recent books are, with Tara Fenwick, *Actor-network theory in education* (2010, Routledge) and, with Tara Fenwick and Peter Sawchuk, *Emerging approaches to educational research: Tracing the Sociomaterial* (2011, Routledge).

Lynn Fendler is an associate professor in the Department of Teacher Education at Michigan State University, USA. In 2010–11, she was Visiting Professor in Languages, Culture, Media, and Identities at the University of Luxembourg. Her research interests include educational theory, historiography, genealogy, and the philosophy of food, and her most recent book introduces the work of Michel Foucault to teachers. Lynn is also interested in the political and epistemological implications of Web 2.0 technologies, and she maintains a wiki to serve as an open, public, and interactive resource on educational theories for teachers and educational researchers. Her current research projects include studies of non-representational theory, methodologies for humanities-oriented research, and the educational problems of aesthetic taste.

Norm Friesen is Canada Research Chair in Curriculum and New Media at Thompson Rivers University in British Columbia, Canada. Dr. Friesen is the author of *Re-thinking e-learning research: Foundations, methods and practices* (2009) and *The place of the classroom and the space of the screen: relational pedagogy and internet technology* (2011). Dr. Friesen is also editor and translator of one of the first books on education to appear in English from post-war Germany:

Klaus Mollenhauer's *Forgotten connections: On culture and upbringing* (forthcoming from Routledge). Dr. Friesen is co-editor of the journal *Phenomenology & Practice* (www.phandpr.org), Associate Editor of the *Journal of Curriculum Studies*, and Director of the New Media Studies Research Centre (http://normfriesen.info).

Deborah Gallagher is Professor of Education at the University of Northern Iowa, USA. Her research interest centres on the philosophy of science as it pertains to research on disability, pedagogy, and policy in education and special education. Among numerous articles and book chapters, she is the lead author of a book entitled *Challenging orthodoxy in special education: Dissenting voices* (2004, Love Publishing Company). In 2006, this book was selected by the European Educational Research Association as one of three key texts for the conference's inclusion strand. She serves as an international advisory board member of the *British Educational Research Journal* and is a founding member of the Disability Studies in Education Special Interest Group at the American Educational Research Association where she has served as its co-chair and program chair.

Lisbeth Lundahl is a professor in the Department of Applied Educational Science at Umeå University in northern Sweden. Her main research interests concern contemporary education politics, youth politics and young people´s transitions from school and work. Her latest research focuses on the thorough transformation of education, professional work and power relations in Swedish schools, resulting from the far-reaching marketization of Swedish education. She is also the PI of a major research project, 'Unsafe Transitions. Dropouts from upper secondary school: individual paths and local strategies in longitudinal perspective'. Lisbeth Lundahl was the Secretary General of European Educational Research Association (EERA) in 2006-2008. She has participated in several European research projects and actively engages in Swedish and European research networks.

Anne M. Phelan is a professor in the Department of Curriculum and Pedagogy, and Co-Director of the Centre for the Study of Teacher Education, at the University of British Columbia, Vancouver, Canada. Her areas of study are teacher education and curriculum studies. Her interests lie in the relationship between language and subjectivity, the dynamic of judgment and responsibility, and the paradoxes of autonomy (creativity and resistance) in teacher preparation and professional life. She has published in journals such as *Pedagogy, Culture and Society; Journal of Curriculum Studies; Teaching and Teacher Education; Curriculum Inquiry* and *Studies in Philosophy of Education*. She is co-editor (with Dr. Jennifer Sumsion, Charles Sturt University) of *Critical Readings in Teacher Education: Provoking Absences* (2008, Sense Publishers).

Thomas S. Popkewitz is a professor in the Department of Curriculum and Instruction, The University of Wisconsin-Madison, USA. His studies are concerned with the systems of reason that govern pedagogical reforms, education sciences and teacher education. His recent publications include *Cosmopolitanism and the age of reform: science, education and making society by making the child* (2008, Routledge); *Schooling and the making of citizens in the long nineteenth century: Comparative visions* (2011, with D. Tröhler and D. Labaree, eds, Routledge); and *Globalization and the study of education* (2009 with F. Rizvi, eds, Wiley). He is currently working on a book about social and education science as a history of the present, examining the historical and political limits of practical knowledge as a project of the social and education sciences.

Alexander M. Sidorkin is Dean of the Graduate School of Education, Higher School of Economics in Russia. Before that, he worked in various universities in the United States as faculty member and dean. He has published four books, including *Labor of learning: Market and the next generation of educational reform* (2009, Sense) and writes a blog, 'The Russian Bear's diaries.' His scholarly interests include educational theory, philosophy and economics of education.

Tomasz Szkudlarek is a professor in the Faculty of Social Sciences, University of Gdańsk, Poland, where he chairs the Department of Philosophy of Educaion and Cultural Studies in the Institute of Education. His interests include cultural and political aspects of education, theories of identity, and discourse theory. His recent research is focused on educational implications of Ernesto Laclau's theory of identity and on the discursive construction of subjectivity. His books include *The problem of freedom in postmodern education*, (1993, Greenwood); *Wiedza i wolność w amerykańskiej pedagogice krytycznej* [*Knowledge and freedom in American critical pedagogy*], (Impuls,1993, 2009); *Media: Szkic z filozofii i pedagogiki dystansu* [*Media. an essay on philosophy and pedagogy of distance*] (Implus, 1998, 2009); and *Dyskursywna konstrukcja podmiotu: Przyczynek do rekonstrukcji pedagogiki kultury* [*The discursive construction of subjectivity: Towards the reconstruction of pedagogy of culture*] (2012).

Daniel Tröhler is Professor of Education and Director of the Research Unit for Socio-Cultural Research on Learning and Development in Languages, Culture, Media, and Identities and of the Doctoral School in Educational Sciences at the University of Luxembourg and Visiting Professor of Comparative Education at the University of Granada, Spain. His latest publications include *Languages of education: Protestant legacies, national identities, and global aspirations* (2011, Routledge, AERA Outstanding Book of the Year Award) and *Schooling and the making of citizens in the long nineteenth century: comparative Visions* (2011, with T. Popkewitz and D. Labaree, Routledge) and he served as guest editor for the special issue *Historicising Jean-Jacques Rousseau: Four ways to commemorate his 300th anniversary* (2012,

Studies in Philosophy and Education). Several of his publications have been translated into different languages.

Robin Usher was Professor of Research Education and Director of Research Training at RMIT University, Melbourne, Australia and now has his own freelance consultancy, 'Thesis Completions' (http://wp.me/P1tBYH-4). His research interests include educational theory, lifelong learning and methodology. Recent books include *Adult education as theory, practice and research: The captive triangle* (2011, with Ian Briant); *Globalisation and pedagogy: Space, place and pedagogy* (2007, with R. Edwards, Routledge) and *Lifelong learning: Signs, discourses, practices* (2007, with R. Edwards, Springer).

Introduction

The theory question in education and the education question in theory

Gert Biesta, Julie Allan and Richard Edwards

Theory plays an important role in educational research and educational practice. But when we ask what kind of role theory plays or should play, and also what kind of theory or theories we actually need, things become more complicated. This has partly to do with the fact that theory plays a number of different roles in educational research and practice. The theory question can therefore never be posed in the abstract but needs to take these differences into account. It also has to do with the fact that the field of educational research – broadly understood as comprising empirical, theoretical and historical studies – has developed differently in different national and linguistic contexts and settings (see Biesta 2011; 2012). Within such different 'constructions' there are different views about the role and status of theory, particularly with regard to the question whether education is a discipline in its own right with its own forms of theory and theorizing, or whether it is an inter- or multi-disciplinary field that relies on theoretical input from 'other' disciplines.

The theory question is not a new question. Questions about theory have at least been raised since education became an academic field of study (see, for example, Thiersch *et al.* 1978; Lagemann 2000; Labaree 2006). In Germany this happened in 1779 when Ernst Christian Trapp became the first Professor of Education at the University of Halle (Ruprecht 1978). Other countries followed (much) later. England, for example had its first Professor of Education in 1873, Scotland in 1876 (see Monroe 1911: 401-409), while John Dewey only became head of the newly opened Department of Pedagogy at the University of Chicago in 1895 (see Dykhuizen 1973: 86).

Discussions about theory have often been conducted in terms of unhelpful dichotomies such as theory *versus* practice, the theoretical *versus* the empirical, or theoretical *versus* useful. Such rhetorical moves have tended to give theory a bad name. There are, however, compelling arguments for the need for theory in educational research. One goes back to David Hume's insight that the only thing that can be empirically established is correlation between observable phenomena, and that theory is needed to generate explanations of underlying causative processes (Hume 1999). In interpretative research a key role for theory lies in deepening and broadening understandings of 'everyday' interpretations and experiences (see, for example, Giddens 1976), while the primary interest of critical theory lies in exposing how hidden power structures influence and distort such interpretations and experiences (see Habermas 1973; Carr and Kemmis 1986). There are also compelling reasons for the need for theory in educational practice, already stemming from the simple observation of what practice would look like if theory were entirely absent.

Within recent discussions there appears, however, to be a tendency to move away from theory. We can see this, for example, in the idea that educational research should focus on generating knowledge about 'what works' – an idea which tends to prioritise the empirical ('evidence') over the theoretical (for a critical discussion see Thomas and Pring 2004; Allan 2008; Biesta 2007; 2010). It is also manifest in more explicit discussions about the value of theory for educational research and practice. Both Carr (2006) and Thomas (2007) seem to be of the opinion that current research and practice are over-theorized and would benefit from less rather than more theory (Thomas) or, in the case of Carr, of no theory altogether. These discussions indicate a need for a more precise analysis of the extent to which and the ways in which educational research and practice are actually over- or under-theorized and why and how this might matter.

This book, which is the first volume in a new series called *Theorizing Education*, aims to make a contribution to this task. It brings together original work on the role of theory in educational research and educational practice, partly documenting existing approaches and ways of working and partly setting out agendas for future work. The chapters in this book cover a range of theoretical orientations and come from authors who work within distinctively different traditions and settings. The chapters not only contain examples of how to 'do' theory, but also provide reflections about the role and status of theory in educational research and practice, both from a historical and from a contemporary perspective. In this introductory chapter we provide a wider 'framing' for the contributions in this book, by placing them in the context of discussions about theory in educational research and practice, and by providing a number of conceptual distinctions that can help to make sense of the wide variety of theories in educational research and practice. We begin with a brief discussion of the different ways in which the field of education has developed and what this implies for the role(s) of theory. We then discuss in more detail the different roles theory can play in relation to educational research and practice. We conclude with a brief introduction to the contributions to this book.

Disciplines and interdisciplinarity in the study of education

Many would characterise educational research as the scientific study of educational processes and practices that occur in designated institutions such as schools, colleges or universities, and that happen in less formal settings such as the workplace or the community. Most of those working in the field of educational research would opt for a rather broad interpretation of what the term 'scientific' stands for, thus encompassing a wide range of methods, methodologies and methodological or 'paradigmatic' orientations. Theory plays an important role in this work and, again, many would highlight the large number of different theories and theoretical orientations that are being used in the conduct of educational research.

A common view in the English-speaking world is that the theoretical resources for educational research stem from a number of academic disciplines – most notably psychology, sociology, philosophy and history – thus giving rise to such subfields as the psychology, the sociology, the philosophy and the history of education (for a recent discussion see Lawn and Furlong 2009; for an earlier account see Tibble 1966). Although over the years other disciplines and approaches have joined the conversation – such as anthropology, economics, cultural studies and feminist theory – and although the relative influence of different disciplines on the study of education has fluctuated over time (see McCulloch 2002), the particular construction of the field of educational research as the inter- or multi-disciplinary study of education has remained relatively constant over time. This has been supported by the social organisation of the field, particularly through the existence of national and international societies and journals devoted to the contribution of particular disciplines to the study of education.

When we look at the role of theory in educational research from this angle it is not surprising to find a wide spectrum of theories with a wide range of different disciplinary 'roots' – and many of the chapters in this book exemplify such an approach. This makes any exploration of the role of theory in educational research exciting but also complex, as it has to navigate different and potentially conflicting disciplinary perspectives and agendas while at the same time having to keep an eye on how this theoretical multiplicity relates to and matters for education. Any attempt to explore the role of theory in educational research therefore not only needs to engage with the question of how theories from a range of different disciplines pertain to the study of education – an angle to which we might refer as *the theory question in education* – but also needs to focus on what it means for particular theories to be used or applied within the context of educational research – an angle to which we might refer as *the education question in theory and theorizing.*

One important aspect of the latter question is whether educational research *necessarily* has to rely on theoretical input from (other) disciplines or whether there are, or ought to be, distinctively *educational* forms of theory and theorizing. This, in turn, raises the question whether education can and should claim to be an academic discipline in its own right or whether it should be understood as an applied field of study, just like, for example business studies or sport studies. While the idea of education as an academic discipline in its own right and with its own forms of theory and theorizing may be rather alien to the English-speaking world, it is an important dimension of the way in which the academic study of education has developed in other settings, particularly under the influence of ideas and approaches developed in German-speaking countries (see, for example, Horn 2003). The influence of this 'construction' of the field has not only impacted on other German-speaking countries in Europe, but also on countries such as Poland, Finland, Spain, Belgium, the Netherlands, Japan, Korea and South Africa.

While in the English-speaking world the field of educational studies is held together through its common *object* of investigation – and makes use of a wide variety of theoretical resources to study this object – the tradition of educational studies that emerged in the German-speaking world, has developed its disciplinary identity much more in terms of a shared *interest* in education as a process that in some way or form should support the emancipation of children towards (a certain degree of) self-determination – and thus has developed forms of theory and ways of theorizing to identify, analyse and promote such processes (see, for example, Oelkers 2001; Benner 2005). Such forms of theorizing are more distinctively educational. This is not to suggest that input from other disciplines is discarded, but it does mean that such input goes through an educational 'filter' so that the questions asked are not, for example, sociological or psychological, but educational in their own right.

Roles and functions of theory in research and practice

Although the word 'theory' is easily used it is actually quite difficult to identify what it refers to not in the least because the meaning of the word has shifted significantly over time (see also Hunter 2005). If we go back to the Greek origins of the word – which, of course, always raises the further question where the Greeks got their words from – theory (θεωρία) had to do with spectatorship: being a spectator of a performance or a festival, including religious festivals, being an official envoy to a festival, consulting an oracle, or making a journey in order to study something. Here, the meaning of theory is firmly located within the domain of the empirical as it is about direct experience and witnessing. With Plato and Aristotle, however, theory became connected to the domain of the *non*-empirical, that is, the domain of Platonic forms and Aristotelian universals. Theory became knowledge of a permanent and unchangeable reality 'behind' the empirical world of change, flux and appearances.

The distinction between empirical and theoretical knowledge gained further prominence with the rise of the worldview of modern science in which the main role of theory became that of the *explanation* of causal connections between empirical phenomena. The need for theory had to do with the insight that while correlations between phenomena can be perceived, underlying causal connections cannot. Theory was therefore needed to account for or speculate about underlying processes and mechanisms. Here, theory transformed into what Gaston Bachelard (1986: 38) has called 'a science of the hidden'. With the rise of hermeneutics and interpretivism in the late 19th century, theory also become a device for *understanding*, that is, for making intelligible *why* people say what they say and do what they do. The role of theory became that of deepening and broadening everyday interpretations and experiences. The primary interest of *critical* theory, developed by the philosophers of the Frankfurt School working in a tradition going back to Marx, lay in exposing how hidden power structures influence and distort such experiences and interpretations. The ambition here was that the exposure of the workings of power can contribute to *emancipation*.

Whereas from one angle there is a clear difference between the role of theory in research that aims at explanation, at understanding or at emancipation, what unites these approaches is that they all deploy theory in order to bring what is strange and not understood into the domain of understanding. This bigger 'gesture' of making the strange familiar has been characterised as a typical modern conception of what research can and should achieve. Here, research is depicted as a process that can help us to get 'better' and 'deeper' insights into the natural and social world. Research can, however, also operate in the opposite direction, that is with an ambition to make what is familiar strange. Such a view has, for example, been espoused by Michel Foucault in his idea of 'eventalization' (Foucault 1991: 76). Here, Foucault argues for an approach that aims at a 'breach of self-evidence' by making visible 'a singularity at places where there is a temptation to invoke a historical constant, an immediate anthropological trait, or an obviousness which imposes itself uniformly on all' (ibid.). Eventalization thus works 'by constructing around the singular event...a "polygon" or rather a "polyhedron" of intelligibility, the number of whose faces is not given in advance and can never properly be taken as finite' (Foucault 1991: 77). Eventalization requires that we complicate and pluralise our understanding of events, their elements, their relations and their domains of reference (see ibid.). While eventalization does not generate the kind of insights that may lead to advice or guidelines for action, Foucault stresses that it is not without practical effect as it can bring about a situation in which people '"no longer know what they do," so that the acts, gestures, discourses which up until then had seemed to go without saying become problematic' (Foucault 1991: 84). This is a situation in which people are spurred into thinking again about what they are doing and what they might do.

Such a practical effect can not only result from work that has its origin in empirical data, but can also stem from more 'autonomous' forms of theorizing that aim at what, after Richard Rorty (1989), we might refer to as the 'redescription' of educational processes and practices. Calling them redescriptions is to highlight the fact that educational processes and practices are always already 'described' in some way by those involved in them. In this mode theoretical work can provide different and alternative descriptions of educational processes and practices. Theory can, for example, 'redescribe' a classroom in terms of information processing, in terms of legitimate peripheral participation or in terms of the reproduction of class and gender inequalities. Theory can redescribe learning as a process of empowerment or a process of control. Theory can redescribe education as knowledge-transfer or as a concern for newness coming into the world. Although such redescriptions can function as hypotheses and therefore as starting points for empirical work, they do not necessarily or exclusively have to be understood as claims to truth. They can also be seen as possible interpretations of what might be the case – interpretations that can inform teachers' perceptions, judgments and actions by opening up possibilities for seeing things in new and different ways.

With regard to the role of theory in empirical research there is a strong emphasis on the ways in which theory can be used for the analysis and interpretation of empirical data. Theory does indeed play a crucial role in making the shift from data to understanding (used here in the broad sense of the word). But theory not only comes in *after* data have been collected, but also plays an important role in the initial phases of research. Two aspects are important here.

First of all theory is indispensable for the *conceptualisation of the phenomenon* one wishes to investigate. While researchers may wish to study learning, it is only after they have engaged with the question how one wishes to conceptualise learning – for example, as information processing, as behavioural change, as acquisition, as participation, as social practice – that they can make decisions about *what* the phenomena are they should focus on and *how* one might go about in doing so (the question of design, methodology and methods). Some researchers, more often those working at the interpretative end of the spectrum, object to bringing in theory at the initial stages of research as they feel it would bias the research findings and would blind researchers from seeing potentially relevant aspects that fall outside of one's theoretical 'frame'. While it is of course always important to be open, this particular objection fails to see that the world never appears unconceptualised, so that *not* to engage with conceptualisation at all runs the risk of uncritically accepting existing definitions and conceptions of the object under investigation.

The second way in which theory plays a role at the start rather than the end of research has to do with the *construction of the object* of research. As an educational researcher one might say that the object of one's research is education – and this is probably the answer most educational researchers would give. But even if one were to agree that the object of research is to be found in schools – albeit that many would question whether education can *only* be found in schools – the question remains: what is it that actually happens within a building with the word 'school' that counts as 'education'? Is it about teachers talking? (And what would one already need to know to be able to identify some of the people there as teachers?) Or is it about teachers talking and students listening? Or about teachers talking, students listening and learning from such talk? Would punishment be part of education? And what about the hidden curriculum that, by definition, is not visible? Questions like these suggest that even the issue of what the object of investigation of the educational researcher and of education as an academic field or discipline is, requires further reflection in which theory has an important role to play.

Starting a conversation

The foregoing attempt to map some of the usages of theory in educational research and educational practice is not meant to be exhaustive but is being presented as a first step towards a more refined discussion about the roles and functions of theory in education. Such a discussion, as is implied in the title of this chapter and the title of this book, not only needs to consider the wide range of theories being used in the educational research and practice – which is the theory question in education – but also needs to address what is distinctively educational about the usages of theory – which is the education question in theory. In the chapters that follow the authors provide a range of different reflections on these questions. The variety that the reader will encounter in the chapters is intended, as our ambition with this book has not been to 'sort out' the discussion about theory in education, but rather to provide a range of different starting points for further exploration and discussion. The authors of the chapters come from a range of different backgrounds – some more clearly located within traditions of educational scholarship that have developed in the English-speaking world; others more strongly rooted in Continental approaches to educational theory and research. Some of the chapters take a more historical outlook in order to develop an understanding of what theory has been doing in educational research and practice (Popkewitz; Tröhler; Friesen). Others engage in contemporary discussions in order to develop new insights in the roles of theory in education (Lundahl; Bellman; Gallagher. Some authors (Szkudlarek; Sidorkin) are quite critical about what theory might achieve and how much it is needed; others make a clear case for particular theories or particular theoretical approaches (Usher and Anderson; Phelan; Fendler). Together the chapters show that questions about theory in education and about the educational dimension in theory remain important, not only for the development of good and meaningful educational research but also for the practice of education itself in all its different forms and manifestations.

References

Allan, J. (2008) *Rethinking inclusive education: The philosophers of difference in practice,* Dordrecht : Kluwer.

Bachelard, G. (1986[1949]) *Le rationalisme appliqué,* Paris: Presses Universitaires de France.

Benner, D. (2005) *Allgemeine Pädagogik.* [*General theory of education.*] Weinheim: Juventa.

Biesta, G.J.J. (2007) 'Why "what works" won't work: evidence-based practice and the democratic deficit of educational research', *Educational Theory* 57, 1-22.

Biesta, G.J.J. (2010) 'Why "what works" still won't work: From evidence-based education to value-based education,' *Studies in Philosophy and Education 29*(5), 491-503.

Biesta, G.J.J. (2011) 'Disciplines and theory in the academic study of education: a Comparative Analysis of the Anglo-American and Continental Construction of the Field,' *Pedagogy, Culture and Society* 19, 175-192.

Biesta, G.J.J. (2012) 'Wanted, dead or alive: educationalists: on the need for academic bilingualism in education', in C. Aubry, M. Geiss, V. Magyar-Haas and D. Miller (Hrsg). *Positionierungen. Zum Verhältnis von Wissenschaft, Pädagogik und Politik*, Weinheim: Beltz Verlag, pp. 20-33.

Carr, W. and Kemmis, S. (1986) *Becoming critical,* London: Routledge.

Carr, W. (2006) 'Education without theory', *British Journal of Educational Studies* 54, 136-159.

Dykhuizen, G. (1973) *The life and mind of John Dewey,* Carbondale and Edwardsville: Southern Illinois University Press.

Foucault. M. (1991) 'Questions of method', in G. Burchell, C. Gordon and P. Miller (eds) *The Foucault Effect: Studies in governmentality*, Chicago: The University of Chicago Press, pp. 73-86.

Giddens, A. (1976) *New rules of sociological method,* London: Hutchinson.

Habermas, J. (1973) *Erkenntnis und Interresse. Mit einem neuen Nachwort,* Frankfurt am Main: Suhrkamp.

Horn, K.-P. (2003) *Erziehungswissenschaft in Deutschland im 20. Jahrhundert. Zur Entwicklung der sozialen und fachlichen Struktur der Disziplin von der Erstinstitutionalisierung bis zur Expansion.* [*The study of education in Germany in the 20th century. On the development of the social and academic structure of the discipline from its original inception until its expansion.*] Bad Heilbrunn: Klinkhardt.

Hume, D. (1999[1748]) *An enquiry concerning human understanding,* edited by Tom L. Beauchamp, Oxford/New York: Oxford University Press.

Hunter, I. (2005) 'The history of theory', *Critical Inquiry* 33, 78-112.

Labaree, D.F. (2006) *The trouble with ed schools,* New Haven: Yale University Press.

Lagemann, E. (2000) *An elusive science: The troubling history of educational research,* Chicago: University of Chicago Press.

Lawn, M. and Furlong, J. (2009) 'The disciplines of education in the UK: Between the ghost and the shadow', *Oxford Review of Education,* 35, 541-552.

McCulloch, G. (2002) 'Disciplines contributing to education? Educational studies and the disciplines', *British Journal of Educational Studies,* 50, 100-110.

Monroe, P. (ed) (1911) *A cyclopedia of education, Volume II.* New York: The Macmillan Company.

Oelkers, J. (2001) *Einführung in die Theorie der Erziehung,* Weinheim and Basel: Beltz.

Rorty, R. (1989) *Contingency, irony, and solidarity,* Cambridge: Cambridge University Press.

Ruprecht, H. (1978) 'Die erfahrungswissenschaftliche Tradition in der Erziehungswissenschaft', in H .Thiersch, H. Ruprecht and U. Herrmann (eds), *Die Entwicklung der Erziehungswissenschaft,* Munich: Juventa, pp. 109-172.

Thiersch, H., Ruprecht, H. and Hermann, U. (eds) (1978) *Die Entwicklung der Erziehungswissenschaft,* München: Juventa.

Thomas, G. and Pring, R. (2004) *Evidence-based practice in education,* Maidenhead: Open University Press.

Thomas, G. (2007) *Education and theory: Strangers in paradigms,* Maindenhead: Open University Press.

Tibble, J.W. (1966) 'The development of the study of education', in J.W. Tibble (ed.), *The study of education*, London: Routledge and Kegan Paul, pp. 1-28.

Section I

The contextual presence of theory

Chapter 1

The empirical and political 'fact' of theory in the social and education sciences

Thomas S. Popkewitz

Introduction

The social and education sciences have never operated without theory. Even with the mantra of educational talk about the theory/practice split or researchers catering to the demands of 'practice' and finding 'practical' and 'useful' knowledge, theories order what is seen, thought about, and acted on. Theories are embodied in the styles of reason that order and classify what is seen and acted on in schooling. They provide the principles generated to order how judgments are made, conclusions drawn, solutions given plausibility, and the existences made manageable. And in these principles of ordering are cultural theses about who the child is and should be.

I focus on the empirical presence of theories in the education sciences through two avenues: Historically, through examining particular psychologies and sociologies related to American Progressive education at the turn of the 20th century; and in contemporary reforms concerned with the 'effective teacher', value-added knowledge, curriculum, and schools as 'markets'. In this sense, I argue that theory is an empirical fact. But, once said, why should we care? The separation of theory and practice elides the historicity of science in construing and constructing what is seen and acted on.

Theories are material, but not in the Marxist sense. Theories just don't stand there to push thought and ideas but are 'actors' in the everyday world. Theories are styles of reasoning that generate cultural theses about modes of living whose principles are not merely about inclusion. They inscribe differences, divisions, and exclusions. The theories of research and pedagogy constitute the political of schooling in making of the subject – who the child is and should be – and the (im)possibilities of change.

My concern with theory is to historicize it by focusing on the styles of reason which orders and classifies what is seen, talked about, and acted on in schooling.[1] The argument explores, first, theories as styles of reason in pedagogy and its sciences. The second section historicizes various cultural principles assembled and connected in 'theories' of schooling through focusing on the notion of adolescence in American child studies, the pragmatism of Dewey, and Chicago

Community Society at the turn of the 20th century. In the third section, I then focus on how theories are 'actors' in the making of practice. I discuss contemporary notions of 'value-added' knowledge about the effective teacher, mathematics education research, and the schools as markets. The discussion considers how these notions of research embody cultural theses about particular modes of life that travel as seemingly self-evident practical and useful knowledge.

The discussion about theory is, ironically, a theory about schooling. The theory, however, is a critical one but in a different sense of the Frankfurt critical theory (see Popkewitz and Fendler 1999). The notion of theory is a strategy of inquiry that looks empirically at the sciences of education as social, historical 'facts' to be investigated. That investigation is to make visible the principles generated to order and classify reflection and action. To talk about research as generating cultural theses is critical through providing a strategy to 'unthink' the common sense of schooling, to denaturalize what is taken-for-granted, and to make fragile the causalities of the present.

'Theory' as styles of thought

There is a common sense about theory that travels in teacher education. 'The Reflective Teacher', a phrase often used in contemporary reforms, is discussed as student teachers write statements about their purposes in teaching. The statements are to serve as a 'theory' to clarify the intentionality of teachers to produce more productive classroom outcomes. This common-sense notion of theory as providing a rational ordering and philosophy in guiding teaching is evident in the more general literature. It is stated in the early 20th century pedagogical 'creeds' of the Russian Markarenko and the American Dewey. These creeds are to give moral significance to education and provide theory as 'tools' that carries the charge of making the righteous through schooling.

Stating 'theories' as a prerequisite for action and judgment is very much a particular mode of thought associated with change in modernity. There is a strong belief that being explicit about one's intent and designing strategies for action are calculative methods that prepare the way for making possible desired futures. This faith in stating desired outcomes comes in many forms. It includes the tasks of school evaluation and assessment. It is also in the calls for justifying reforms through providing 'scientific evidence' that the reforms will work and will continue to do so. It is also ironically embodied in the theories of human agency that provide the *a prior* assumption in designing curriculum to teach children how to problem solve in order to bring a logic to their everyday life.

This notion of theory has residues in an earlier trust in European philosophy as the pinnacle of all knowledge. Philosophy was given the enlightenment task to make visible the possibilities of the future through an analysis of the present. In the French and English Enlightenment thought of the late 18th and 19th centuries, philosophy was considered as the highest form of knowledge that had the power and the task of shaping life through the analyzing and dissecting of the things of the world (Cassirer 1932/1951: viii). This focus on the present and future was to replace prior notions about knowledge as bringing fulfillment, identifying the origins of things, and about the finality and teleology of all things of nature and humanity. From Germany, Kant's (1784) 'What is Enlightenment?' asks about the philosophical meaning of present reality of which the philosopher belongs and in which he can situate himself as an actor of change.

The past faith in philosophy has, for the most part, given way to the empirical social sciences. Theorizing is embodied in conceptualizing to order and classify the present that would provide paths to the future. This epistemological mainstay of the contemporary education sciences and philosophy leaches into the everyday life of classroom as a 'theoretical' principle in the designing the reflection of 'the reflective teacher' and school evaluation and accountability.

I am not sure this faith in organizing the future has empirical validity or has been helpful by itself (except to the theorists) (Popkewitz, 2011). But the promise of the future embodied in the notions of reflection has limits in thinking about change, a conclusion that at first might seem paradoxical. One central limit in such formal theorizing is that it leaves unexamined the political of schooling.

First, this instance of theory assumes that change can be tamed through conscious and rational efforts. At one level, that seems reasonable as a strategy to produce a more progressive society. But the particular logic of change accepts rather than challenges the distinctions and divisions that order and classify the present. Change becomes more about activity and motion than about change (Popkewitz 1984). Second, the planning to change social conditions is directed to 'designing' the life of others, an odd prescription when thinking about democracy. Third, the desire to shape and fashion the future elides the comparative quality of the theories that inhabit pedagogical practices. That is, travelling with the hope of making particular kinds of people are distinctions and divisions. In contemporary social policy and schooling, for example, research is directed to produce a particular mode of living called the 'lifelong learner'. This kind of person is presumed to make possible the knowledge and innovative societies of the future. But when examined closely, the representations are also of its 'Others': immigrants, the poor, and ethnic and racial populations as kinds of people feared as endangering that future (Popkewitz 2008).

It seems to me, if I pursue this argument about the particular ways of ordering the present and the future as embodied theories about people, the contemporary challenge of the sciences of schooling is not to articulate theories that stand as external guides for action. The challenge of the sciences of schooling is to hold up for scrutiny the theories that order what is seen and acted. Change, I will argue, is not to forecast the future but to make fragile what is taken as natural and thus to open spaces to make alternatives possible that are outside of what is given as the order of things. The latter, the designing of alternatives in a democracy, should not rest in the inscriptions of an expertise that pretends to know both the future, its kinds of people, and the paths for its realization.

I take this task of historicizing the theories in the education sciences through borrowing from Ian Hacking's notion of styles of reason. The focus on styles of reason directs attention to the principles that shape and fashion the how *we* find out, recognize, and distinguish the kinds of people that pedagogy (teaching and learning) is to act on. The people to act on in schooling are called children (gifted, adolescent, at-risk, among others) and the agents of change (and kinds of people) are teachers. But the objects of change and the agents of change are made possible through particular rules and standards of reason that generate principles about "seeing", thinking, and acting in schooling.

To consider theories as cultural theses about kinds of people, I focus on the social and education sciences. Turning to the title of this chapter, oddly and paradoxically, theories are an empirical fact of educational practices. They embody systems of classification and distinctions about what is noticed and acted on as the qualities and capabilities of children and the possibilities of their change. This way of thinking about theories, then, is not about their formal characteristics and declarations about intent and purpose. It is to make visible the cultural theses that populate the social and education sciences as they intersect with the everyday life of schooling.

Practical knowledge as historically inscribed 'theories' about kinds of people

The idea of practical knowledge often circulates as helping the teachers and children plan their lives to find a better, more successful and beneficial future. This planning is often called 'learning' and the successful child is talked about as 'responsible' and 'motivated'. But when this planning is thought of historically, the ways of thinking and acting to effect this planning are not something merely there to implement through words that sound good such as 'learning'. What is acted upon as the practices of pedagogy are made possible through a grid of historical principles. These principles form theories about what is to be done, and about the child who is to do it in the processes of schooling. In this section, I explore the grid of principles that order the 'theories' of pedagogy. The notion of adolescence in child studies, John Dewey's notion of the problem-solving child, and the notion of community are explored as cultural theses or theories about who the child is and should be.

The adolescent as a cultural thesis about a kind of child

The notion of adolescence can be thought of as the time in the life of a child who is making the transition to adulthood and learning about the moral obligations of living in a community. This kind of person – yes, we can call it a kind of person – did not always exist as a way of thinking about the child and schooling. It emerges at the turn of the 20th century as a theory about childhood that produces a particular cultural thesis about modes of living.

If a little tracing is done, the concept of adolescence first worked in the context of religious feelings and was then (re)visioned in the new universe often associated with industrialization and urbanization at the turn of the 20th century. The American Progressive psychological sciences of child study, for example, gave expression to the notion of the child as an adolescent. *The notion of the child as an adolescent is a theory.*[2] It was a fiction, created at the turn of the century to think about particular populations and their children who started to come to the common school in America. G. Stanley Hall (1904) proposed adolescence as a way to respond to this new kind of child who came to the mass schooling. The influx of southern and eastern European immigrants and African Americans freed from slavery into the city produced new sets of issues related to health and perceived moral disorder of the city given attention in the reforms of American progressivism.

The hope of inscribing Progressivism cosmopolitan values was that 'reason, true morality, religion, sympathy, love, and aesthetic enjoyment in the child would prevail' (Hall 1928: xiii). The hope of psychology was to combat the fears about the 'danger of loss' in 'our urbanized hothouse' that 'tends to ripen everything before its time' where '[t]here is not only arrest, but perversion, at every stage, and hoodlumism, juvenile crime, and secret vice seem not only increasing, but develop in earlier years in every civilized land' (Hall 1904: xiv).

Hall's psychology inscribed these principles as part of school reform given direction by the new psychological science. Psychology, he asserted, would provide the guidance to social and individual development that would contribute to the development of the Christian 'soul':

> The new psychology (of the child), which brings simply a new method and a new standpoint to philosophy, is I believe Christian to its root and centre; and its final mission in the world is not merely to trace petty harmonies and small adjustments between science and religion, but to flood and transfuse the new and vaster conceptions of the universe and of man's place in it…with the old Scriptural sense of unity, rationality, and love beneath and above all, with all its wide consequences.
>
> (Hall, in Ross 1972: 140)

Adolescence, however, was never merely about the natural qualities of the child. It served as a metonym that condensed a grid of different practices into a particular kind of person. This grid included, for example, pastoral notions about the virtues of rural life, cosmopolitan notions of the civilized person, religious salvation themes drawn for Calvinist reformism about correcting the causes of moral disorder of urban life (see, Tröhler, 2011, Popkewitz, 2008). The grid of different historical practices is called Progressivism in US history. The progressive reforms were, as I argue later, embodied theories about saving the soul and the body. The challenges to the soul were described as alcoholism, family disintegration, delinquency among youth, and prostitution, the breakup of the urban family and the disintegration of community. The sciences of the child were the medium of change that inscribed theories that were to link values and norms of collective belonging and root out the pathologies.

Pragmatism as a historical event and making peoples

Particular strands of Progressivism were to provide for the political and social health of the republic by bringing scientific thought into everyday life (Jewett 2003). People were to learn the *generalized* processes of science as a way to think effectively in social settings and to liberate the individual through commitments to experimental investigation and theoretical explanation. Dewey's pragmatism embodied this faith in science. The anthropological psychology gave expression to plans to liberate the human spirit that brought enlightenment notions of cosmopolitan reason and rationality into the everyday life of schooling. The methods of science would resolve conflicts about beliefs and revise ideas in response to experience. Dewey's notions of 'intelligent action', community, problem solving, and scientific methods embodied the characteristics of this kind of person. The mode of living entailed formulating working hypotheses tested by the consequences in actual life situations (Ryan 1997: 38). Action and problem solving were to teach children how to rationally order their activities to enable them to act wisely in a life of continuous change.

The notions of action and problem solving brought into pedagogy a mix of different historical practices. It entailed a Protestant reformism that (re)visioned Puritan notions of salvation about the good works of individuals into a political theory of the citizen and democracy that gave the nation a sacred place in the world (Popkewitz 2008). Science became the highest point of reason that would calculate and plan changes in the conditions of social life and to provide guidance to what it was possible for people to do. But science was to act as a mode of ordering everyday life. Dewey saw science as a continual pursuit or method through which individuals would enact their life. That enactment was to enable human agency in the process of change. 'Command of scientific methods and systematized subject-matter liberates individuals; it enables them to see new problems, devise new procedures, and, in general, makes for diversification rather than for set uniformity' (Dewey 1929: 2). The laboratory school of the university placed science with the transcendent presence in the reason of progress.

If I bring back Hall with Dewey, the two different psychologies about the child were given plausibility within a grid of historical practices. Dewey, as well as Hall, was among the generation of professors in the new scientific university who gave expression to the new hope of science as the apotheosis of reason that would pursue the enlightenment dreams of progress. The new university disciplines of philosophy, science (psychology), and pedagogy gave focus to notions of community, discussed later, and the social conditions that would foster and hinder the cosmopolitanism of the citizen.

The theories and methods of the social and educational science were to provide professional expertise that was 'in service of the democratic ideal' (McCarthy 1912). Dewey saw his Lab School in the university as similar to those of biology, physics, or chemistry. It was the place where principles of pedagogy would be tested and demonstrated (Popkewitz 2011). The laboratory was an experimental site that merged the wisdom attained with philosophy as a conviction of moral values with a social psychology to develop a culture of 'critical action in which to overcome obstacles, dispose of predicaments, and settle problematic situations' (in West, 1989, p. 86).

Scientific and technological changes in the US were placed in a cultural dialogue about the nation and the liberation of the human spirit in 'a prosperous and egalitarian' cosmopolitan society whose landscape and people had a transcendent presence (Nye 2003: 5). The new scientific and technological landscape of the nation was seen to embody the enlightenment's cosmopolitan reason. The power of Niagara Falls, Edison's electric lights, and the different progressive social and education sciences captured the cultural role of science in what Nye (2003) called 'the technological sublime'. Science and technology were to provide the expertise in the making of the New Individual of the Republic and the civic obligations of the citizen. And the technological sublime also served as cultural theses in the learning theories of the school about how to order life and plan for the future. Dewey's pragmatism, for example, combined philosophy and social psychology to talk about scientific methods. The pedagogical project was related to what the University of Chicago progressive educator Parker talked about as teacher education to make 'earnest' and 'devoted' people in the governing of the democracy.

The Progressive sciences were to respond to The Social Question. The Social Question concerned the economic and moral conditions of urban life. Science was to counter the perceived disintegration and decay. Ideas of childhood, child rearing and family were interwoven with the moral questions shaping public health programmes, urban planning and schooling. The social and psychological sciences were to plan to change the conditions of urban life through the expert knowledge provided.

But at the same time were fears that travelled in the hopes of pragmatism. Dewey's 'habits of the mind' brought a cultural thesis about the mode of life that was to counter the debilitating effects of urban modern life. 'The existence of scientific method protects us also from a danger that attends the operation of men of unusual power; dangers of slavish imitation partisanship, and such jealous devotion to them and their work as to get in the way of further progress' (Dewey 1929: 11). The systematic training in 'thinking' was to prevent 'the evil of the wrong kind of development [that] is even greater...the power of thought...[as it] frees us from servile subjection to instinct, appetite, and routines' (23).

The language of salvation and redemption drew from Calvinist reformism that circulated in Progressivism and the emergence of the modern scientific universities. The president of the University of Chicago Harper where Dewey was a professor called the university 'the priest' of society. Dewey saw no difference between a universalized notion of Christian values about the good works of the individual and the democracy of the nation. Dewey spoke of democracy as revelation that expressed the ethics of a generalized Christianity (Calvinism) to the progressive revelation of truth (Dewey 1892/1967-1990). The 'Christian Democracy,' as Dewey called it in his early writing, emphasizes the rationality of science, the qualities of the democratic citizen, and a Protestant notion of salvation (see, for example, Childs 1956; also Westbrook 1991):

> I assume that democracy is a spiritual fact and not a mere piece of governmental machinery...If God is, as Christ taught, at the root of life, incarnate in man, then democracy has a spiritual meaning which it behooves us not to pass by. Democracy is freedom. If truth is at the bottom of things, freedom means giving this truth a chance to show itself, a chance to well up from the depths. Democracy, as freedom, means the loosening of bonds, the wearing away of restrictions, the breaking down of barriers, of middle walls, of partitions.
>
> (Dewey 1892/1967-1990: 8)

Embodied in this grid was a particular cultural thesis embodied in the social or anthropological psychology. It was to design life as a continuous progression that could be rationally ordered. The life to be imitated was that of science in planning individual development. The problem-solving child of Dewey or the adolescent of Hall were brought into the planning of teaching as modes of living drawn from universalized philosophy of science that overlapped with psychologies of the child (Rudolph 2005). Models of action were imagined analytic notions of the experimental method of the natural sciences that had no anthropological or empirical basis for understanding science itself.

Community sociology

The pastoral image of community was brought into the city to vitiate the effects of urbanization associated with The Social Question. The cathedral of community was evoked to stress a moral imperative of self-responsibility. In literature, politics, and science was a romantic desire to build organic values into an increasingly specialized and mechanized urban, industrial, scientific civilization (Ross 1972: 335-37). To participate in a community was to provide the social relations through which individuals lose the passions, greed, lust, and pride that work against the common good.

The city was the sociological laboratory or 'living textbook' in which the scientific mind could promote an experimental life, with philosophy as an experimental science (Menand 2001: 320). The trilogy of urban child, family and community in the new human sciences provided the social technologies for intervening and mediating the abstract relations of modernity. The pastoral images of 'the community of God' was recreated as a theory of moral order and the collective belonging in the 'home' of the city. Dewey talked about 'community' to think about 'the incarnation of God in man (man, that is to say, as the organ of universal truth) becomes a living, present thing, having its ordinary and natural sense' (Dewey 1892/1967, 1990: 9). Hall's synthetic transformation of the earlier ideas into the modern concept of adolescence, as well, owed much to the social setting of the 1890s in America and the Protestant reformism and its ideas of community as developing collective norms in individuality.

Early 20th century American community sociology adapted the German sociologist Tönnies' theory about what differentiated the pastoral community (Gemeinschaft) where neighbors, prior to modernity, come closest to nature and God, with that of modern society. The latter, society (Gesellschaft) was built on abstract relations where the moral or ethical grounding of the memorialized pastoral images of Christianity were lost. Charles Horton Cooley, a founder with George Herbert Mead of what later was called 'symbolic interactionism,' directed attention to the remaking of the urban moral order by linking the self to community. The center for the development of social organization, social consensus, and order was the urban family and its environment. The interpersonal interactions of the family and community (Gemeinschaft) were urbanized in American sociology. Community was to bring love and sympathy into the industrial world of abstract relations that defined modern society (Gesellschaft). The patterns of small town community face-to-face relations were (re)visioned as interactional patterns and communication networks of urban life.

The insertion of community was not only about the hope of the future by reimagining the pastoral in urban life. Community gave expression to the dangers and dangerous people of the urban trilogy. As Chamberlin and Gilman (1985) suggest, 'hope was looked after by progress and seemed as the tenor of the times, but fear was contagious' (p. xiii). Elaborate symbols of corruption, degeneracy, and the fall of the republic were expressed, if, for example, the development of childhood was not controlled (Krug 1972; also Rodgers 1998; Tröhler 2000, 2006). The movements of the US Settlement House to assimilate immigrants that Dewey was associated with, for example, combined reform Protestantism and the social gospel of Victorian critics of industrialism into urban reforms. Jane Addams, a leader of the Settlement Movement in Chicago's Hull House and close colleague of John Dewey, thought that the influx of foreigners brought people who were 'densely ignorant' of American customs and institutions (cited in Lybarger 1987: 181). Addams searched for ways 'to transform social relations and establish patterns of thinking so that increasing numbers of people, from increasing numbers of cultural traditions, could live together in crowded, urban conditions and still maintain a sense of harmony, order, beauty, and progress' (Lagemann 2000: 55).

Pragmatism was a theory about the relation of the social, community and individuality. It provided a mode of living that was 'to inculcate [immigrants] with American civic and cultural norms in a setting where their particular national heritages were acknowledged and respected' (Menand 2001: 399). Dewey likened the urban conditions of the city to a place where 'all hell turned lose and yet not hell any longer, but simply material for a new creation' (in Menand 2001: 319).

To this point, I have explored how certain common-sense categories of teaching (adolescent, problem-solving, and community) embody particular ways of reasoning or theories about the child. The objects of schooling are made possible through the intersection of different historical principles to generate cultural theses about who children are and should be. But theories order and classify what become the objects of 'experience' of schooling and its performances. In this historical sense, theories empirically act to shape and fashion spaces of freedom. In the next section, I move from this examination of the empirical 'fact' of theories to how the ordering principles of practice perform as actors in interning and enclosing the possibilities of schooling.

Theories as actor

The theories operating in the distinctions and differentiations of schoolings are not merely ideas or about thought processes. The principles enter into social life as 'actors' in which cultural theses are generated about what to do and how to administer the lives of children; and for the children to act on their daily lives. This section focuses on this 'other' side of theories: as actors that order conduct. Reform related to 'value-added' knowledge in teacher reforms, curriculum models in mathematics education, and the markets as remedy for school improvement are exemplars in this argument. These exemplars are explored as particular styles of reason that acts indirectly on the actions of people through shaping and fashioning the boundaries of 'freedom'.

The 'value-added' effective teacher as an actor

One of the current efforts to improve teaching is to identify the 'value-added' knowledge of the effective teacher. Value-added knowledge is to identify statistically the variables that increased student achievement beyond what would be predicted through correlations of social class indicators and age. A recent article in a leading educational research journal, for example, focused on teacher effectiveness as providing an integrated 'wholist, nuanced understanding of teachers' work and lives' beyond achievement scores (Day, Sammons, and Gu 2008: 330). Inscribed in the discourses about research is planning – planning to find more effective schools and teaching, planning to erase the achievement gap; planning by finding the value-added knowledge of teaching.

The 'value-added' knowledge seems merely to be a descriptive effort to identify and then use that knowledge to improve the skills and expertise of the teacher. But to identity what is value-added, the techniques of research created an abstraction about the effective teacher. That abstraction entailed achievement scores, children's age, and social economic status linked to something the researchers called life phases of the teacher. The life phases were 'a value-added measure', an abstraction whose quantities and qualities embody a particular kind of teacher. The research then went out to collect data about this teacher and thus to make that abstraction into an empirical 'fact' of reform. The characteristics embodied in the measurements were given as what the good *real* teacher was. The given qualities were bound to the procedures of measurement and were not something that were discovered. The abstractions, paradoxically, became an actor as the research proclaims it was for 'the *discovery and delineation* of key findings' about the qualities of effective teaching and the effective teacher (330-331; italics added).

My concern here, however, is not with the internal adequacy of the techniques applied for measurement or the instrumentations that were applied as its 'methods'. The effective teacher identified through 'value-added' knowledge is the making of kinds of people; its principles of ordering and classifying are taken as a determinate category about who the teacher is and should be. This occurs, in part, through giving the abstraction of the effective teacher magnitudes and correlations by the calculations of the numbers. Citing sample choices (100 schools and 300 teachers studied for three years) gives the abstraction about the teacher uniformity and standardization as the object and subject of study. The subject of teacher is *stabilized* through numerical categories of age, experience, gender, teaching of the school subject matter, specialization, and the years of working as a teacher (service). Charted as the Teacher Profession Life Trajectories, the different categories of the teacher are correlated with student background rendered numerically through figures about age, gender, ethnicity, English as the first language, special education, eligibility for free school meals, and prior achievement levels.

The language of certainty about what constitutes the effectiveness of the teacher is expressed through the use of numbers to identify 'the value-added' qualities. The numbers suggest a model of scientific rigor: the abstraction is given materialization as the effective teacher that has the 'contextual value added using multilevel models [334] that identifies differential qualities that relate to sustaining commitment, (n=189, 61%) or sustaining commitment despite challenging circumstances (n=39, 13%)' (335).

To understand these teacher qualities as practices of governing, we need to consider numbers as defining a problem space for standardizing its subject and object. The inscription of numbers is a social technology that seems to instantiate a consensus and harmony in a world that otherwise appears to be uncertain, ambiguous, and contentious. The uniformity given by numbers brings unlike orders in social life into a system of magnitudes that regularize relations among social and psychological components (Rose 1999: 206). By correlating the statistical magnitudes of the characteristics of teachings to achievement levels of children, numbers perform as technologies to chart, compare and give direction to what should be in schooling.

The representations and their magnitudes in the numbers are 'acted' as real to describe schools and guide change. The numbers are never just numbers, but embody cultural principles. They act as in a grid of historical practices to order how judgments are made, conclusions drawn, rectification proposed, and the fields of existence made manageable.

The belief in the truth-telling capacity of numbers to establish values about social and personal life has not always been the case. Prior to the 18th century, truth was told through the manners and rhetorical qualities of the speaker that established one's social position (Poovey 1998). For example, considerable numerical information was collected by the British government in the first three-quarters of the 18th century. That data, however, was not collected in the context of coherent theory about statecraft (Poovey 1998: 214). In Sweden, numbers were an official part of governing through registering the reading ability of the population. That register about numbers was individual and without the probability reasoning for ordering populations that appeared in the 19th century. The emergence of large group statistics and probability theories occurred in different and unrelated areas as part of changes that traversed economy, statecraft, and culture during the 19th century. It is possible to trace these changes in the meaning of statistics as in the 18th century where it was a literary term; the numerical part of the description of the state in the 19th century, and by the 20th century it was tied to mathematical techniques for numerical analysis of data whatever type (Desrosirères, 1993/1998): 200).[3]

Curriculum models as an actor: mathematics education

If we turn to the field of curriculum and current reforms, 'theories' are empirically there to circulate in the models in the selection, organization, and evaluation of school subject knowledge. If I turn to mathematics education, the programs about children's learning are theories about particular kinds of children. The theories tell about how to think and act in using particular forms of mathematical knowledge to access and confirm the reality of the external world and to arbitrate what is truth and what is falsehood.

This making truth and the kinds of people who have access to that knowledge is embodied in current mathematics education reforms. The reforms call for greater pedagogical content knowledge of teachers. This knowledge enables classroom instruction to have a closer proximity with what is found in the academic discipline of mathematics. Teacher education reforms begin with an assertion that teachers 'should possess deep knowledge of the subjects they teach' (Grossman and Schoenfeld with Lee *et al.* 2005: 201). That deep knowledge of school subjects is to capture the cultural norms of the discipline of mathematics in classroom instruction. Speaking of standards reform, 'Classrooms are mathematical communities writ small and key reform documents envision the classroom as a mathematical culture governed by roughly the same norms of argument and evidence as govern discourse within communities of scholars in the disciplines themselves' (Nelson, Warfield, and Wood 2001: 6–7).

When we begin to look more closely at the models of curriculum that order and classify the mathematics in teaching, it is not a pedagogy about mathematics. It is pedagogy about changing children and making human beings. A key term in this change process is 'problem-solving'. Problem-solving is posited as learning to deal with the uncertainty of the future that embodies unspoken norms and values about the obligations of the individual in a democracy. The problem-solving of mathematics, in one research text, is the 'modern social answer to the need to enable children to become citizens – that is, members of a society who have access to both a shared culture and who are empowered with intellectual and emotional tools to face problems within the workplace and everyday life' (Sutherland and Balacheff 1999: 2).

Problem-solving mathematics is a cultural theses about how children should live that has little to do with mathematics as a disciplinary field. The narratives about children constructing knowledge and learning about the world embody, in particular, the political values about a cosmopolitanism that are tied, at least in the American research, to images of the responsibilities and obligations of the citizen. Ball (2001), for example, uses a narrative about her own teaching as a research 'site of practice.' The teaching is narrated as an exemplar of children using their everyday lives and interests in learning to problem solve and working in a community through which students ideas, interests and lives are interpreted to 'respect who they are, as well as who they can become' (13).

This apparent report of children's experiences is in fact an enactment of a political theory about a particular cosmopolitanism embodied in American liberalism. The 'democracy' of the classroom where children participate and learn to be responsive entails a mode of life associated with American liberal political notions of participation and collaboration. That reason of learning mathematics becomes a modeling procedure where children are to use mathematics to test and judge what is 'real'.

'The reason' of learning is also about what the possibilities of life itself are, which has little to do with the culture of learning mathematics, a stated if unfilled goal. Participation links the child's 'expertise' in solving problems to the iconic stature of professional knowledge in an ordered and manageable physical world. Children's participation and problem-solving are organized to learn the majesty of the procedures, styles of argument, and symbolic system that assert the truthfulness of mathematics as a way of modeling the world.

Markets as actors

My last exemplar is market as a theory about social life that has much currency in educational reforms and contemporary policy. Market is an 'actor'. For conservatives, it is a cultural thesis about how society works and, if properly invested in, will usher in the knowledge society and the human kind that makes that society possible. That kind of person is entrepreneurial, innovative, and flexible – they are called the lifelong learner. For the left, market is a way to order society and define humanity that foregoes the commitments to the common good and which reproduces inequities.

But if the category of markets is *historicized*, it is a particular way of ordering things of the world that is given a material existence. The category of markets presupposes the notion of systems brought into social theory by Scottish Enlightenment historians and experimental moral philosophers. The notion of system was embodied in the work of David Hume; Hume, the Scottish Enlightenment philosopher was concerned with the explanation of phenomena through natural causes and laws (Poovey 1998). Hume's naturalist philosophy was not interested in empirically exploring the effects of that system (264). Hume and other political economists 'saw notions of equity and equivalence between objects that were less questions of knowledge than of justice with respect to the law governing market exchange. Numbers did not play a part in deciding justice and equity.

Adam Smith's *Wealth of Nations* (1776), in contrast, was to probe the effects of the metaphor of system to see how the theoretical entities of philosophy (and moral economy) could actually work by measuring and quantifying things such as rents, profits, and wages as influenced by commodity prices (Poovey 1998: 237). The heart of Smith's moral economy was the 'market system'. Markets, however, were not something there to uncover its 'reality' in order to gauge human interest and/or its processes to bring progress. Markets were a method of thought, a grid of economic and sociological analysis, an imagination, and a method of governing. Numbers were applied to create a way to think about the system to which numbers were applied that 'embodied [Smith's] a priori assumptions about what the market system *should be*' (Poovey 1998: 216).

For Smith, the magnitudes of numbers were to compare differences expressed as the 'invisible hand' of wealth and society. It connected 'the individual pursuit of profit with the growth of collective wealth; and to show the incompatibility between economic development and the governmental procedures' (Foucault 2004/2008: 321). Numbers did not exist prior to Smith to prove the abstraction of markets. Smith set up ways of measuring and calculating 'as if they did exist, to say something about wealth and governing' (Poovey 1998: 240–1). The sciences of markets would 'solve' the problem of studying the particulars observed so as to standardize phenomena in a manner that could be projected into the future. The historical schema focused on the intersection of subjectivity and sociality. It gave importance to domesticity, manners, women, and commercial society as 'the most sophisticated incarnation of human sociality through which the human mind would be collectively revealed' (Poovey 1998: 227).

The categories and their magnitudes provided by the numbers became an historical agent of 'human nature', a philosophical universal that could be named and quantified to determine the effects of the abstraction of markets (Poovey 1998: 247). The abstraction of markets performed as a cultural thesis about certain kinds of people. Its 'second order abstractions such as labor and happiness...was no longer a universal claim but a 'non-rhetorical (nonsuasive) place for a kind of representation that described what could be as if this potential was simply waiting to materialize' (Poovey 1998: 248).

Today, market is no longer a way to think or theorize in its formal sense. It is treated as having a real existence, the cause of things to happen and the pathway to change. But markets are about what kinds of people 'we' are and ought to be. Market is theory that generates cultural theses about modes of living.

Going forward by returning to the beginning: historizing theory as an empirical 'fact'

To move forward to the question of the future of theory is to return to the beginning. Theory is of course important. It is difficult to argue against trying to articulate that a rational, orderly, and progressive path that brings our intentions and purposes into actuality in the name of schooling and pedagogy. But once that is said, this need for such a rationality that organizes the present for the future comes against another notion of theory that inhabits such futures. This notion of theory is not what is expressed and applied as the visions in the present in teacher education programs or philosophy. Theory, in its sense of this discussion embodied styles of thought that generate cultural theses about who 'we' are, should be, and the fears of those who are 'not' us.

To think of the empirical presence of theory through the styles of reason is to engage critically the politics of schooling. The obligation of research is posed as not to accept people who 'claim to be representative, who make a profession of speaking for others, and they lead to a division of power, to a distribution of this new power which is consequently increased by a double repression; or they arise from the complaints and demands of those concerned' (Foucault 1977: 208-209). Deleuze, in the same conversion with Foucault, suggests that 'theory is exactly like a box of tools. It has nothing to do with the signifier. It must be useful. It must function, and not for itself'.

The issue of 'theory' as styles of thought is to provide ways of unthinking to rethink what is given as practical and useful. The investigation of theory is to make visible the rules and standards that produce what is seen, thought, and acted on. It is to historicize as effects of power that which is given as consensual and practical. The 'usefulness' of this notion of theory, if I can play with the word, is to disturb the causality that interns and encloses the possibilities of the present.

Notes

1 I draw on this notion from Hacking (1992). Danziger (1997) in *historicizing* how psychology makes its subject, that focuses on the presuppositions of the subject matter of a discipline that are applied in the categories that order what is seen and acted on in exploring empirical findings (9).
2 It is not merely one theory but for argument's sake I am using the single form.
3 The term of statistics as a numerical expression of human activity emerged from 18th century German 'cameral statistics' as a science of the description of the varied aspects of the State. Later and through successive (re)visioning of the word, 'statistics' separates the political management of people from the scientific management of things and the autonomy of statistics as a field of knowledge.

References

Ball, D. (2001) 'Teaching with respect to mathematics and students', in T. Wood, B. S. Nelson and J. Warfield (eds) *Beyond Classical Pedagogy: Teaching Elementary School Mathematics,* Mahwah, NJ: Lawrence Erlbaum.

Cassirer, E. (1932/1951) *The Philosophy of the Enlightenment,* trans. F. Koelln and J. Pettegrove, Princeton, NJ: Princeton University Press.

Chamberlin, J. E., and Gilman, S. L. (eds) (1985) *Degeneration: The Dark Side of Progress,* New York: Columbia University Press.

Childs, J. L. (1956) *American Pragmatism and Education: An Interpretation and Criticism,* New York: Henry Holt and Co.

Danziger, K. (1997) *Naming the Mind: How Psychology Found its Language,* London: Sage.

Day, C., Sammons, P., and Gu, Q. (2008) 'Combining qualitative and quantitative methodologies in research on teachers' lives, work, and effectiveness: From integration to synergy', *Educational Researcher,* 37: 330-42.

Desrosirères, A. (1993/1998) *The Politics of Large Numbers: A History of Statistical Reasoning,* trans. C. Naish, Cambridge: Harvard University Press.

Dewey, J. (1929). Philosophy and the social order. In J. Dewey, *Characters and events: Popular essays in social and political philosophy: Vol. II* (J. Ratner, ed.), New York: Henry Holt and Company.

Dewey, J. (1892/1967-1990) 'Christianity and democracy,' in *The collected works of John Dewey, 1882-1953. The early works of John Dewey, 1882-1898.* Electronic Edition. (This database is based on the 37-volume printed edition The Collected Works of John Dewey, 1882-1953, published by Southern Illinois University Press, 1967-1990 (edited by Jo Ann Boydston). Available at: http://www.nlx.com/collections/133.

Foucault, M. (1977) 'Intellectuals and power: Language, counter-memory, practice', in D. F. Bouchard (ed.) *Selected Essays and Interviews,* Ithaca, NY: Cornell University Press.

Foucault, M. (1977) *Language, Counter-Memory, Practice: Selected Essays and Interviews,* Ithaca: Cornell University Press.

Foucault, M. (2004/2008) *The Birth of Biopolitics. Lectures at the Collège de France 1978-1979,* trans. G. Burchell, New York: Palgrave Macmillan.

Grossman, P., Schoenfeld, A., *and* with Lee, C. (2005) 'Teaching subject matter', in L. Darling-Hammond *and* J. Bransford (eds) *Preparing Teachers for a Changing World: What Teachers Should Learn and Be Able to Do,* San Francisco: Jossey-Bass.

Hacking, I. (1992) ''Style' for historians and philosophers', *Studies in the History and Philosophy of Science,* 23: 1-20.

Hall, G. S. (1904) *Adolescence: Its Psychology and its Relation to Physiology, Anthropology, Sociology, Sex, Crime, Religion, and Education (Vol. 1),* New York: Appleton and Co.

Jewett, A. (Fall, 2003). Science *and* the promise of democracy in America, *Daedalus*. Pp.64-70.

Kant, I. (1784/1996) 'An answer to the question 'What is enlightenment?', in L. Cahoone (ed.) *From Modernism to Postmodernism: An Anthology,* Oxford: Blackwell.

Krug, E. (1972) *The Shaping of the American High School, 1920-1941* (Vol. 2), Madison: University of Wisconsin Press.

Lagemann, E. C. (2000) *An Elusive Science: The Troubling History of Education Research,* Chicago: University of Chicago Press.

Lybarger, M. (1987) 'Need as ideology: Social workers, social settlements, and the social studies', in T. Popkewitz (ed.) *The Formation of the School Subjects: The Struggles for Creating an American Institution,* New York: Falmer Press.

McCarthy, C. (1912) *The Wisconsin Idea,* New York: Macmillan.

Menand, L. (2001) *The Metaphysical Club,* New York: Farrar, Straus, and Giroux.

Nelson, B. S., Warfield, J., and Wood, T. (2001) 'Introduction', in T. Wood, B. S. Nelson and J. Warfield (eds) *Beyond Classical Pedagogy: Teaching Elementary School Mathematics,* Mahwah, NJ: Lawrence Erlbaum.

Nye, D. E. (2003) *America as Second Creation: Technology and Narratives of New Beginnings,* Cambridge, MA: MIT Press.

Poovey, M. (1998) *A History of the Modern Fact. Problems of Knowledge in the Sciences of Wealth and Society,* Chicago: University of Chicago Press.

Popkewitz, T. (1984) *Paradigm and Ideology in Educational Research, Social Functions of the Intellectual,* London and New York: Falmer Press.

Popkewitz, T. (2008) *Cosmopolitanism and the Age of School Reform: Science, Education, and Making Society by Making the Child,* New York: Routledge.

Popkewitz, T. (2011). The Past as the Future of the Social and Educational Sciences. D. Tröhler *and* R. Barbu (eds), *Education Systems in Historical, Cultural, and Sociological Perspectives,* Rotterdam: Sense Publishers.

Popkewitz, T. and Fendler, L. (eds) (1999) *Critical Theories in Education: Changing Terrains of Knowledge and Politics,* New York: Routledge.

Rodgers, D. T. (1998) *Atlantic Crossings: Social Politics in a Progressive Age,* Cambridge, MA: Belknap Press of Harvard University Press.

Rose, N. (1999) *Powers of Freedom: Reframing Political Thought,* Cambridge, MA: Cambridge University Press.

Ross, D. (1972) *G. Stanley Hall: The Psychologist as Prophet,* Chicago: The University of Chicago Press.

Rudolph, J. L. (2005) 'Turning science to account: Chicago and the general science movement in secondary education, 1905-1920', *Isis,* 96: 353-89.

Ryan, Alan (1997). *John Dewey and the high tide of American liberalism,* New York: W.W. Norton *and* Company.

Smith, A. (1776) *An Inquiry into the Nature and Causes of the Wealth of Nations,* London: Methuen and Co., Ltd.

Sutherland, R., and Balacheff, N. (1999) 'Didactical complexity of computational environments for the learning of mathematics', *International Journal of Computers for Mathematical Learning,* 4: 1-26.

Tröhler, D. (2000) 'The global community, religion, and education: The modernity of Dewey's social philosophy', *Studies in Philosophy and Education,* 19: 156-96.

Tröhler, D. (2006) 'Max Weber and the Protestant ethic in America', paper presented at Pestalozzianum Research Institute for the History of Education, University of Zurich.

Tröhler, D. (2011). *Languages of education: Protestant legacies in educationalization of the world, national identities, and global aspirations* (T. Popkewitz, Foreword), New York: Routledge.

West, C. (1989). *The American evasion of philosophy: A genealogy of pragmatism*, Madison: University of Wisconsin Press.

Westbrook, R. (1991) *John Dewey and American Democracy*, Ithaca, NY: Cornell University Press.

Chapter 2

Challenges of educational theory in the age of knowledge capitalism

Lisbeth Lundahl

In the welfare states that emerged in most capitalist countries after World War II, the public institutions were complementary to and interacted with the market, with the double aims of benefiting economic growth and social cohesion. Their relationship to the economy was indirect to large extent, providing, for instance, schools, universities and their professionals with a certain degree of autonomy and legitimacy. In the so-called knowledge economy or knowledge capitalism the State, rather than retreating which sometimes has been argued, plays a new vital role vis-à-vis the economy; we witness the transition to a competition state or liberal Schumpeterian state which actively seeks to boost economic growth by supporting innovation, enterprise and flexibility (Ball 2007; Jessop 2006). 'The economy' is extended to include a range of factors that previously were regarded as external, education among them. In consequence, education and research have become directly linked to the economy at all levels, and are subject to active reconstruction accordingly (Apple *et al.* 2005; Peters 2003; Jessop *et al.* 2008). Equally notable, a global social imaginary of education policy has emerged, permeated with neoliberal ideas and concepts (Rizvi 2006).

In this chapter it is argued that social and educational theory is essential in order to grasp and analyse the present state of education and to envision its possible future/s, and that the neoliberal reconfiguration of education, education governance and research challenges such a task in multiple ways. Two consequences of the neoliberal and global context are discussed: (a) the thorough reshaping of the preconditions and nature of educational phenomena as such means that theories probably have to be rethought and reconstructed in more and other ways than has hitherto been the case; (b) the obvious clash between theories with an aim of understanding and critical questioning that are largely used in educational and social science today and the assumptions and theories underlying the strong, sometimes vehement demands of 'valid knowledge' and 'valid research' under knowledge capitalism.

The 'new' mission of education

Under the latest stage of globalisation, education and research are assigned crucial functions in the accelerating international flow of capital, labour and ideas. Education becomes subject to closer scrutiny and evaluation by the state, a discourse of quality and excellence dominates, and various control techniques are installed in the name of quality assurance (Peters 2005; Power 1997). International comparisons of performance and outcomes become increasingly important (Henry *et al.* 2001; Grek 2008) and Ball and Youdell (2008) speak of this as a hidden privatisation, often preceding a more direct one. The latter, meaning marketization and commercialisation of education, indicates a weakened relationship to the state and increasing subordination to the market and its theories, methods and values (c.f. Ball 1998). Education becomes redefined as a private rather than common good, valued mainly as a crucial capital for successful competition and economic growth, while the democratic and cultural functions of education tend to become obscured. A modernisation or re-shaping of the curriculum is formulated accordingly, stressing outcomes of education and the fostering of responsible, self-governing, problem-solving and enterprising individuals. The collective base is increasingly dominated by performance modes, at all educational levels (Young, 2009; Young and Muller, 2010). This transformation is far from smooth; it presupposes a radical makeover of allegedly heavy-footed and old-fashioned schools, curricula, teachers and educational management (Dale and Robertson, 2003, p. 7). Hereby markets, competition and choice are seen not only as the goals to be reached, but also as the magic wands by which all this will happen.

The example of the 'novel Swedish model'

The Swedish education system provides a telling, even provocative, example of the strengthening links between education and economy under knowledge capitalism. It displays most of the characteristics of internal, 'hidden' marketization discussed above, but has also developed an extensive tax funded for-profit free-school sector within the last two decades (Lundahl 2002). Until the early 1990s, when vouchers and generous conditions for alternatives to the public schools were introduced, private schools were very rare in Sweden. In the early part of 2010, almost one fourth of all students at upper secondary level attended free-schools, around half of the students in the three biggest cities. The proportions are lower at preschool and compulsory levels, but will probably rise due to hardening competition at upper secondary level. Within a short period of time, the free-school sector has changed into being a business like any else. School trade is attractive as it is profitable and relatively safe. In 2011 almost nine out of ten free-schools were joint-stock companies. Ownership is increasingly concentrated to large groups of companies, commonly venture capital companies, by national and international purchases and mergers (Arreman and Holm 2011; Lundahl 2011). This new 'Swedish model' has received considerable international attention, especially in Britain (see, for example, Hatcher and Jones 2011), but also for example in the US. This was certainly not the model former Swedish school and Prime Minister Olof Palme was referring to in the early 1960s when he talked about the Swedish school being a spearhead into the future.[1]

Free schools constitute the most eye-catching aspect of the new market situation in Sweden, but the whole school system is reshaped by it. In our research project 'Upper secondary school as a market' we found that practically all upper secondary schools – public and free schools – were affected by the need to attract and retain students. Competition influences teachers' and students' working tasks and working conditions, the courses and programmes offered, and the resources available. The market situation affects self-images and images of the competing other/s. The pupils encounter a veritable jungle of courses and programmes at upper secondary level and often find this situation extremely difficult and stressful. Almost nine out of ten schools actively market themselves through a range of channels. Four out of ten invest considerable resources on marketing. Many schools try to have tempting offers, for example attractive programme profiles and fringe benefits such as free driving classes, discounts at a gym and free laptops. Other research has shown that grades (in Sweden teachers alone do the grading) are affected by the competition; high grades and few dropouts constitute a selling argument.

The introduction of choice and competition in Swedish education was motivated both with references to international declarations of parental rights and expectations of general quality promotion, raised educational performance and lowered costs. The actual outcomes are nowhere near this vision, however. On the contrary, the attainment of Swedish primary and secondary schools show a declining trend since the 1990s. Even more worryingly, there is a clear tendency of growing social and ethnic segregation between schools, which is related to the aforementioned choice and market reforms, even if this is not the sole factor (see, for example, Östh *et al.* 2010; Allen 2010).

Possible theoretical implications

In his essay *Vertical and Horizontal Discourse* on the languages of different knowledge structures ('theories'), Basil Bernstein (1999) noted that the languages of the social sciences tend to have an inbuilt redundancy. As a consequence, and particularly at times of rapid transformation, social phenomena are not describable or are only inadequately describable with the language of the past. The present stage of knowledge capitalism means a powerful and rapid reconfiguration of education – its functions, work, institutions and actors – and the knowledge to be transmitted by schools and other institutions. I would argue that this profound change of the basic structures and nature of education and schooling requires a revision and development of our theoretical tools in a number of ways, and I want to substantiate this argument with a few examples. In the last of them, implications of Basil Bernstein's notion of the de-centred market position is further concretized and illustrated by democracy learning in market-oriented schools.

The understanding of how of the school market works is still lacking to a considerable degree. This is not merely a question of lacking empirical data; in order to understand the dynamics of the privatisation of education, it is equally important that it is *conceptualised* and theorized. The marketization process is not devoid of underlying assumptions and theories, but these too often remain implicit and unchallenged. They are the neoliberal ideas of rational choice and utilitarianism, the economic and self-interested man, competition as a universal driving force of development and the all-encompassing transformation of social acts to market transactions.[2]

Relatively little attention has been paid to the construction, contents and functions of school curricula in the age of knowledge capitalism, in particular in relation to the creation of a transnational education space (Grek and Lawn 2009; Lawn and Grek 2012). Are existing curriculum theories sufficient when we want to grasp and critically analyse a 'European educational curriculum', as mediated by recurrent international evaluations (PISA, TIMSS *etcetera*) for example, and the framework of key competencies for lifelong learning (EC 2006), are they sufficient to examine how such an international curriculum enters the national ones? What kind of curriculum theory is needed when global organisations like the OECD increasingly advocate assessment and accountability systems rather than or instead of formalised curriculum-making (Karseth and Sivesind 2010)?

Even if the restructuring of education has led to considerable revision and reconstruction of theories of teacher work, it may be time to formulate a more comprehensive theory of the new occupational roles and relations that are emerging in schools exposed to the market (Mahoney and Hextall 2000, Beach 2010). More generally, theories of professions and professionalization need to be rethought and reformulated. According to earlier critical theories, professions are legitimized by their relations to allegedly neutral and objective knowledge and to the State; occupations with a close connection to the market, for example, the economic and engineering occupations, have not been considered as professions precisely because of this (Sarfatti Larson 1977). Traditionally, neo-institutional theory has characterised schools as isomorphic institutions (i.e. having similar features regardless of their location) that are loosely coupled with other institutions and administrative bodies. Marketization challenges precisely such assumptions; schools are now expected to become both more sensitive and accountable to stakeholders, and, at least in certain segments of the school market, to appear as 'unique' in one aspect or another in order to successfully compete for students.[3]

Basil Bernstein's (2000) outline of a theory of pedagogic identities still remains to be developed and refined. 'Pedagogic identity' refers to internal sense making and external relationships in time, space and context (Bernstein and Solomon 1999: 271). Bernstein spoke of four positions that are constructed from the dimensions of retrospective-prospective and centred-decentred, positions from which pedagogic identities emanate. He labelled one of them the Decentred-Market position (DCM). Bernstein assumed that the pedagogic identity related to the DCM position would be oriented towards the optimisation of the exchange value in the market, towards short term rather than long-term gains, and extrinsic rather than intrinsic values.

When we seek to develop Bernstein's notion of the DCM, we not only regard it as a novel foundation of pedagogic identities, but also as a new framing or governing of education and relationships between teachers and students. This is fully in line with Bernstein's argument:

> Imagine an educational institution which has considerable autonomy over the use of its budget, the organisation of its discourse, how it uses its staff, the number and type of staff, the courses it constructs, provided (1) it can attract students who have a choice of institution, (2) it can meet the external performance criteria and (3) it can optimise its position in relation to similar institutions. The basic unit of the institution (…) will also have autonomy over its position in the market: that is to optimise its position with respect to the exchange value of its products, namely the students. Thus the pedagogic practice will be contingent on the market in which the identity is to be enacted.
>
> (Bernstein 2000: 69)

When Bernstein wrote this, the DCM was a position still to be realised, and one that might be difficult to recognise, he argued. Interestingly, we can now rather easily recognise it in Sweden, less than 20 years later.

Two main actors can be identified at the de-centred market: the market-oriented school on the one hand and the student on the other. We would expect their aims, strategies and actions to increasingly focus firstly on the actor's freedom, in the case of the student freedom of what to choose, in the case of the school freedom of what to offer, and secondly, on individual rather than collective agency. Thirdly, we would find an increased focus on behaviours or activities that may enhance the individual student's and/or school's performance and competitiveness, and fourthly, an emphasis on image management with the aim of enhancing the visibility and attractiveness of the individual and/or school. A re-analysis of recent ethnographic studies of formal and informal democracy education and students' democracy learning in Swedish upper secondary schools (Beach and Dovemark 2011; Öhrn *et al.* 2011; Hjelmér 2013; Wyndhamn forthcoming) has supported these assumptions. We found that young people's democracy learning is affected by their new roles and power positions in the market-led school. Students are influential as customers when choosing school and programme, since the upper secondary schools intensively compete to attract them. Later, students embody a 'capital' of the school, which will face economic consequences if they leave. The students are also valuable by contributing to the marketing of the school as school ambassadors. However, there seems to be little opportunity to have a voice or to practise or experience influence over the concrete everyday aspects of education. Such initiatives risk being perceived as obstacles to effectiveness and performance, both by competitive students and schools (Lundahl *and* Olson forthcoming). This is a picture of what a school, student and democracy is about that clearly contrasts with what we are used to seeing, and it illustrates well the depth of the market transformation of education.

A battle against 'useless' and 'weak' research

> How is strong research to trump weak research in a marketplace that is unsophisticated with regard to research quality? There has to be an entity that vets research on program effectiveness for practitioners and policymakers using *rigorous* scientific standards. And it has to become the preeminent source for such information, effectively muting the cacophony of conflicting claims and assertions that arise from those who advocate with numbers or draw conclusions based on methods that cannot support causal conclusions.
>
> (Institute of Education Science 2008: 14)

Even the academic landscape, including tertiary education and research, has been transformed in the so-called knowledge-based economy, earlier and in some respects more radically than education at primary and secondary levels. The links between money, markets and universities have three distinct elements: the steering of the knowledge to be produced, the work and organisation of academics, and the control and exploitation of knowledge products (c.f. Boden and Epstein 2006). Here I will focus on the first of these aspects. Today, the pressure 'to deliver' knowledge of the 'right kind' is particularly strong within the humanities and social science research, which previously had low funding priority, but still enjoyed a certain academic freedom to choose research questions, theories and methods. In the late 1990s and early 2000s, research aiming at critical analysis and understanding rather than instrumental explanation and prescription for policy and practice has been downgraded, criticized and even attacked for being 'weak' and of little use (Oancea and Pring 2008). 'Education research was found lacking in all aspects that were high on the official agenda: relevance; cumulativeness and coherence; methodological rigour; and cost effectiveness.' (Ibid.: 16) Research related to the public welfare sector and its occupations (e.g. social work, nursing and teaching) has been actively pressed to provide social work, care and education with scientific knowledge of 'what works' – or to perish.

The basic assumptions of what counts as valid research have been taken over, lock, stock and barrel, from leading parts of the natural sciences; the 'golden standard' consists of carefully conducted (quasi) experiments, randomly controlled trials and cohort studies. Hence, rather than acknowledging the need for employing varying theoretical and methodological approaches related to research foci and phenomena addressed, only technical-instrumental research and a few accompanying methodologies are accepted as valid (c.f. Hammersley 2001; Pirrie 2001). It is assumed that studies in social science, as in natural and engineering sciences, could and should be cumulative and comparable to a large degree and that social research designed accordingly will give clients, practitioners and policymakers general, reliable and valuable information. Finally, quality and quality assessment are externally defined and managed rather than by the research community (Oancea and Pring 2008). The underlying assumptions of evidence-based social research and systematic reviews have been subject to extensive and relevant critiques, for example by Atkinson (2000, 2004); Hammersley (2001); Oancea and Pring (2008); Pirrie (2001); and Popkewitz (2004).

In Britain, the nature and quality of educational research was attacked in the 1990s; such research was said to give poor value for money (Hargreaves 1996; Pirrie 2001; Oancea and Pring 2008). In 2002, in the US, the Institute of Education Sciences (IES), based on the 2002 the 'No Child Left Behind' Act[4] and the Education Sciences Act, espoused similar underlying ideas regarding the strength of some educational research approaches, and the paucity of others. Swedish educational research was questioned on the same grounds some years later (see below). So-called research clearinghouses were to become important in providing 'research maps' of various fields, finely adjusting the measurement tools of the gold standard, collecting evidence-based research and diagnosing the state of research. The British EPPI centre (The Evidence for Policy and Practice Information and Co-ordinating Centre) was founded in 1993, and the Campbell collaboration in 2000, with an aim to 'help people make well-informed decisions by preparing, maintaining and disseminating systematic reviews'00 in education, crime and justice, and social welfare.[5]

In the following section I give some concrete examples of the efforts to combat 'weak' research in the 'unsophisticated marketplace' of educational and social science, and of a discourse which risks becoming totally dominant. Finally, I discuss possible consequences and strategic responses for researchers.

IES and the promotion of 'scientifically valid research'

The Institute of Education Sciences (IES) was established, under the aegis of the US Department of Education, through the US Education Sciences Reform Act (2002), according to which the Institute's aims are to support and disseminate the findings of 'scientifically valid research activities', and promote the use, development, and application of knowledge gained from such research activities. The Education Sciences Reform Act of 2002 contains a detailed definition of scientific research standards and valid research – the latter directly relating to the former.[6]

In his 2008 report to the US Congress, the retiring Director of IES Grover J. Whitehurst described, and commented on, its history and development. He described how IES had successfully transformed education into an evidence-based field by supporting research and evaluation projects using 'scientifically rigorous' designs, especially randomized design. The work of IES was guided by the definition of scientific research (see above) as opposed to:

> … the dominant forms of education research in the latter half of the 20th century: qualitative research grounded in postmodern philosophy and methodologically weak quantitative research. Whereas questions of what works are paramount to educators, there was declining interest in those questions in the education research community prior to IES. Quantitative research on program effectiveness was replaced, frequently, by activities in the tradition of postpositivism and deconstructivism in the humanities. These approaches are based on philosophical assumptions that question the existence of a physical reality beyond what is socially constructed….In the context of declining interest in studies of the effectiveness of education programs, the ascendance of postmodern approaches to education research, and the frequent use of weak methods to support strong causal conclusions, IES took a clear stand that education researchers needed to develop interventions that were effective in raising student achievement and to validate the effectiveness of those interventions using rigorous methods. (Ibid.: 6).

Whitehurst added, that these measures had challenged 'the old guard', researchers whose interests were threatened by the IES research policy and now hoped for a return to the time in which virtually anything passed as credible education research.

The 57 research projects funded in 2012 by the National Center for Education Research (NCER) are fully in line with the 'what works' philosophy. They all focus on practical utility-development of programmes and evaluating or assessing their effectiveness or efficacy. There is clearly no room for historical, philosophical or, more generally, critical studies.

Swedish educational research put in the corner

In 2010, the Swedish National Board of Health and Welfare evaluated about 1,400 Swedish doctoral theses in seven disciplines, including social work, psychology and education, in order to assess the extent to which they measured effects of social interventions. Thirteen per cent had such an orientation, of which only a third (four per cent of the total) were judged to be of high quality, that is: following the 'golden standard' (Sundell and Stensson 2010). This caused the board to send a warning letter to the universities, underscoring the gravity of the situation, an exceptional measure which was met by protests from leading researchers in social work. In an interview in the journal of the Swedish school leaders, *Skolvärlden* (trans. 'The School World') under the headline 'The Swedish school fiasco', one of the authors of the aforementioned report criticised educational research on the basis of the same investigation, using additional publication statistics. Sundell related the downward trend of Swedish pupils' attainments in international evaluations to the incapacity of educational researchers to provide teachers with validated methods. Some months later, his critique resonated in the largest daily newspaper in Sweden. In a series of long articles, journalist Maciej Zaremba presented a critique the Swedish education system, a narrative with distinct heroes and villains: decentralisation reforms and ignorant municipalities, the grading system, teacher education, bad teachers and school leaders (with notable exceptions). Last but not least, the researchers, allegedly living in an isolated world far from the needs of children, teachers and parents, were attacked. The articles received great attention and probably had considerable impact, but unlike their colleagues in the US and Britain, Swedish educational researchers remained surprisingly passive in this media turmoil. One important reason may be the lack of a strong educational research association at national level that could serve as a platform for information and debate. Swedish educational researchers are commonly organised in the Nordic Association of Educational Research, but also in several other, more specialised associations.

Final comments

I want to emphasise that I am not negative about quantitative and experimental methods as such. They may be highly appropriate for addressing some research problems, although I argue that the scope for conducting experiments or quasi-experiments in teaching and learning environments is clearly limited. However, I am highly sceptical about the idea that research can, or should, guide or actually replace education policy-making and politics. The school is a highly complex social setting, and the connection between evidence and policy is highly questionable. What I actively oppose is the elimination of theoretical perspectives and methodological approaches that are necessary to tackle the whole spectrum of educational matters, from educational philosophy, history of education and education policy to ethnographic studies of classrooms and other settings of education and learning. There is an obvious risk that we will end up with a research mono-culture that is capable of covering only narrow aspects of the central educational problems (cf. Lareau and Barnhouse Walters, 2010). As Biesta has argued, technological models of professional action are insufficient or even misleading as education is rather a process of symbolically mediated interaction (Biesta, 2007).

Having said this, some self-critical reflections are not out of place. There is a need to take some of the criticisms of educational research seriously, including, for example, a sometimes unclear relationship of conclusions to evidence (in a broad sense), low accessibility to those outside the research community, and insufficiently addressing the problems that trouble decision-makers and teachers. This, however, does not imply that an impoverishment of what counts as research solely in terms of 'what works' is acceptable (Oancea and Pring, 2008, p. 34). We should more frequently consider the obvious difficulties in communicating and conversing across diverse social and educational theories. How can we actively promote translation and conversation between our theories? Moreover, the language of educational qualitative research is often abstruse, even for researchers in their own field. As a consequence, we often have considerable problems communicating our research and findings to teachers, parents and decision-makers outside our scientific communities. Bernstein (1999) noted 'an obsession with language' in the horizontal discourse, and advocated more focus on the empirical analysis than with taking space with the language as such. Maybe this something to consider in our reporting when going outside the rather exclusive, 'excellent' journals that we, according to the market logic, are supposed to publish in.

I started this chapter by emphasising the importance of social and educational theory being able to grasp and analyse the state of education in the stage of knowledge capitalism and to envision its future development. The evidence-based 'gold standard' research is obviously not the best one to do so. Theoretically strong research is not externally prescribed; it is instead characterized by autonomy and integrity. It does not emanate one-sidedly from a utility interest to evaluate and control social phenomena; equally it may well have the aim of understanding and/or critically questioning such phenomena. Theoretically strong research has the capability to widen the scope of inquiry; narrowing its focus must not be the sole aim.

Notes

1 Speech 25 May 1962, two days after the parliament decision on the general introduction of the nine-year compulsory, comprehensive school. Available at: <http://www.olof-palme.org/>.

2 Neoliberal ideology, with the individual, choice and protection of market as its cornerstones, constitutes the basis for economic and institutional theory: monetarism and theories of institutional restructuring, such as public choice theory, agency theory and transactional cost economics (see, for example, Olssen, Codd and O'Neill, 2004).

3 Such assumptions of neo-institutional theory have been tested on cases of public schools, private elite schools and new private sector school in Ontario, Canada (Aurini, 2006; Davies and Quirke, 2007).

4 Oancea and Pring (2008) note that the 'No Child Left Behind' (NCLB) Act of 2001 included over 100 mentions of 'scientifically-based research' as the desirable basis for education, and in detail defined its attributes, namely those of the 'gold standard' (ibid.: 18).

5 http://www.campbellcollaboration.org/about_us/index.php.
6 (18) SCIENTIFICALLY BASED RESEARCH STANDARDS.
(A) The term 'scientifically based research standards' means research standards that:
(i) apply *rigor*ous, systematic, and objective methodology to obtain reliable and valid knowledge relevant to education activities and programmes; and
(ii) present findings and make claims that are appropriate to and supported by the methods that have been employed.
(B) The term includes, appropriate to the research being conducted;
(i) employing systematic, empirical methods that draw on observation or experiment;
(ii) involving data analyses that are adequate to support the general findings;
(iii) relying on measurements or observational methods that provide reliable data;
(iv) making claims of causal relationships only in random assignment experiments or other designs (to the extent such designs substantially eliminate plausible competing explanations for the obtained results);
(v) ensuring that studies and methods are presented in sufficient detail and clarity to allow for replication or, at a minimum, to offer the opportunity to build systematically on the findings of the research;
(vi) obtaining acceptance by a peer-reviewed journal or approval by a panel of independent experts through a comparably *rigour*ous, objective, and scientific review; and
(vii) using research designs and methods appropriate to the research question posed. (the U.S. Education Sciences Reform Act of 2002).

References

Allen, R. (2010) 'Replicating Swedish 'free school' reforms in England', *Research in Public Policy*, Summer: 4-7.

Apple, Michael W.; Kenway, Jane and Singh, Michael (eds) (2005) *Globalizing Education: Policies, Pedagogies and Politics,* New York: Peter Lang.

Arreman Erixon, I., and Holm, A.-S. (2011) 'Privatisation of public education? The emergence of independent upper secondary schools in Sweden', *Journal of Education Policy*, 26: 225–243.

Atkinson, E. (2000) 'In defence of ideas, or why "what works" is not enough', *British Journal of Sociology of Education*, 21: 317–330.

Atkinson, E. (2004) 'Thinking outside the box: An exercise in heresy', *Qualitative Inquiry*, 10: 111–129.

Aurini, J. (2006) 'Crafting legitimation projects: An institutional analysis of private education businesses', *Socio-logical Forum*, 21: 83–111.

Ball, S. J. (1998) 'Big policies/small world: An introduction to international perspectives in education policy', *Comparative Education*, 34: 119–130.

Ball, S. J. (2007) *Education Plc: Understanding Private Sector Participation in Public Sector*, New York, NY: Routledge.

Ball, S. J., and Youdell, D. (2008) *Hidden Privatisation in education*, Brussels: Education International. Available at: <http://download.ei-ie.org/docs/IRISDocuments/Research%20Website%20Documents/2009-00034-01-E.pdf>. (Accessed July 1, 2011.)

Beach, D. (2010) 'Neoliberal Restructuring in Education and Health Professions in Europe Questions of Global Class and Gender', *Current Sociology*, 58: 551–569.

Beach, D. and Dovemark, M. (2011) 'Twelve years of upper-secondary education in Sweden: The beginnings of a neo-liberal policy hegemony', *Educational Review,* 63: 313-327.

Bernstein, B. (1999) 'Vertical and horizontal discourse: An essay', *British Journal of Sociology of Education*, 20: 265–279.

Bernstein, B. (2000) *Pedagogy, symbolic control and identity: Theory, research, critique*, Lanham, MD: Rowman and Littlefield Publishers. Available at: <http://www.timescapes.leeds.ac.uk/secondary-analysis>.

Bernstein, B., and Solomon, J. (1999) 'Pedagogy, identity and the construction of a theory of symbolic control': Basil Bernstein questioned by Joseph Salomon', *British Journal of Sociology of Education*, 20: 265–279.

Biesta, G. (2007) 'Why "what works" won't work: Evidence based practice and the democratic deficit in educational research' *Educational Theory*, 57: 1–22.

Boden, R., and Epstein, D. (2006) 'Managing the research imagination? Globalisation and research in higher education', *Globalisation, Societies and Education*, 4: 223–236.

Dale, R., and Robertson, S. L. (2003) 'Editorial: Introduction', *Globalisation, Societies and Education,* 1: 3–11.

Davies, S., and Quirke, L. (2007) 'The impact of sector on school organizations: Institutional and market logics, *Sociology of Education*, 80: 66–89.

European Commission (2006) 'Annex. Key Competences for Lifelong Learning – A European Reference Framework' *Official Journal of the European Union* 31.12.2006. L 394/13. Available at: <http://eur-lex.europa.eu/LexUriServ/LexUriServ.do?uri=OJ:L:2006:394:0010:0018:EN:pdf>.

Gough, D. and Elbourne, D. (2002) 'Systematic Research Synthesis to Inform Policy, Practice and Democratic Debate', *Social Policy and Society*, 1: 225–236.

Grek, S. (2008) 'From symbols to numbers: The shifting technologies of education governance in Europe', *European Educational Research Journal*, 7: 208–218.

Grek, S., and Lawn, M. (2009) 'A short history of Europeanizing education. The new political work of calculating the future', *European Education*, 41: 32–54.

Hammersley, M. (2001) 'On "systematic" reviews of research literatures: A "narrative" response to Evans and Benefield.' *British Educational Research Journal*, 27: 543–554.

Hargreaves, D. H. (1996) 'Teaching as a research-based profession: possibilities and prospects', Teacher Training Agency annual lecture 1996. London: Teacher Training Agency. Available at: <http://www.bera.ac.uk/files/ resourcesfiles/educationalresearch/hargreaves_1996.pdf>. (Accessed April 3, 2011.)

Hatcher, R. and Jones, K. (eds) (2011) *No country for the young: Education from New Labour to the Coalition*, London: Tufnell Press.

Henry, M., Lingard, B., Rizvi, F., and Taylor, S. (2011) *The OECD, globalisation and education policy*, Oxford: Pergamon.

Hjelmér, C. (2013) '*Leva och lära demokrati? En etnografisk studie i två gymnasieprogram* [Live and learn democracy? An ethnographic study of two upper secondary education programs]', PhD thesis. Umeå University, Sweden.

Institute of Education Sciences, US Department of Education (2008) 'Rigour and relevance redux: Director's biennial', Report to Congress (IES 2009–6010). Washington, DC. Available at: <http://ies.ed.gov/director/pdf/20096010.pdf>. (Accessed 12 May 2010.)

Jessop, B. (2006) 'State- and regulation-theoretical perspectives on the European Union and the failure of the Lisbon Agenda', *Competition and Change*, 10: 141–161.

Jessop, B., Fairclough, N., and Wodak, R. (2008) *The Knowledge-Based Economy and Higher Education in Europe*, London: Sense.

Karseth, B. and Sivesind, K. (2010) 'Conceptualising curriculum knowledge within and beyond the national context', *European Journal of Education*, 45: 103-120.

Lareau, A., and Barnhouse Walters, P. (2010) 'What counts as credible research?' *Teachers College Record*. ID number: 15915. Available at: <http://www.tcrecord.org>.

Lawn, M. and Grek, S. (2012) *Europeanizing Education: Governing a New Policy Space*, Oxford: Symposium Books.

Lundahl, L. (2002) 'Sweden: Decentralisation, deregulation, quasi-markets – and then what?' *Journal of Education Policy*, 17: 687-697.

Lundahl, L. (2007) 'Swedish, European, global: The transformation of the Swedish welfare state', in B. Lingard and J. Ozga (eds), *The RoutledgeFalmer Reader in Education Policy and Politics*, London: RoutledgeFalmer.

Lundahl, L. (2011) 'The emergence of a Swedish school market', in R Hatcher and K Jones (eds), *No Country for the Young: Education from New Labour to the Coalition*, London: Tufnell Press.

Mahoney, P. and Hextall, I. (2000) *Reconstructing Teaching: Standards, Performance and Accountability*, London: RoutledgeFalmer.

Oancea, A. and Pring, R. (2008) 'The importance of being thorough: On systematic accumulations of "what works" in education research', *Journal of Philosophy of Education*, 42: 4-15.

OECD (2011) *The OECD Skills Strategy*. Paris: OECD Publishing. Available at: <http://www.oecd.org/dataoecd/58/28/47769132.pdf>. (Accessed May 15, 2012)

Öhrn, E., Beach, D. and Lundahl, L. (eds) (2011) *Young people's influence and democratic education. Ethnographic studies in upper secondary schools*, London: Tufnell Press.

Olssen, M., J. Codd, J. and O'Neill, A.-M. (2004) *Education policy: Globalization, citizenship and democracy*, London: Sage.

Östh, J., Andersson, E., and Malmberg, B. (2010) 'School choice and increasing performance difference: A counterfactual approach', *Stockholm Research Reports in Demography* 2010:11. Available at: <http://www.suda.su.se/SRRD/SRRD_2010_11.pdf>. (Accessed May 3, 2011.)

Peters, M. A. (2003) 'Classical political economy and the role of Universities in the New Knowledge Economy', *Globalisation, Societies and Education*, 1: 153–168.

Peters, M. A. (2005) 'The new prudentialism in education: Actuarial rationality and the entrepreneurial self', *Educational Theory*, 22: 122–137.

Pirrie, A. (2001) 'Evidence-based practice in education: The best medicine?' *British Journal of Educational Studies*, 49: 124–136.

Popkewitz, T. S. (2004) 'Is the National Research Council committee's report on scientific research in education scientific? On trusting the manifesto', *Qualitative Inquiry*, 10: 62–78.

Power, M. (1997) *The Audit Society: Rituals of verification*, Oxford: Oxford University Press.

Rizvi, F. (2006) 'Imagination and the globalisation of educational policy research', *Globalisation, Societies and Education*, 4:193-205.

Sarfatti Larson, M. (1977) *The rise of professionalism. A sociological analysis*, Berkeley: University of California Press.

Sundell, K., and Stensson, E. (2010) 'Effektutvärderingar i doktorsavhandlingar (Effect evaluation in doctoral theses)', Stockholm: The Swedish National Board of Health and Welfare (in Swedish). Available at: <http://www.socialstyrelsen.se/Lists/Artikelkatalog/Attachments/17970/2010-3-24.pdf>. (Accessed May 2, 2010.)

US Congress (2002) Education Science Reform Act of 2002. H. R. 3801–8. Available at: <http://www2.ed.gov/policy/rschstat/leg/PL107-279.pdf>. (Accessed May 2, 2010.)

Wyndhamn, A.-K. (forthcoming) *'Tänka fritt, tänka rätt. En studie om värdeöverföring och kritiskt tänkande i gymnasieskolans undervisning* [Thinking free, thinking right. A study about values transmission and critical thinking in upper secondary school's teaching]', PhD thesis, Gothenburg: Department of Education

Young, M. (2008) *Bringing Knowledge Back In. From Social Constructivism to Social Realism in the Sociology of Education*, London: Routledge.

Young, M., and Muller, J. (2010) 'Three educational scenarios for the future: Lessons from the sociology of knowledge', *European Journal of Education*, 45: 11–27.

Chapter 3

Between universally claimed theory and common understanding

Theoretical knowledge in education

Daniel Tröhler

Introduction

Before educational theories were formulated explicitly as theories, education had become recognized as a core element of social life. According to traditional appraisals, this increased recognition emerged in the eighteenth century, and usually this emergence is equated with education becoming modern. As a rule, this ascription of modernity is based on the assumed discovery of childhood as a more or less independent stage of life in Jean-Jacques Rousseau's novels *Julie ou la Nouvelle Héloïse* (1761) and *Emile* (1762). Certainly, it is not the discovery of childhood *per se* that is believed to make education modern, for education had been discussed intensely ever since the end of the seventeenth century, most notably by paediatricians (Mercier 1961). Rather, it was the connection between 'childhood' on one hand and specific social expectations of the future adult as citizen on the other hand that allowed the change in claims about education. It was this connection that was pertinently described in the first three books of Rousseau's *Emile* and certain passages of *Nouvelle Héloïse*. The incredible success of Rousseau's novels proves that Rousseau obviously hit a nerve of the times, serving a public desideratum that had emerged out of particular interpretations of the social transformations of the eighteenth century.[1]

This desideratum had become tangible predominantly in Protestant parts of Europe, where people were experiencing difficulties integrating their interpretations of the social and economic transformations around and after 1700 in their worldview (Tröhler 2011a). At the outset was the shift that Western Europe experienced in its economic structures, which challenged the traditional common good-oriented and anti-commercial ideals of political philosophy (Hirschman 1977; Pocock 1985). Within the frame of these traditional political ideals, the social shifts triggered by the economic developments evoked public criticism. Commerce was accused of inciting the passions of the commercial men, leading them to promote their private interests rather than the common good. This interpretation dominated especially in those Protestant parts of Europe devoted to classical republicanism, and thus in those influenced by the Swiss Reformation (Calvin and Zwingli). It was here that education was first formulated as solution to these challenges. In order to transcend the problem of the passions in the context of the commercializing society, these passions had to be separated ideologically from commerce and thus made accessible to a concerted human intervention called education. The aim of this education was to strengthen the soul[2] of the young in order to overcome the temptations of commerce, wealth and power. It is this educational paradigm—educationalizing social problems—that successfully and enduringly promised to safeguard the modern world against possible dangers of modernity. Henceforth, and continuing up to today, ideas of progress and concepts of education have been closely connected (Tröhler 2006a, 2008).

To make the soul accessible to education, childhood as a more or less independent stage of human life had to be constructed, and it is no surprise that it was a Swiss Protestant man deeply embedded in classical republicanism—Rousseau—who presented this concept to the public in wonderful and passionately and seductively written novels (Tröhler 2012). The quality and success of Rousseau's novels can be deduced from the fact that the educational concept was adopted beyond the ideological limits from which they had emerged. The German Lutheran readers in particular—the German 'philanthropinists' in education[3] had all studied Lutheran theology—believed to have discovered the solution to their contest with the changing world. However, whereas the Reformed Protestants (Swiss Protestantism) believed that this kind of education was able to strengthen the soul to secure progress against its very own hazards, the Lutherans professed to have found a solution against the concrete world altogether. It is in this context that shortly after the philanthropinists' heyday (1770-1790), which ended definitively with the perception of a disastrous French Revolution (that is, even before the *terreur* from June 1793 to June 1794), that the idea of Lutheran inwardness was emphasized even more and radicalized to become the ideology of *Bildung*, an emerging educational notion pointing to the vision of an inner harmonious totality beyond the world (Horlacher 2004; Tröhler 2011d).

The overall and fundamental cultural importance that was attributed to education towards the end of the eighteenth century—the educationalized world—triggered two different but programmatically connected developments. One development was a process in which education had to be grasped intellectually, that is, theoretically clarified. This theoretical clarification included a system of statements that explain education as a distinct social and cultural practice to plan the future and to formulate recommendations for educational practices. However, the starting position of this theorizing process was by no means what might be constructed nowadays as empirical practice; it was instead a merger of idealism and practice: The real had to be ideal, a perception that mirrored the dawn of German idealism. Accordingly, in the process of formulating an educational theory, it was not empirical practices that were at issue but crucial concepts (*Begriffe*). If—and this was the basic idea—education is a practice of its own (and around 1800 there was no doubt anymore that it was a practice of its own, and one on which the future as a whole depended), it had to have central concepts (*Begriffe*) that would form a theoretical frame of education in which the soul of the child was the centre. The particular perceptions of the soul in relation to the empirical world—indebted to denominational preferences—and the semantic of the central terms functioned as a grid of what became an educational theory, and the construction of this grid proved to be extremely sustainable.

In this chapter I will first reconstruct how (the perception of) the soul became crucial in formulating theories of education, and I will hint at different educational theories resulting from different perceptions of the soul. In another section, I address how educational theories were legitimized and formulated and in a third section I look at how the aspiration of educational theories was universalized. In a final, larger section, I examine how these educational theories dealt with practices, and in a short outlook I reflect on the condition of educational theory.

The perceptions of the soul and its relation to the world: Germany and Switzerland

The French Revolution and its consequences were decisive for the development of an explicit educational theory in Germany. The movement of the German 'philanthropinists' in education (around 1770-1790) came to an end when the exponents of this movement started to realize that their political prerequisite—the power structure of the state as not being at issue—was untenable after the French Revolution (Trapp 1792: 6) and that there was a realm called the 'public' that was not identical with the state: 'The state must not see itself as a society for the promotion of the common best', the philanthropinist Trapp wrote, 'but within the state many things have to be done for the promotion of the common best'. That is to say, the promotion of the common good was not a task of the state but of the 'public': Public schooling, for instance, was open to anybody interested in learning what was being taught at school (Trapp 1792: 4). With regard to this kind of 'general useful' education, Trapp continues, the state may have 'no influence' (Trapp 1792: 5, freely translated here).

In the very same year, 1792, Wilhelm von Humboldt, then 25 years old, published a series of articles in several journals, including 'What Should be the Limits of the Government's Concern for the Well Being of its Citizens?' that much later jointly appeared under the title *Versuch die Grenzen der Wirksamkeit des Staates zu bestimmen* (*The Spheres and Duties of Government*) (Humboldt 1854). In this typical German response to the French Revolution—Humboldt had visited Paris together with this former private tutor, the philanthropinist Campe, during the Revolution in 1789—Humboldt limited the power of the state in order to emphasize the 'cosmopolitical' 'true end of men': 'The true end of Man, or that which is prescribed by the eternal and immutable dictates of reason,...is the highest and most harmonious development [*Bildung*] of his powers to a complete and consistent whole. Freedom is the grand and indispensable condition' (Humboldt 1792/1864: 64), whereas *Bildung* is understood as inward transformation of the soul to a harmonious whole. A year later, in 1793, Humboldt argued that all activities of human beings are directed by the purpose to give themselves 'value and duration'. Precisely and only because the 'pure form' of the soul, the 'pure idea', needs material to practice, the human being needs a 'world outside of himself' in order to form himself. The only aim of encountering the world is his 'inward improvement and purification' (Humboldt 1793/1960: 235, freely translated here).

This decidedly inward turn of the German intelligentsia in 1792/1793 found an echo with Pestalozzi in Switzerland but with some important nuances. In his analysis of the French Revolution and the *terreur*, Pestalozzi concluded that political freedom could only be enjoyed if every single person had a 'longing for inward purification of himself' (Pestalozzi 1793/1931: 163, freely translated here). The similarities with the German discussion are obvious, but there are important differences. Pestalozzi does not ask primarily for the limited role of the state (freedom) with regard to the inward purification but rather for the role of the inward purification for the benefit of political freedom. True freedom, Pestalozzi concludes, is not the political right to do whatever one wants to do as long as it is not explicitly forbidden by law—this would be a classical liberal idea that may be applied (to some degree) to Trapp or Humboldt. According to Pestalozzi, true freedom is 'a formed force of the citizen to do what makes him happy and to prevent what makes him unhappy as a citizen' (Pestalozzi 1793/1931: 149, freely translated here). In accordance with the Swiss Reformation, Pestalozzi's ideal is the happy citizen in his country, whereas the German (Lutheran) ideal is the fulfilled human being living in a (any) country.

A year later, in 1794, after the end of the *terreur*, Pestalozzi (1794/1931) concludes with regard to the *sans-culottes* in the French Revolution: 'Sans-Culottism, in the political sense, is heresy, for human being as citizens must not "let loose" [question the true principle of it] when it comes to property rights'. Any desire to obtain a neighbor's property must be combated by the public authorities, and the very sources of these desires to obtain a neighbor's property have to be distracted by public education. However, Pestalozzi adds, within the civic realm there is something like a moral 'let loose'—questioning the true principle of it—and that is with regard to one's own property (and only then): One may renounce the right of property if it is one's own property, and this 'let loose' or renouncing ennobles or purifies humans in their interior. With regards to *his own* property a person may subordinate his rights to love for others, which is 'undoubtedly the spirit of Christianity': We may never take what is not ours, but we may always give what is ours. In other words: 'The first Christians lived obviously in a form of moral Sans-Culottism, that is, they gave what the political Sans-Culottism steals—they let themselves be killed; the political Sans-Culottism kills others' (Pestalozzi 1794/1931: 266, freely translated here). The social state of life depends on just laws, but because these laws are not sufficient to guarantee a happy life; the social state of life depends also on the moral ennoblement of the people wanting to be good citizens of the state.

The difference between Switzerland and Germany is not obvious at first sight,[4] but it is relevant, as can be seen in one of the most important publications with regard to Protestantism toward the end of the eighteenth century. It was written in 1799 by Friedrich Ernst Daniel Schleiermacher, a Lutheran minister who was himself son of a Lutheran minister and army preacher, and who later became president of the new university in Berlin (designed by Humboldt). In *Über die Religion: Reden an die Gebildeten unter ihren Verächtern* (*On Religion: Speeches to Its Cultured Despisers*) (Schleiermacher 1799), Schleiermacher emphasized that religion means contemplation in the universe, (allegedly) free from metaphysics and from morality. This universe is found in the interior of the human being, and only a 'toilsome way into the depths of man's spirit' (Schleiermacher 1799/1893: 12) leads the individual to his interior ('his inmost emotions'). Religion was developed as a 'sense and taste for the Infinite' (Schleiermacher 1799/1893: 278), guiding practice as art and speculation as science. Every particular element of the world is part of a sacred universal whole that can be estimated by the educated soul (*Bildung*). The universal totality is recognizable by the inward totality of the soul of the individual, and religion is the key to the mutual connection: 'It is neither thinking nor acting, but intuition [*Anschauung*] and feeling [*Gefühl*]. It will regard the Universe as it is' (Schleiermacher 1799/1893: 277).[5]

Whereas in the Swiss case Pestalozzi asked for inward purification of the citizen to realize the 'happy' and virtuous republic and while he oriented the educational idea of intuition (or 'sense-impressions'; Pestalozzi 1801/1894: 33) (*Anschauung*) to textbooks designed along the line of the (allegedly) eternal process of human development, the German colleagues reduced the influence of the state in order to realize the divinely designed analogy of the inward wholeness and universal wholeness by intuition (*Anschauung*) of the totality of the world or the divine Universe.[6] This conception of an inwardly backed-up universal wholeness and cosmopolitanism became transformed after the defeat of the Prussian troops against Napoleon in 1806; Schleiermacher's revision of his 1799 publication *On Religion: Speeches to its Cultured Despisers* (in 1806) was much more national: The inward purification became more and more related to the (idea of the) German nation. In 1808, German idealist Johann Gottlieb Fichte[7] spoke accordingly in his famous *Addresses to the German Nation* (Fichte 2008): He proclaimed the need for a 'complete reform of the current educational system as the only means of preserving the existence of the German nation' (Fichte 2008: 17). This education was to consist of a spiritual-intellectual (*geistig*) part and an emotional part.

In the spiritual-intellectual part of Fichte's education, young men were to be led to recognize the archetype of a good life, and in the emotional part they were to gain strength to implement this archetype in real life (Fichte 2008: 21ff.). The archetype is not empirical but metaphysical: 'Thus, at its very commencement this education gives rise to a knowledge that truly surpasses all experience, that is supersensuous, strictly necessary and general, that embraces in advance all subsequently possible experience' (Fichte 2008: 28). Whereas the old and bad education had to motivate the young to learn by promising 'that this knowledge would be useful in the future', true education does not want to be the 'servant of one's sensuous wellbeing', for this would produce immoral people (Fichte 2008: 29). Fichte was ideologically supplemented by Humboldt, the founder of the University of Berlin (*Alma Mater Berolinensis*), in 1809, one year after Fichte's *Addresses*:

> All the schools in the hand of the nation or the state have to aim at a general education for mankind (*allgemeine Menschenbildung*). Whatever the needs of a concrete life, or of a concrete trade, they have to be separated and be taught after the fulfillment of general education. If both are mixed up, we will end up with neither of them, neither complete humans nor complete citizens in their social classes.
>
> (Humboldt 1809/1964: 188, freely translated here)

Educational theory as theory of the art of education

Shortly after 1790, a universal cosmopolitanism maneuvered the educational turn of German Protestantism, and some 15 years later it was the (transcended idea of the) German nation that stood behind the educational endeavors to renew the cultural identity in a world that had become uncertain in many respects: political revolutions, industrial revolution, the steep rise of the modern sciences, natural right theories, and democracy. All of these developments were interpreted to be foreign to the Germans, and they irritated the Germans deeply across the century. One hundred years later Thomas Mann, the famous Nobel Prize winner, would express it this way in *Reflections of an Unpolitical Man*:

> The political spirit, anti-German as spirit, is necessarily Germanophobic as politics...Democracy, politics itself is foreign and poison to the German essence...I confess myself deeply convinced that the German people never will love political democracy, for the simple reason that the ill-reputed authoritarian state is the proper state for the German people.
>
> (Mann 1918/1983: 22, freely translated here)

'Germanness', Mann concluded, 'is culture, soul, freedom, art, and *not* civilization, society, vote, literature'. Germanness is 'spirit (*Geist*), not politics; the former is cosmopolitan, the latter international'. However, the true citizen 'is cosmopolitan, *because* he is German' (Mann 1918/1983: 23).

The immense German expectations towards education around 1800—universal cosmopolitan salvation in a changing world—led almost 'naturally' to the development of educational theories designed to direct educational practice. The concerned German reformers in mass education, who were almost all of them either sons of Lutheran ministers or themselves Lutheran ministers, had agreed that the immensely important (in their eyes) practice or 'art of education' needed guidance, called a 'theory of education'. Christian Weiss, German philosopher and son of a Lutheran minister, noted explicitly in 1803 that the 'noble art of education' needed to be conducted with prudence and therefore treated academically (*wissenschaftlich*). The art of education and theory of education were defined as follows:

> I call art in the larger sense the skill to treat a given according to its purpose, or to depict the idea of an object; [and I call] academic, also in the larger sense, the systematic knowledge of the laws of this art, or, which is the same, the art when it is completely understood.
>
> (Weiss 1803: 8, freely translated here)

In the same year, 1803, Immanuel Kant's lectures on education (Kant 1803/2003) were published by Friedrich Theodor Rink, Lutheran doctor of theology and head pastor of Trinity Church in Danzig. In accordance with the idealistic conception of an educational theory, Kant—deeply embedded in German pietism—said that a "theory of education" had to be:

> ...a glorious ideal, and it matters little if we are not able to realise it at once. Only we must not look upon the idea as chimerical, nor decry it as a beautiful dream, notwithstanding the difficulties that stand in the way of its realization. An idea is nothing else than the conception of a perfection which has not yet been experienced.
>
> (Kant, 1803/2003: 8)

The German intelligentsia agreed that in order to create this *Erziehungswissenschaft*—the academic rationalization or the theorization of the art of education—one needs simply to develop the central terms of the art of education systematically (Weiss 1803: 8), which results in the theory of education.

This idea or procedure of developing an educational theory was used in 1806 by the German philosopher Johann Friedrich Herbart, who in *Allgemeine Pädagogik* (Herbart, 1806) on a generalized educational theory started from the assumption that the educational field is largely independent of any other contexts. This idea of 'educational autonomy' would prove to be a successful ideological prerequisite in formulating all educational theories in Germany up to today; the most prominent of the recent advocators was Heinz-Elmar Tenorth in 2004 (Tenorth 2004). Herbart's ambition in *Allgemeine Pädagogik* was systematic clarification of the 'indigenous terms' in the educational realm (Herbart 1806: 13). According to Herbart, education as a theory has two parts. One is the elaboration of the general idea, an 'ideological' map, that tells the educator *what* to do; the second part, psychology, explains the possibility of education and the limitations of real circumstances in a theoretical way, or *how* to do (Herbart 1806: 16). *Allgemeine Pädagogik* published in 1806 covered the first, general part; Herbart's 1841 *Umriss pädagogischer Vorlesungen* (*Outlines of Educational Doctrine,* Herbart 1901) dealt with psychology. In the later work Herbart stated that the central concept of the educational theory (*pädagogik*) is *bildsamkeit* (formability, educationability) and that education as academic theory had two dependencies, namely, 'practical philosophy and psychology'—the *what* and *how* to do (Herbart 1841/1902: 69). Whereas practical philosophy aims at virtue understood as the permanently realized idea of 'inward freedom' (Herbart 1841/1902: 71), psychology is outlined as early developmental and cognition psychology (Herbart's formal phases), according to which the teaching of school subjects had to be designed: preparation, presentation, association, generalization, and application. Combined with the appropriate arrangement of the school subjects—the curriculum—the student would be enabled to understand the total unity of the universe and to build a harmonious analogy between being educated (*gebildet*) and the totality of the world.

In the German-speaking part of Europe[8] of the first half of the nineteenth century, we find three somewhat dominant educational theories that may have been understood as consecutive models, although they all claimed to be far-reaching or even universal.[9] Whereas Pestalozzi was interpreted to have laid the basis of elementary education for children up to the first school years, Herbart was regarded to have founded the formal organization of learning during elementary and secondary schools, and Humboldt was seen as having designed higher education. However, their aspirations were quite different. Pestalozzi aimed at harmonious development of the intellectual, physical and (religious) moral or emotional 'forces' under the leadership of the latter, guaranteeing a socially responsible person characterized by public virtues. Herbart and Humboldt aimed less at public-relevant virtues than at 'inward freedom' (Herbart) or 'inward *Bildung*' (Humboldt) facing the total universe rather than a clear sphere of life, Herbart focusing in his 'rational' approach more on knowledge than Humboldt in his 'neo-humanistic' approach. However, all three formulated their theories of education as prescriptions or instructions on how to deal with the potentiality of the human soul and mind in a changing world.

Universal theory

For a long time the intellectuals had come to formulate not only a theory of education with universal claims but even more so a universally acceptable theory of education. The different value systems across the denominations and the multiple cultures and nations had triggered doubt that educational theory should follow a specific political philosophy or philosophical ethics. At the same time, as these doubts grew, a new academic discipline emerged that suggested a way out of the *aporia*, and it is no surprise that the science of the soul— psychology—seemed to provide the light.[10] Hardly anyone concerned with education had doubted that the human soul was key in both aspects of the educational endeavors, in the process and in the goal. The first results of the aspiring psychology were immediately 'educationalized'—that is, made useful in the efforts to formulate a universal theory of education.

Psychology as an academic discipline was developed almost exclusively by sons of Protestant ministers of different denominations. In addition (or in competition) to traditional theology, psychology began more and more to represent the academic tool for understanding the soul, which had become the object of education back in the eighteenth century. It was only a question of time until education was to be based mainly on psychology. Pragmatism was one of these educational theories that struggled with the theological origins of their understating of the soul and their idea of congregation (Tröhler 2011b). In Germany it was Wilhelm Dilthey, son of a German Calvinist minister, who first developed educational theory based on an understanding of the soul that was different to that of the Pragmatists. In an exemplary way, Dilthey demonstrates how psychology had become the lynchpin of an academic educational theory with a universal claim. There was no underlying political philosophy leading Dilthey's considerations nor was there a system of philosophy; instead, Dilthey's assumption was of a soul that had its end in itself (Tröhler 2011c).

According to the German dualistic tradition, Dilthey's philosophy not only separated the human soul from the outer world but also virtually opposed it to the outer world. German education was focused on this inner world, which Dilthey called *Seelenleben*, or inner (or spiritual) life, and much less on ('mere') knowledge. Some years later, Dilthey's disciples would attack Herbartianism with its focus on 'mechanically' structuring the learning of knowledge. In 'Über die Möglichkeit einer allgemeingültigen pädagogischen Wissenschaft' [Feasibility of a universally valid educational science] published in 1888 (Dilthey 1888/1962), Dilthey distinguished three different faculties of the human soul that were identified as the target of educational intervention. These faculties were: perception, the emotional transformation of perception, and the will to act (Dilthey, 1888/1962: 63f.). The three faculties are interconnected to characterize human *Seelenleben* as a psychological process. In accordance with the simple stimulus-response psychology that had been promoted by Wilhelm Wundt and his forerunners Ernst Heinrich Weber and Gustav Theodor Fechner (all three of them sons of Lutheran ministers), Dilthey locates at the beginning of the psychological process impulses that stimulate the soul, and at the end of the process, the human will to act. However, in contrast to Wundt, Weber and Fechner's rather simple stimulus-response model, Dilthey advocates a kind of a black box between the first and the last step. According to Dilthey, in this black box impulses are transformed into emotions, which will eventually constitute the individual's determination to act. By virtue of this black box, the psychological process is not mechanical, and the appropriate research method is therefore not experimental but spiritual (*geistig*); it is 'hermeneutics'.[11] The three faculties are not static either, for they strive for development. This development is characterized by a twofold teleology. First, the faculties are designed to perfect themselves, and second, they can become perfect only in mutual calibration.[12] According to Wilhelm Dilthey, education is the tactical effort to perfect the teleological structure of these three elements of the soul (perception, transformation, will to act) *regardless* of what kind of impulses the soul is exposed to. A theory of education seeking to be granted general (or universal) validity, therefore, does not examine contents or contexts but is instead oriented towards 'formal perfection' of the constitutive elements of the soul (Dilthey 1888/1962: 69).

Even if this result of an encompassing or universal theory of education seems to be a disappointment, Dilthey's theory of education is a somewhat logical consequence of the aspirations that were formulated 100 years earlier: to find a response to a changing world by means of (the Protestant) assumption that the inward life or the soul (in Protestantism, after all, the place of salvation) had to be the place of the educational interventions, with the aim of mastering the empirical world. The educational theory had found what it was looking for, an alleged natural organism of the soul as a point of reference. If the 'outer' world was changing and was even threatening, and if the 'inward' life of a person was the solution to these challenges, and if the potential of this inward life was to be implemented by education, what else could an educational theory rely on other than building on the structures of the soul?

The delusion of a universal educational theory: *geisteswissenschaftliche Pädagogik*

Since its earliest attempts, the German endeavor to formulate an educational theory was either in opposition to the empirical world, or—similar to this—it simply ignored it: The aim was the moral character of the soul, and the educational guidance was defined by the structure of the soul. The dualism between the world and (the theory of) education shows up in concentrated form in an essay by Herman Nohl[13] in 1926. This was during the Weimar Republic, when the vast majority of the German intelligentsia mourned the loss of the empire and began to admire Italy's leader Mussolini as having universal ideas. Nohl's paper, 'Die Einheit der Pädagogischen Bewegung' [The unity of the educational movement] (Nohl 1926), is probably the shortest, most succinct summary of the *geisteswissenschaftlich* educational theory that would prove to be the most sustainable theory in Germany throughout the twentieth century.

In the essay, Nohl (1926) discusses several reform movements in education, that is, the different aspects of German progressive education and the debates on a new education law that were unleashed at a School Conference (*Reichsschulkonferenz*) of the Weimar Republic in 1920. These debates about the role of education in society in general and the ordering of the school in particular had been intensively pursued, and they unmistakably represented different views about the ideal of education and the purpose of schooling. This plurality of opinion was—for most of the German intelligentsia—unacceptable, for it juxtaposed the ideal of unity prescribed by the Divine Universe. Rather than interpret the different opinions as characteristic of democracy, Nohl strives to find a common base behind the warring parties. He does so by using the classical dualism in Lutheran Protestantism, according to which empiricism and *Geist* (mental-internal unity), plurality and unity, and outward and inward are distinguished: The juxtaposition is between 'plural, external reality' and the 'inward unity of *Geist*, or mental-internal unity'. This distinction is descriptive as well as normative, because it clearly favors the inward unity of *Geist*.

Along the line of the grid of this dualism Nohl concludes that the seemingly different positions in the debates only differ from each other on an outer, superficial level. But if one goes deeper, the picture changes: *If* these diverse educational movements represent something that is *true and alive*, Nohl argues, then there *must* be ultimate unity among them. The notion of truth that Nohl mentions refers to the idea of truth in German philosophy at the time; it is idealistic, national and non-empirical, and it stands in explicit contrast to the pragmatic idea of knowledge as dependent upon experience. The contemporary conception of life (*Leben*) that was common by 1900 was also not empirical, as in modern science, but instead expressed the notion of the mystic-holistic experience of life, which Dilthey, Nohl's teacher, had contrasted against the natural sciences. The unity that Nohl (1926) proposes to discern in the diverse reform movements from 1900 onwards is the 'unity of a new ideal of the German man' (Nohl 1926: 58, freely translated here). This not only homogenizes the multifarious forms of progressive education but also narrows them down nationally. Nohl thus trims and cuts progressive education to allow it to be utilized for the development of a national doctrine of *geisteswissenschaftliche Pädagogik*.

In the late 1920s Nohl started a project to publish a handbook on education (*Handbuch der Pädagogik*); it was published in five volumes between 1928 and 1933. The last volume to be published was designed as the first volume, and it was dedicated to 'the theory and development of the education system' (*Theorie und Entwicklung des Bildungswesens*). The first lemma, 'Theory of Education' (*Bildung*), was written by Nohl himself. It starts out with the question of a universally valid theory in education. Nohl argues that, at least so far, there are three reasons why no educational theory of universal validity has been formulated. The theories have been dependent on different ideologies (*Weltanschauungen*), according to which the art of education is seen either as a technical-causal art in the sense of the natural sciences, as ethical art based on ethics or as an aesthetical art based on aesthetics. Furthermore, there had been no agreement on what Nohl calls the function of education: Is its purpose to create a gentleman, a humanist or a social person? And finally, Nohl adds with reference to Dilthey, in different historical epochs different ideals of education had been valid, but none of them could claim universality.

Dilthey's solution to maximize the individual functions of the soul is not defended by Nohl, with the argument that this system does not even know whether it produces a perfect criminal or a perfect man (Nohl 1933: 8), and Nohl refuses to rely on the 'mechanical' psychology in the sense of the natural sciences, because the human mind or spirit (*Geist*) is not accessible by a 'causal psychology' (Nohl 1926: 11) that analyzes rather than aims to understand the unity of the soul. This unity is the 'last secret of the spiritual' in which the pluralistic world finds its universal interpretation of its meaning—meaning not constructed socially but transcendentally. In other words, what has so far been offered as the starting point of a universal theory of education is invalid and the situation is an 'expanse of ruins' (Nohl 1926: 12). Nohl concludes that an educational theory had to start from somewhere else, from an undisputable point of reference, namely, from 'the fact of the educational reality (*Erziehungswirklichkeit*) as a meaningful whole' (Nohl 1926: 12) with its procedures and institutions and rules that are (ideally) governed 'by an idea of its own'.

The educational theory has to orient itself to the structures of the spiritual existence of the soul with its twofold structure, a horizontal and a vertical structure. The horizontal structure has three layers, whereby Nohl follows Plato. Each of these layers—the body, the *Thymos* (emotions, desire, mental energy) and the *Nous* (higher intellectual sense)—has its needs for an education of its own, but the layers must be set in a hierarchical order, with the upper layer, the *Nous*, as the dominant layer. This horizontal structure is owed to Dilthey and depicts three elements: impression, inward transition and reaction. The conceptual link between the two different structures of the soul describes the foundation of the educational theory: Any psychological process (impression, transition, reaction) is an educational process, if it serves the individual layers in their hierarchical order of the human soul (Nohl 1933: 44ff.).

The perception of the human soul, its presumed structure, its assigned *telos* and its interrelation to the empirical and social world obviously defined the framework conditions in which educational theories were designed in the last two centuries. This phenomenon is not restricted to Germany or the German-speaking part of the world but is to be found, with some nuances, in the United States in the frame of pragmatism, in which liberal reformed Calvinism (Congregationalism, Baptism) was based on a perception of the soul that essentially depended on social interaction and cooperation. Within this framework the educational theory of pragmatism evolved, whereas in the more traditional Calvinism (Presbyterianism) and Methodism the idea of the soul was envisaged as more open for the development of cognitive psychology with its own educational theories.

The interface between theory and practice: the education of teachers

Because of the alleged necessity to formulate an educational theory as intellectual legitimation and as instruction for educational practices, the educational theories preponderantly focused on specific ideas of the soul in its adjudicated role to the empirical world. However, the organization of both the school and its related institutions as well as the education of their actors, foremost teachers, was the second consequence (after the need of formulating theories of education) of the educationalization of the social world around 1800, and the schools followed an agenda of their own between political guidelines, professional policy and by learning from their own experiments. This agenda was by nature more pragmatic than the theories of education were.

The interface between the practice of (organizing) teaching and educational theory was foremost the ideal of teacher education, for teachers were meant to implement the theoretical ideas.[14] In contrast to the English-speaking world, where issues of educational theory were foremost developed from the empirically evident necessities of teacher education, the German discourse around education theory was more an emanation of German (Protestant) idealism (see also Biesta 2011). Some philosophers of education were even themselves devoted to educate the main actors of the educational field,[15] but as a rule the organization of both—mass education and teacher education—was left to a different expertise for which theory aimed at providing the ideological guidelines. Consequently, discourse on teacher education did not focus so much on knowledge or questions of 'classroom management' as on the formation of an ideal teacher, that is, of an ideal character of the teacher. The molding of the teacher's soul was to be achieved by what could be called an early form of 'best practice', and 'best practice' was to be found in the big heroes of education who were described in the genre 'history of education' that was developed foremost in Germany after 1871, copied in France 10 years later and disseminated in the Western world by the end of the nineteenth century.

By the last third of the nineteenth century it was a foregone conclusion that teacher education needed knowledge about the 'chief authorities' in education, as the British school reformer Robert Herbert Quick said in 1868; stating regrettably that pertinent books in history of education were written in German: 'I have found that on the history of Education, not only good books but all books are written in German, or some other foreign language' (Quick 1868/74: iiif). At this time professionalization had become organized moralization, most of all nationalistic moralization. The pertinent textbooks on the history of education were written to mold the character of the prospective teachers by providing morally valuable examples that were nationalistically focused—a symptomatic combination at a time when one's own nation had become sacred. The formal structures of these national textbooks were all strikingly similar, for they represented the very same ideology about national progress and the values of the nationally-minded teachers within this endeavor. But the characters in these heroic histories altered dramatically according to the national provenance of the authors of the textbooks (Tröhler 2006). These national distinctions became apparent not only with their nationally different heroes but also with the notion describing the aim of higher education.

In Germany, the aim was the *Persönlichkeit*, the (untranslatable concept) inwardly strong personality. *Persönlichkeit* was not a global but rather a national aim of education. An impressive testimonial of this ideology became apparent when William James compared the English and German universities in his essay *Talks to Teachers* (James 1899/2001). As James wrote, whereas the German university focused almost exclusively on scientific progress, the English university tended 'to teach an Englishman how to be an Englishman' (James 1899/2001: 16). In an (unrequested) response, the German philosopher Günther Jacoby wrote:

> The German university does not make it its task to teach a German *Herr* how to *behave* as a German *Herr*. In our tradition, that is exclusively a matter for the nursery. In contrast, the German university, to an outstanding extent, makes it its task to educate the German student to become a *Persönlichkeit*—a fact that William James, of course, does not take into account but that is nonetheless important and true. England is the land of gentlemen; Germany is the land of *Persönlichkeiten*. Gentleman and *Persönlichkeit*, however, stand essentially in hostile opposition to one another. This does not at all mean that a gentleman cannot have something *Persönliches* about him or that a *Persönlichkeit* cannot be a gentleman. But the ideal of the gentlemen clashes with the ideal of the *Persönlichkeit*, and the ideal of the *Persönlichkeit* clashes with the ideal of the gentleman.
>
> (Jacoby 1912: 217, freely translated here)

Indeed, two years later, the contradictory European ideals clashed with traumatic effect until 1945. However, this did not alter the deep faith in education. On the contrary, after the Second World War the turn to education became more popular than ever before, especially against the background of the challenges of the Cold War (Tröhler 2010, 2011e.). It was in this context that education became an academic discipline, although it was never clear what the basis of this discipline was meant to be. In Germany, *geisteswissenschaftliche Pädagogik* rose from the dead as if nothing had happened in between, and the pronounced empirical turn following Heinrich Roth's inaugural lecture at the University of Göttingen in 1962, 'Die realistische Wendung in der pädagogischen Forschung' [The realistic turn in educational research] (Roth 1962), had little effect for a long time. The alleged enemies of *geisteswissenschaftliche Pädagogik* were not the empiricists but the neo-Marxists clustered around the notion of 'critical education' (Herwig Blankertz, Andreas Gruschka, Wolfgang Klafki, Klaus Mollenhauer), who derived their theoretical assumptions from their study of the advocates of 'critical theory' (Theodor W. Adorno, Max Horkheimer, Jürgen Habermas) and who aimed via the method of critique of ideology (that was assigned only to the others) for self-determination of every individual. It is here that the traditional idea of *Bildung* had a new renaissance as educational theory (Horlacher 2012). It is only with the supranational organizations such as the OECD that the leitmotivs have changed on the basis of a 'cognitive revolution' in the education of professional educators, eliminating the sacred cow of educational history in teacher education by promoting an ahistorical and fundamentally decontextualized educational ideology (Rohstock and Tröhler in press).

Outlook

Educational theories as a response to the Protestant idea of educationalizing the social world have traditionally been developed along the line of denominational idiosyncrasies, with their pertinent ideas on the soul and their visions of ideals of social organization. Today, we do not know enough about these path dependencies, and rather than continuing to multiply discourses of salvation in the clothing of theory, we might be better advised to historicize and contextualize educational theories and to compare them across the different religions and nations. Historization means that theories are not theoretical in the sense of timeless validity, and contextualization is the attempt to understand why certain 'theories' were developed, accepted, challenged or ignored at a certain time. And making this comparison means that during similar periods of time totally different ideas or theories could be promoted, advocated or demonized. Combining these three research strategies, educational theory will address, for instance, the (later) German mandarin Eduard Spranger mocked Dewey's pragmatism as 'despicable kitchen and handyman utilitarianism' that had to be countered by the German 'theory of the ideal *Bildung*' (Spranger 1966: 37). There were different Protestant denominations and different ideals of the social life. Whereas Dewey advocated a form of social rather than political democracy, Spranger—as did most of the German intelligentsia at the time—concluded that dictatorship was the logical consequence of democracy as seen in Russia and Italy. However, Spranger (1928) supported the Italian dictatorship (Mussolini), for it had brought a 'sort of redeemer' to the head of the country, for 'whoever has the great idea of the state, the real leader (*Führer*), should govern. It is the idea that is of utmost importance' (Spranger 1928: 30).

Theory of education—if there is any—needs to emancipate itself from both the Protestant ideas of educationalizing social problems and the theories derived from Protestant interpretations of the soul and its relation to the world; or one should re-integrate education into Protestant theology. Its starting point—if there is any—is not any kind of (necessary or unnecessary) idealism but rather historical (not philosophical) emanations of educational arguments and institutions across time and space. It has to collect these cultural data in order to understand how education has been envisaged as a technology to solve alleged problems and to plan an envisaged future and to see how obstacles and systems of professional or public feedback have modified theory (less likely) or organization (more likely). Maybe by extracting and gathering modes of resistance in practices across time and space and their effect on organization and curriculum, we might find something like a grammar not of schooling but of education, which then might serve as the basis of an educational theory. Meanwhile, though, we will be busy enough deconstructing the different salvation narratives before aspiring to build a new temple with dubious components. A (new) temple of that kind would be deconstructed rather soon and will therefore not meet the claims of the (new) dogma of sustainability. This is not discouraging, and certainly not for some of the Protestants, if we follow the legend of Luther. When asked about his faith and energy when facing a possible end of the world, Luther allegedly answered: 'If I knew that tomorrow was the end of the world, I would plant an apple tree today!' It is important to know, however, that the first written evidence of this saying dates from 1944.[16]

Notes

1 I am deliberately not talking about the effects of Rousseau (*Wirkungsgeschichte*) and not even about the readings of Rousseau (*Rezeptionsgeschichte*), but of Rousseau as the 'right man' in the 'right place' at the 'right time'.

2 The identification of the soul as the main target in education (and policy in general) towards the end of the eighteenth century was also emphasized by Michel Foucault in *Discipline and Punish: The Birth of the Prison* (Foucault 1977). By neglecting Scottish, Swiss and German sources Foucault restricts his interpretation mainly to the French discussions and comes to somewhat different conclusions, especially with regard to the arising educational theories after 1800, which in France was dominated after 1816 for a few years by what is called Bell-Lancaster method (see Nique 1990). Nevertheless, Foucault acknowledges that the soul had become the crucial element of governing or planning the people (Popkewitz 2008).

3 Johann Bernhard Basedow (1724-1790), Christian Gotthilf Salzmann (1744-1811), Ernst Christian Trapp (1745-1818), Joachim Heinrich Campe (1746-1818).

4 The difference becomes even more evident when the 'travelling libraries' (Marc Depaepe) are examined. The reading of Shaftesbury's philosophy helped the Germans to develop their inward theory of *Bildung*, whereas the same texts had a completely different, much more political reading in Switzerland (see Horlacher 2004).

5 *Anschauung*—literally: the looking at [something]— is a core concept in the educational discussion of the time. In the traditional dualistic Lutheran worldview it meant, on the

one side, to look at concrete objects in order to learn them not only by description or definition but with the sensual aid of the eyes. On the other side, it indicated an 'inner eye' looking at the infinite and divine Universe, the merger of the individual's soul and God. The result of the former is 'only' knowledge; the result of the latter is *Bildung*.

6 In the tradition of Swiss Reformation Pestalozzi presents a different solution towards *Anschauung* than the Lutherans. Organizing the educational experience of the child along the lines of its own natural development means starting from external objects and ending with morality. With that Pestalozzi still represents a certain Protestant dualism between the inner and the outer world, but he sees an evolutionary line between the two, also, a line that can be realized by a 'natural' education under the condition that the learning materials are composed along the line of the child's development. 'All instruction of man is then only the Art of helping Nature to develop in her own way; and this Art rests essentially on the relation and harmony between the impressions received by the child and the exact degree of his developed powers' (Pestalozzi 1801/1894:26).

7 Johann Gottlieb Fichte would become the first elected president of the newly founded *Alma Mater Berolinensis* (today: Humboldt University of Berlin) in 1811/1812, Schleiermacher the fifth (1815/1816).

8 In the French, Spanish and English-speaking parts of Europe we find for one or two decades another successful educational technology rather lacking of theoretical foundations, the 'monitorial system' developed independently by Joseph Lancaster and Andrew Bell. It is the one that Foucault (see endnote 2) relied on in his analysis of the rise of educational institutions.

9 Pestalozzi remained the hero of public education of mass schooling throughout the nineteenth century in the whole Western world, Herbart was popular in Germany and, at the end of the nineteenth century in the United States (where in 1895 the National Herbart Society was founded that in 1901 was converted to the National Society for the Study of Education with prominent members such as John Dewey or Nicholas Murray Butler), and Humboldt has remained, up to today, the epitome of a free research university almost all over the world.

10 In some sense, ever since the rise of psychology as an academic discipline in Germany in the last third of the nineteenth century, there has been a struggle for domination concerning 'how to explore the soul'. The traditional way was the philosophical-hermeneutic interpretation of the soul as not-measurable essence, and the new way was to conduct experiments in order to detect the formal procedures of *logos* of the *psyche*. This debate led to the foundation of the GEBF in 2012 (*Gesellschaft für Empirische Bildungsforschung*), as an alternative (or competition) to the major DGFE (*Deutsche Gesellschaft für Erziehungswissenschaft*) [GERA, German Research Association].

11 Dilthey developed his theory of hermeneutics as a method to understand the spiritual (*geistig*) processes as a further development of the hermeneutical elaborations by Friedrich Daniel Ernst Schleiermacher, who had constructed the art of understanding from the metaphysical assumption that every writer and every reader is (also) part of a non-individual, transcendent spiritual (*geistig*) world that is being developed in world history. Both attempts, Schleiermacher's and Dilthey's, remained unfinished.

12 The teleological character of the soul corresponds to four dimensions of human life: (a) preservation and (b) progression of individual existence, and (c) preservation and (d) progression of humankind (see Dilthey 1888/1962: 63).

13 Herman Nohl was born into a family with either Lutheran ministers or teacher training college teachers, and he studied with Wilhelm Dilthey in Berlin.

14 This holds true especially for the time before the Cold War. There had been some curricular interventions such as the propaganda for local studies (*Heimatkunde*) in the realm of the *geisteswissenschaftliche Pädagogik* (Spranger 1923) or of arts and craft within pragmatism (Dewey, 1899), but the systematic penetration of the school curriculum

from particular educational theories became a central issue only after the Great War (Tyler 1949; OECD *et al.* 1966; Robinsohn 1967).

15 Herbart, for example, had a sort of seminary in his private house in Königsberg, where he took over Kant's chair of philosophy at the university in 1808.

16 See http://www.luther.de/en/baeume.html (Accessed 12 November 2012).

References

Biesta, G. (2011) 'Disciplines and theory in the academic study of education: a comparative analysis of the Anglo-American and Continental construction of the field', *Pedagogy, Culture and Society,* 19:175–92.

Dilthey, W. (1888/1962) 'Über die Möglichkeit einer allgemeingültigen pädagogischen Wissenschaft', in *Wilhelm Dilthey: Gesammelte Schriften, VI. Band,* Göttingen: Vandenhoeck and Ruprecht.

Fichte, J. G. (2008) *Addresses to the German Nation,* Cambridge, UK: Cambridge University Press. (Original work published in German 1808)

Foucault, M. (1977) *Discipline and Punish: The Birth of the Prison,* New York: Pantheon Books. (Original work published in French 1975).

Herbart, J. F. (1806) *Allgemeine Pädagogik,* Göttingen: Johann Friedrich Röwer.

——(1901) *Outlines of Educational Doctrine,* New York: The Macmillan Company (Original work published in German 1841)

Hirschman, A. O. (1977) *The Passions and the Interests: Political Arguments for Capitalism Before Its Triumph,* Princeton: Princeton University Press.

Horlacher, R. (2004) '*Bildung* – a construction of a history of philosophy of education', *Studies in Philosophy and Education,* 23:409—26.

——(2012) 'What is *Bildung*? Or: Why *Pädagogik* cannot get away from the concept of *Bildung*', in P. Siljander, A. Kivelä, and A. Sutinen (eds), *Theories of* Bildung *and Growth: Connections and Controversies Between Continental Educational Thinking and American Pragmatism,* Rotterdam: Sense Publishers.

Humboldt, W. (1854) *The Sphere and Duties of Government,* London: John Chapman. (Original work written in German 1792, published 1851)

——(1960) 'Theorie der Bildung des Menschen' in W. von Humboldt, *Werke in fünf Bänden, Band I* (pp. 234–40), Darmstadt: Wissenschaftliche Buchgesellschaft. (Original work written in German 1793)

——(1964) 'Der Königsberger und der Litauische Schulplan', In W. von Humboldt, *Werke in fünf Bänden. Band IV* (pp. 168–95), Darmstadt: Wissenschaftliche Buchgesellschaft. (Original work written 1809)

Jacoby, G. (1912) 'William James und das deutsche Geistesleben', *Die Grenzboten. Zeitschrift für Politik, Literatur und Kunst,* 71:212—20.

James, W. (1899/2001) *Talks to Teachers on Psychology and to Students on Some of Life's Ideals,* Mineola: Dover Publications.

Kant, I. (2003) *On Education,* Mineola: Dover Publications. (Original work published in German 1803)

Mann, T. (1983) *Betrachtungen eines Unpolitischen,* Frankfurt: Fischer Verlag. (First published 1918)

Mercier, R. (1961) *L'enfant dans la société du XVIIIe siècle (Avant l'Émile),* Dakar: Université de Dakar.

Nique, C. (1990) *Comment l'école devint une affaire d'état,* Paris: Nathan.

Nohl, H. (1926) 'Die Einheit der pädagogischen Bewegung', *Die Erziehung,* 1: 57-61.

Nohl, H. (1933) 'Theorie der Bildung', in H. Nohl and L. Pallat (eds), *Handbuch der Pädagogik, vol I,* Langansalza: Beltz.

OECD, Stoke, H. W., Löwbeer, H., and Capelle, J. (1966). *Modernizing Our Schools: Curriculum Improvement and Educational Development,* Paris: OECD Publishing.

Pestalozzi, J. H. (1894) *How Gertrude Teaches Her Children: An Attempt to Help Mothers Teach their Children,* London: Swann Sonnenschein. (Original work published in German 1801)

——(1931) 'Ja oder Nein? Aüsserungen über die bürgerliche Stimmung der euro-peischen Menschheit in den oberen und unteren Stenden, von einem freyen Man', in *Pestalozzis Sämtliche Werke, Band X,* Berlin: De Gruyter. (Written in 1793)

——(1931) 'Über Sansculottismus und Christentum', in *Pestalozzis Sämtliche Werke, Band X,* Berlin: De Gruyter. (Written in 1794).

Pocock, J. G. A. (1985) 'The mobility of property and the rise of eighteenth-century sociology', in J. G. A. Pocock (ed), *Virtue, Commerce, and History: Essays on Political Thought and History, Chiefly in the Eighteenth Century,* New York: Cambridge University Press.

Popkewitz, T. (2008) *Cosmopolitanism and the Age of School Reform: Science, Education, and Making Society by Making the Child,* New York: Routledge.

Quick, R. H. (1874) *Essays on Educational Reformers,* Cincinnati: Robert Clarke and Co. (First published London 1868).

Robinsohn, S. B. (1967) *Bildungsreform als Revision des Curriculum,* Neuwied: Luchterhand.

Rohstock, A. and Tröhler, D. (in press) 'From the sacred nation to the unified globe: changing leitmotifs in teacher training in the Western world, 1870-2010', in R. Bruno-Jofré, and J. S. Johnston (eds), *Teacher Education in a Transnational World,* Toronto: University of Toronto Press.

Roth, H. (1962) 'Die realistische Wendung in der pädagogischen Forschung', *Neue Sammlung. Göttinger Blätter für Kultur und Erziehung,* 2: 481–90.

Rousseau, J.-J. (1758/1995) 'J.-J. Rousseau, Citoyen de Genève, à M. d'Alembert ...: Sur son article Genève dans ce VIIe Volume de l'Encyclopédie et particulièrement, sur le projet d'établir un théâtre de comédie en cette Ville', in S. Baud-Bovy (ed.), *Oeuvres complètes V,* Paris: Gallimard.

——(1762/1969) 'Émile ou de l'éducation', in B. Gagnebin and M. Raymond (eds), *Œeuvres complètes de Rousseau, Volume IV,* Paris: Gallimard.

Schleiermacher, F. D. E. (1799) Über die Religion: Reden an die Gebildeten unter ihren Verächtern, Berlin: Unger.

——(1806). *Über die Religion. Reden an die Gebildeten unter ihren Verächtern,* Berlin,Germany: In der Realschulbuchhandlung (2nd ed).

——(1893) *On Religion: Speeches to its Cultural Despisers,* J. Oman (trans), London: Kegan Paul, Trench, Trübner and Co. Ltd. (Original work written in German 1799)

Spranger, E. (1923) *Der Bildungswert der Heimatkunde,* Berlin: Hartmann.

——(1928). *Der deutsche Klassizismus und das Bildungsleben der Gegenwart,* Erfurt: Kurt Stenger Verlag. (First published1926)

——(1966). Letter sent to Georg Kerschensteiner on 14 March 1915, in L. Englert (ed.), *Georg Kerschensteiner [–] Eduard Spranger. Briefwechsel 1912-1931,* Munich: Oldenbourg.

Tröhler, D. (2006) 'The formation and function of histories of education in Continental teacher education curricula', *Journal of the American Association for the Advancement of Curriculum Studies,* 2. Available at: <http://www2.uwstout.edu/content/jaaacs/vol2/trohler.htm>. (Accessed 25 July 2012).

——(2006a) 'History and historiography of education. Some remarks on the utility of historical knowledge in the age of efficiency', *Encounters on Education / Encuentros sobre Educación / Rencontres sur l'Éducation,* 7: 5–24.

——(2010) 'Harmonizing the educational globe: world polity, cultural features, and the challenges to educational research', *Studies in Philosophy and Education*, 29: 7–29.

——(2011a) 'The educationalization of the modern world: progress, passion, and the Protestant promise of education', in D. Tröhler, *Languages of Education: Protestant Legacies, National Identities, and Global Aspirations*, New York: Routledge.

——(2011b) 'The 'Kingdom of God on Earth' and early Chicago pragmatism', *Educational Theory*, 56: 89–105. (Newly published in D. Tröhler (2011) *Languages of Education: Protestant Legacies, National Identities, and Global Aspirations*, New York: Routledge.)

——(2011c) 'The becoming of an educational science: the Protestant souls and psychologies', in D. Tröhler, *Languages of Education: Protestant Legacies, National Identities, and Global Aspirations*, New York: Routledge.

——(2011d) 'The German *geisteswissenschaftliche Pädagogik* and the ideology of *Bildung*', in D. Tröhler, *Languages of Education: Protestant Legacies, National Identities, and Global Aspirations*, New York: Routledge.

——(2011e) 'The global language on education policy and prospects of education research', in D. Tröhler and R. Barbu (eds), *The Future of Education Research: Education Systems in Historical, Cultural, and Sociological Perspectives*, Rotterdam: Sense Publishers.

——(2012) 'Rousseau's Emile, of the fear of passions', *Studies in Philosophy and Education*, 31: 477–89.

Tyler, R. W. (1949) *Basic Principles of Curriculum and Instruction: Syllabus for Education 360*, Chicago: University of Chicago Press.

Weiss, C. (1803) 'Über die Nothwendigkeit, die Erziehungskunst wissenschaftlich zu behandeln', *Beiträge zur Erziehungskunst, zur Vervollkommnung sowohl ihrer Grundsätze als ihrer Methode*, 1: 1–26.

Chapter 4

The changing field of educational studies and the task of theorizing education

Johannes Bellmann

Introduction

During the 1990s *Bildung* became a buzzword again in Germany, and this remains the case today. A former president raised *Bildung* to a mega-issue, while chancellor Merkel wants to turn Germany into a '*Bildung*srepublik', a republic of education. In this booming business of *Bildung* educational studies are prospering as well. And understandably enough, they set great value on running under the banner of *Bildung* too. This is why the new term *Bildungswissenschaften* is gaining centre-stage while at the same time superseding the older term of *Erziehungswissenschaft*. The notion of *Erziehungswissenschaft* (singular) usually stands for a differentiated discipline of its own, a phenomenon that some observers hold to be characteristic of the way the academic field of educational studies has usually been structured in German-speaking countries (Lochner 1969). The notion of *Bildungswissenschaften* (plural), however, stands for a heterogeneous field of various disciplines doing research on education, which comes fairly close to the way the academic field is structured in English-speaking countries (Tibble 1971; see also Biesta 2011).

Erziehungswissenschaft is now faced with the fact that it is not only characterized by a high degree of internal differentiation, but that it is only one of many *Bildungswissenschaften*. Knowledge about education is increasingly produced outside the discipline of *Erziehungswissenschaft* and, in addition to that, the knowledge produced in fields such as educational psychology or neuroscience is often found to be more reliable and useful for guiding educational reform initiatives. This renews the question as to what the distinctive contribution of *Erziehungswissenschaft* to the wider field of *Bildungswissenschaften* might be. I will argue that to deal with this question, one has to take up the task of theorizing education from a disciplinary perspective, i.e. one has to conceptually reconstruct the scientific object of *Erziehungswissenschaft*.

After addressing some indicators for the rise of *Bildungswissenschaften*, I will discuss two contrasting interpretations of this development and some open questions that are not addressed in either of these interpretations. Exposing these deficits, I will turn to the main part of my chapter, sketching what it might mean to reconceptualise education from a disciplinary perspective.

The changing field of educational studies in Germany

To begin with, I will briefly refer to some empirical evidence for changes in the field of educational studies in Germany.

Germany's major research association for educational science, the *Deutsche Gesellschaft für Erziehungswissenschaft*, has recently experienced a severe split-off, or one might say, an outsourcing, of a majority of its empirical researchers, who decided to found a new research association under the name Gesellschaft für Empirische *Bildungs*forschung[1] (Association for Empirical Educational Research).

A new term has been introduced in teacher education programmes as well. Formerly, the part of the programme that is studied next to one or more academic subjects was called *Erziehungs*wissenschaftliches Begleitstudium (Concurrent Educational Studies). Here, various disciplines were involved but *Erziehungswissenschaft* had the biggest share. When the new Bachelor-Masters system was introduced in Germany, the teacher education programmes were restructured as well and adapted to this system. In many teacher training institutions, educational psychology seized the opportunity to take greater responsibility or, if you like, greater control in these restructured teacher education programmes. And, most strikingly, a new name was introduced that served as a generic term for all disciplines involved in teacher education, namely *Bildungswissenschaften* (Terhart 2012: 25).

Interestingly enough, it is not only teacher education programmes but also Master's programmes that are increasingly to be found under the term of the interdisciplinary notion of *Bildungswissenschaften*. In the past, one could enrol in *Erziehungswissenschaft* as a discipline of its own. Now, at many universities, one enrols in *Bildungswissenschaften*, which is understood as a field study (Terhart 2012: 26).

The change of terms in the context of academic institutions comes as no surprise. Since the 1970s educational science has undergone a tremendous internal expansion. A discipline that formerly focussed on education as an intergenerational practice has evolved into a discipline that is concerned with education over the lifespan, from early childhood education to the education of the elderly. Given this development, the name of the discipline caused some discomfort, as in German the term *Erziehung* is usually associated with the upbringing of children or their moral correction, at least in a non-scientific usage. But even in the scientific discourse the term *Erziehung* is now only rarely used as a generic term for any form of interaction between teaching and learning. This is why some scholars proposed it was time for a change of the discipline's name from *Erziehungswissenschaft* to *Bildungswissenschaft* (Liebau 2002).

My last piece of evidence for changes in the academic field of educational studies is the fact that new players have surfaced in the field. In recent times, prominent exponents of neuroscience have written bestsellers on *Bildung*, one of them being a volume entitled *Bildung Braucht Persönlichkeit: Wie Lernen Gelingt* (Bildung *Needs Personality: How learning succeeds*) (Roth 2011). Another is entitled *Medizin für die Bildung: Ein Weg aus der Krise* (*Medicine for* Bildung*: A way out of the Crisis*) (Spitzer 2010). Notably, both neuroscientists present themselves as '*Bildungs*wissenschaftler' and as scientists who do research on 'what works' while attacking the poor quality of existing educational research. In the media, they often show up in the white coat of a physician and talk about *Bildung* and educational reform. Using the term *Bildung*, they are not only able to profit from the term's humanistic tradition (see the book Bildung *needs personality*); they are also able to address the big picture, issues where the country's future is at stake. Against this, the term *Erziehung* usually addresses issues that are much less glamorous. When talking about *Erziehung* in the public discourse, one is usually not addressing the big picture but rather the unpleasant behavioural problems of individual cases. Given this background, the name of the scientific discipline I work in has become outmoded. Thus, many scholars in my field wish they could be '*Bildungs*wissenschaftler' too.

At the present time, we cannot judge the state of affairs between *Erziehungswissenschaft* and *Bildungswissenschaften* conclusively. For some, it appears that both are arriving at some kind of peaceful coexistence, where *Erziehungswissenschaft* survives as a distinctive discipline within the wider field of *Bildungswissenschaften*. For others, it appears to be rather a hostile takeover, in which *Bildungswissenschaften* is not just a new generic term for a family of scientific disciplines but rather an alternative term that takes the place of the older notion of *Erziehungswissenschaft* and at the same time changes the field of educational studies altogether.

Two contrasting interpretations of the changes in the field of educational studies

In this section I will discuss two contrasting interpretations of the changes in the field of educational studies just mentioned. The first interpretation takes a decidedly critical stance towards these changes, while the second, on the whole, sympathises with this development.

The critics place the rise of the *Bildungswissenschaften* in the context of recent publications by the OECD that highlight the relevance of neuroscience for a new understanding of learning (Casale *et al.* 2010). An influential OECD report from 2002 is entitled 'Understanding the brain: Towards a new learning science' (OECD 2002). According to the critics, the term 'learning science' is part of the OECD's agenda setting to restructure the field of educational studies. This agenda has an international outreach, but at the same time is recontextualised into different cultures of educational research. So the critics claim that in the case of German-speaking countries the term 'learning science' was simply translated into '*Bildungswissenschaft*' (Casale *et al.* 2010: 50). The critics describe this as an artifice by which fundamental differences between the notion of *Bildung* and a neuropsychological understanding of learning are concealed.

In my view, this interpretation has several problems. So far I have not been able to find any evidence for the claim that 'learning science' has been translated into '*Bildung*swissenschaft'. Secondly, by interpreting the rise of *Bildungswissenschaften* as an external dictate of the OECD, one underestimates the fact that this development is also triggered by the internal expansion of *Erziehungswissenschaft* to a discipline concerned with lifelong learning, having thereby grown out of its conceptual framework. Thirdly, the critics one-sidedly emphasize the differences between the new learning science and modern theories of *Bildung*. On a deeper level, however, an important affinity between both might be discovered. I will return to this below.

Sympathisers of the term *Bildungswissenschaften* are anxious to show that it does not indicate any new development at all (Terhart 2012). Rather, the term is interpreted as the late but necessary acknowledgment of the fact that the field of educational studies has always been an interdisciplinary endeavour. These sympathisers call for a friendly coexistence amongst various *Bildungswissenschaften*, in which the discipline of *Erziehungswissenschaft* can continue to play an important role. Interestingly, we are not told what this role might be and how the distinctive contribution of *Erziehungswissenschaft* might be conceived. The sympathisers welcome the fact that academic programmes, institutes or the entire field of research are given a new name that captures the interdisciplinary nature of the field more adequately. Following this interpretation, then, the term rather indicates a process of normalisation of the German way to organize the field of educational studies and thus catch up with international conventions (Terhart 2012: 32-33).

Charming as it may be to catch up with international conventions, from my point of view this interpretation has its problems as well. Regarding the current developments as a process of normalisation and internationalization conceals that fact that a disciplinary understanding of *Erziehungswissenschaft* has never been established in the English-speaking world (Biesta 2011). Such an orientation towards international conventions would come close to giving up the tradition and its sources for theorizing education from a disciplinary perspective. Sympathisers avoid discussing this unsettling consequence. By suggesting that everything will remain unaffected, they actually try to silence the debate.

Open questions

Having sketched two competing interpretations and their pitfalls I will now turn to some open questions that neither the critics nor the sympathisers have addressed. The first open question is why a new umbrella term for the field of educational studies is needed at all. The fact of the matter is that before the new umbrella term *Bildungswissenschaften* was introduced, another umbrella term existed that was at least implicitly agreed upon: social sciences (Wulf 1983). This tacit consensus had been present since the 1970s at least when the philosophically-oriented 'Geisteswissenschaftliche Pädagogik' was no longer the leading paradigm and educational science underwent a pervasive process of modernization due to a stronger orientation towards social science. So today one might wonder why a discipline that recently learnt to be a social science is in need of a new umbrella term at all.

One explanation comes from the non-scientific environment. By renaming their academic programmes, institutes and universities try to profit from the booming business of *Bildung*. Studying or doing research in a field labelled 'learning sciences' might be much more attractive than in a field labelled 'social science'. A more profound explanation, however, would claim that it is not just about an exchange of terms. The fact is that within educational science, those fields of research that are not prepared to be readily subsumed under the category of social sciences, like educational psychology, became more important. Furthermore, *Bildung* has become an issue that is increasingly treated in research fields outside the discipline of educational science as well, among which neuroscience is much noticed. This means that *Bildungswissenschaften* as a new umbrella term is needed because the emergent fields within educational studies, such as educational psychology and neuroscience, regard themselves as sciences in a unified sense of the term, but not as social sciences in particular.

So the change of the generic term indeed indicates a changed understanding of the field.

A good example for this changed understanding might be the rise of evidence-based education (Bellmann and Müller 2011). Derived from evidence-based medicine, this paradigm is located in a framework of unified science. Studying effective interventions in education, medicine, agriculture or other fields, the social or non-social nature of the object of study is a negligible factor. That is why, in a strict sense, there is no need for a theory of education in evidence-based educational research, let alone a theory of education as a social phenomenon.

This leads to the second open question that was left by the competing interpretations of the current changes in the field of educational studies. The tremendous success of *Bildungswissenschaften* might not only be due to the reorientation of the field away from humanities and social sciences towards science in the unified sense of the term. It may also be due to the fact that on a deeper level there is a decisive affinity between the new learning sciences and modern theories of *Bildung*. This affinity consists in the individualist framework that both theories of learning and theories of *Bildung* share. The mainstream of psychological theories of learning unmistakably has an individualist outlook. Learning is understood as a process of acquisition and adaptation that results from the interaction of an individual with its environment, while no generic difference is made between the physical and the social environment (Illeris 2010).

An individualistic outlook can also be attributed to modern theories of *Bildung*, which concentrate on personal self-governance and self-formation (Koselleck 2006). The modern term *Bildung* primarily refers to a self-reflexive experience of the individual human being. Theories of *Bildung* were developed in the framework of the modern philosophy of the subject that put the individual in the centre of actions and acts of consciousness.

Irrespective of their differences, theories of learning and theories of *Bildung* share a significant deficit in social theory. Social phenomena are conceptualised as statistical aggregates or as a context, not as emergent phenomena on their own terms. Given this affinity between the new learning sciences and modern theories of *Bildung*, it is difficult or nearly impossible to criticize the current changes in the field of educational research that come along with a further phase of individualization. In a way, the new learning sciences and modern theories of *Bildung* are like distant relatives – different, but of the same kind.

This, however, means that the orientation of educational science towards the social sciences has not had any far-reaching effects on educational theory. This orientation was indeed associated with an elaboration of research methods and with closer attention to the social contexts of learning and education too, but a new conceptualisation of education, as the central scientific object of study, has not been formed. Oddly, turning to the social sciences, the deficit in social theory has remained unaffected, with consequences that can be felt in current debates.

The scientific object of *Erziehungswissenschaft*

Following my critical appraisal of the changes in the field of educational studies in Germany, I now turn to what it might mean to reconceptualise education from a disciplinary perspective. I want to argue that this perspective can only be approached by dealing with the main deficit that both the modern tradition of philosophy of education and the emerging *Bildungswissenschaften* have in common, namely its inability to understand education as a social phenomenon on its own terms, an interaction order *sui generis*.

Of course, I do not claim that there is no tradition at all that conceptualises education as a social phenomenon on its own terms, but these traditions such as research on classroom interaction in the vein of symbolic interactionism and ethonomethodology (Breidenstein 2010: 872-73[2]) had their heyday some decades ago. Furthermore, due to their focus on research methods their impact on a changed understanding of the foundations of a science of education altogether was limited and non-sustainable. So far, there are only few scholars who have tried to develop a social-theoretical approach to education as a distinct alternative to long-prevailing individualistic approaches.[3]

As a first step to a social-theoretical approach to education, it is important to stress that it is not *Bildung* but *Erziehung* that is the specific scientific object of *Erziehungswissenschaft*. This is a point that cannot be made easily in the English language. For *Bildung* there are no clearly defined disciplinary boundaries and responsibilities (Tenorth 2011). That is why many scientific disciplines feel competent talking about *Bildung*. Consequently, the new term *Bildungswissenschaften* only makes sense in the plural, if it makes sense at all. The same is true for subject matters like learning. Neither subject matter can be attributed to a specific scientific discipline. They rather constitute interdisciplinary fields of research like the so-called 'learning sciences' (Sawyer 2006). Both *Bildung* and learning are universal and ubiquitous processes that do not necessarily depend on education as a specific interaction order.

The focus on learning has also been reflected in major strands of anthropology. In particular, continental anthropology of education was fascinated with the human-specific ability and necessity to learn (e.g. Roth 1966). From there it was just a few steps to conclude that human beings are not only educable but that they have to be educated. But while the human-specific ability to learn might well be a necessary condition for education it cannot be regarded as a sufficient condition for education. This also means that anthropology of education cannot be based solely on the fundamental fact of learning; its starting point must be found in a specific, socially situated operation.

Insights from evolutionary anthropology

A promising starting point can be found in the field of evolutionary anthropology that has emerged over the last decades. Especially the research of Michael Tomasello, a developmental psychologist who works at the Max Planck Institute for Evolutionary Anthropology in Leipzig, can be regarded as an important contribution to a social-theoretical approach to education (Tomasello 1999; 2009). In his comparative research with young human children and chimpanzees, Tomasello found that the major specifically human trait might not be a specific form of learning but, above all, a basic form of teaching.

> Although both chimpanzees and young human children help others in some situations, there is one special form of helping in which only children engage: providing needed information. Importantly, this is not depended on language. Human infants inform others as early as twelve months of age, pre-linguistically, by pointing. Chimpanzees and other apes do not point for one another at all, and, I will argue, they do not use any other means of communication to helpfully inform one another of things either.
>
> (Tomasello 2009: 14).

As a specifically human gesture, pointing requires the other person to have the ability to understand the referential character of these gestures, i.e. the communicative intentions of those who are pointing. Understanding the referential character of pointing gestures presupposes the ability of 'joint attention' in some kind of 'triadic interaction' of at least two persons with an object of interest. Tomasello and his colleagues found that humans are not born with this ability, but that this ability emerges in the so-called 'nine-month revolution'.

> (A)t around nine to twelve months of age, a new set of behaviors begins to emerge that are not dyadic...but are triadic in the sense that they involve a coordination of their interactions with objects and people, resulting in a referential triangle of child, adult, and the object or event to which they share attention.
>
> (Tomasello 1999: 62).

Although Tomasello's research does not address issues of educational studies, the insights into the entanglement of pointing and learning, of communication and cognition, are an important impulse to understand education as a social phenomenon (Kraft 2007). It can be concluded that the ability of understanding pointing gestures in forms of triadic interaction can be regarded as the fundamental anthropological and developmental precondition for education. In this perspective, education can be understood as a way of staging joint attention, which makes clear that, right from the outset, education is characterized by a specific form of sociality in which agents share propositional attitudes towards objects of interest and in which their operations are temporarily synchronized. The advantage of this framework is to define education not with reference to its aims but with reference to the specific operations that are involved and coordinated in educational practices.

Towards an understanding of education as an emergent phenomenon

These anthropological prepositions, however, are not sufficient to understand the sociality of education as an emergent phenomenon. There are approaches in German philosophy of education that indeed emphasize the significance of pointing as the basic operation in education but nevertheless depict education as a composite phenomenon that consists of the educators' operations of pointing on the one side and the operations of learning by those addressed on the other side. Thus, education is conceptualized as a 'bi-subjective activity' that consists of two partial operations: teaching or imparting on the one side, learning or acquisition on the other side (Prange 2005; Sünkel 1997). The dominant approaches suggest that the phenomenon of education is sufficiently understood if one understands the activities and 'inter-actions' of those involved in it. The primal scene of education is the dyad of educator and learner. This indicates that the mainstream of modern educational theory is characterized by an astonishing social theoretical deficit.

If we compare this unfortunate state of affairs with that of sociology, the situation is by no means unambiguous. It is well known that methodological individualism is not only the prevalent approach in psychology but also pervades major strands of sociology. Ironically, 'mainstream social science' (Bernstein 1979: 22) also suffers from a social theoretical deficit. Nevertheless, there are alternative approaches to social phenomena that can be found in the work of Emile Durkheim (1953), Georg Simmel (1968), or Norbert Elias (2009). Here, social phenomena are conceptualised as emergent phenomena that cannot be adequately understood by investigation into the individuals that are involved in it. With reference to the emergent character of social phenomena Durkheim simultaneously tried to defend the autonomy of social science, first and foremost against competing claims of psychology. For Durkheim the 'independence of social facts' means that the whole surpasses the parts.

> If one can say that, to a certain extent, collective representations are exterior to individual minds, it means that they do not derive from them as such but from association of minds, which is a very different thing. No doubt, in the making of the whole each contributes his part, but private sentiments do not become social except by combination under the action of the sui generis forces developed in association. In such a combination, with the mutual alteration involved, they become something else. (...) The resultant surpasses the individual as the whole the part. It is in the whole as it is by the whole. In this sense it is exterior to the individuals. No doubt each individual contains a part, but the whole is found in no one.
>
> (Durkheim 1953: 26).

Compared to Durkheim's insights in the autonomy of social sciences based on the independence of social facts, one might doubt whether educational science and its scientific object of study has ever reached a similar status of independence. Even in Germany, where a specific discipline of *Erziehungswissenschaft* emerged in the 20th century, this discipline might merely have attained the external features of a 'normal science' such as professorships, journals, conferences, research societies and so on, while the primary features such as theories, concepts, methods and the systematic order of knowledge are chronically disputed (Vogel 1991). Certainly, there are various reasons for that; one of them might be that so far no consensus has been reached about the social nature of education as the primary scientific object of study.

With regard to the current changes in the field of educational studies under the banner of *Bildungswissenschaften*, one cannot be optimistic that a remedy for the social-theoretical deficit of educational theory is within reach. On the contrary: this restructuring of the field signifies an even stronger orientation of educational studies towards individualist approaches. Without doubt the dominant discipline within the wide range of *Bildungswissenschaften* is educational psychology, which tends to turn every aspect of the educational world into variables, so that even teaching is nothing but a context variable of learning. The mainstream of this research uses variable analysis as its most important research procedure and this seems to yield a universal scheme that can be applied to various social settings.[4] The characteristics of education as an emergent social phenomenon, as an interaction order sui generis, are not taken into account, and neither is the question as to which theories and methods might be adequate to approach a phenomenon like this.

The figure of the third in educational settings

Another symptom of the social-theoretical deficit in educational theory is its dyadic conception of educational settings. As previously mentioned, the primal scene of education is the dyad of educator and learner. The 'third factor' is usually conceptualised as the subject matter of instruction and learning, like in the classical instructional triangle. What is missing in this setting, oddly enough, is a third person by which a new dynamic enters into the social figuration of education. Usually, the triadic interaction of at least two persons with an object of interest takes the existence of a third person or a third party into account, even if this third is not necessarily present. Georg Simmel (1968) has shown that the third can be neither reduced to another alter ego nor to the position of an object. Rather, the third is characterized by his independent relations to alter and ego, so that social relations gain the quality of non-transient social facts.[5] Interestingly, Simmel's crucial insight into the significance of triads for social theory has been taken up by current social network analysis, which opened up new theoretical and methodological approaches to social settings.[6]

What does this mean regarding education? Focussing on triads instead of dyads, we can much more clearly describe how teaching and learning enter into a process of recognition (Ricken 2009). The impositions of teaching and learning and the intelligibility of what is supposed to be taught and learnt have to stand the test before the eyes of a third party. It is only due to the third that a subject matter taught and learned can gain the independence of a social fact. In this perspective teaching and learning are permanently dealing not only with cognitive problems but also with problems of recognition. That's why the peer culture in the classroom is not something external to the realm of instruction. Rather, cognition and recognition are internally related in educational settings. This is apparent particularly in formal educational settings, in which teaching and learning are often unsettling, in which habits already learnt in informal settings often have to be put at stake and in which the motivation to learn can consequently not simply be taken for granted. Precisely in these formal settings it depends on the third whether or not a learner is prepared to get involved with the impositions of teaching.

The third can take different roles in an educational setting: she can be the one who has already gained some understanding of the subject matter, thus signalling that it is not an unacceptable imposition. She can, however, also be the ally of those who do not understand, who do not want to understand or who understand in a different way – thus forcing the teacher to revise his methods. In educational settings the third is not necessarily another learner, but can also be another teacher. The fact that in education we are always confronted with a plurality of teachers has been well known since Rousseau, but its significance for a social theory of education is often overlooked. In teaching, every teacher is aware that his pupils shift between different educational settings and that his lessons are actually or potentially checked by other teachers. In any case, it is only through the third that one begins to realise that the subject matter can receive independent recognition beyond the educational dyad.

A 'triadic turn' would have another advantage not only in social theory but also in educational theory: it draws attention to the missing link between the interactional and the institutional level of education (Fischer 2010: 144). In dyadic interactions of alter and ego, rules can be agreed upon and changed at discretion; but only if rules are followed by a third party do they emerge as a reality of their own. The missing link between the interactional and institutional level of analysis is quite noticeable in educational theory in particular. Sociological approaches to schooling such as Parsons' long-dominant structural functionalism often try to explain interaction in the classroom directly by taking recourse to the function schooling has for society (Breidenstein 2010: 871). Thus, they fail to analyse the internal functioning of the specific interaction order in the classroom, an order that can neither be explained with reference to dyadic interaction nor with reference to society on the whole.

An interim result of my comments on a social-theoretical approach to education might be put like this: everything that gains significance in the world of education has to gain this significance in and through an interaction order that has an independent status and functioning towards those engaged in it (Vanderstraeten and Biesta 2006). For instance, the meaning of authority, of competence or of a certain element of a curriculum cannot be deduced from individual traits of a teacher, cognitive accomplishments of the learner or objective qualities of a subject-matter. Their meaning has to be generated in education as a specific interaction order, and neither organization nor society can reach any educational objectives by passing over their mediation through interaction.

Conclusion: the main obstacles to theorizing education as a social phenomenon

In this final section I will draw attention to the main obstacles to theorizing education as a social phenomenon.

(1) The first obstacle that has already been mentioned is the *framework of a modernist 'philosophy of the subject'*, in which major contributions to educational theory have been made. Especially in the founding period of continental educational theory around 1800, we find a strong individualist theoretical

framework, in which the emergent qualities of social phenomena could not be conceptualised. Historically this deficit is no surprise since social theory as a distinct field of its own didn't emerge until the end of the 19th century. Prior to this, social theory was dealt with in the context of moral philosophy or political philosophy but not as a field of its own (Bedorf 2010: 14). Educational theory, however, was for a long time shaped by the individualist premises of its formative period.

Certainly, there are counter movements in 20th century educational theory, especially in the context of pragmatism and critical theory. Both share a deeper understanding of the priority of intersubjectivity over subjectivity, which was signalled by core concepts such as interaction, taking over another's perspective and communication. Critical pedagogy began to conceptualise education as 'communicative action' (Mollenhauer 1972) and in the German discourse of the 1970s and 1980s a 'Pedagogy of Communication' (Schaller 1987) was developed, which placed education in an ontological primordial sphere of intersubjectivity, while combining this reconceptualisation with a trenchant critique of the individualism of idealistic philosophies.

This is not the place for a detailed discussion of these counter movements. Therefore, only two short queries are appropriate: first of all, it is disputable whether these approaches really abandon the framework of the modernist philosophy of the subject. Particularly with regard to the communicative turn in educational theory, it looks as if the new vocabulary fits smoothly into the old framework of the philosophy of the subject. In critical pedagogy, the effect is that educational settings are characterized by two subjects and two intentionalities, while the emergent quality of education as a social phenomenon is not realized (see Masschelein 1991). Given the distinction between action, interaction and transaction that can be found in the later works of Dewey and Bentley (1989), we might conclude that critical pedagogy conceptualised education in terms of interaction but not in terms of transaction, i.e. critical pedagogy was still focusing on interacting subjects and their intentions, while education as a social figuration in its own right was not adequately captured. Thus, the communicative turn in educational theory was carried out inchoately and should not be mistaken for a relational turn, which is still an unaccomplished project.

This deficit is linked to another feature of critical pedagogy, namely its normative approach to core concepts such as communication and interaction. Concepts like these are far from being used as descriptive instruments of social theory, by which specific characteristics of education as a social figuration might be captured and made accessible to empirical investigation. On the contrary: concepts such as communication and interaction were closely linked to normative claims of emancipation and autonomy, which were usually given priority, while options for descriptive or empirical approaches were left unexploited. A similar query can be made with respect to Deweyan pragmatism, in which the concept of communication is also far from being used as a descriptive instrument of social theory. In fact, the concept stands for a functional equivalent for the religious ties of community (Bellmann 2007).

(2) This leads to a second obstacle to theorizing education as a social phenomenon, namely the *dominance of normative approaches to education*. There is a strong consensus across different traditions of educational theory that the distinctive feature of education can only be captured with reference to its inherent normativity, emancipation and responsibility being the crucial normative categories. Some schools of thought also agree that the normativity of education has to correspond to the normativity of educational theory as a form of practical theory that is concerned with 'what ought to be the case' in educational practice (Hirst 1966: 42). This assumption seems to be a common ground for diverse traditions in educational theory such as analytic philosophy and the German tradition of *Geisteswissenschaftliche Pädagogik* (Osterloh 2004). Educational theory has been preoccupied with value judgements and principles of legitimate forms of education. The question as to what education ought to be has overridden the question of how education is possible. In consequence, investigations on the procedural character of education as a specific interaction order have not been taken up or left to sociologists. Strikingly, normativity itself has been conceptualised in the traditional framework of the philosophy of the subject – e.g. in terms of autonomy and responsibility – thereby one-sidedly emphasizing the asymmetrical character of educational relationships. The consequence is a peculiar fascination with paradoxical theoretical accounts of education as a correlation of freedom and coercion. This normative approach, however, has little time for the question how these paradoxes are dealt with and resolved in the process of education.

The dominance of normative approaches in educational theory has also become apparent in recent controversies about evidence-based education. As an example, I will briefly touch upon a recent contribution by Gert Biesta (2010) in this debate. While Biesta can be credited with major contributions to a social-theoretical understanding of education, in his recent papers, he expounds the problems of the dominance of 'what works' questions in educational research with reference to the 'teleological character of education' (Biesta 2010: 500). It is not instrumental questions concerning effective means, but rather normative questions concerning legitimate ends that are supposed to have priority in education. Normativity – in the guise of rather heterogeneous terms such as 'telos', 'aim', 'purpose', 'values' (Biesta 2010: 500-501) – is regarded as constitutive of education. Without reference to a normative orientation, one could not even identify a practice as an educational practice. Thus Biesta calls for a reorientation of the current debate: 'from Evidence-Based to Value-Based Education' (Biesta 2010: 500).

Strikingly, the question 'How is education possible', which had been highlighted in Biesta's earlier works (Vanderstraeten and Biesta 2006), is now fading into the background as befits the question as to what education ought to be. Consequently, an important option in the debate with evidence-based education is left unexploited: the pretensions of 'What works' might more convincingly be rejected with reference to the *social* character of education as an emergent phenomenon instead of hinting at the *teleological* character of education. This holds true especially when this teleological character itself seems to be explained as a property of actors and their 'decisions' (Biesta 2010: 500) instead of a property of educational practices, i.e. a 'teleoaffective structure' (Schatzki 2002: 80) of educational practices that goes beyond the decisions of those involved in it. In the debate with evidence-based education a closer relationship of educational theory and social theory is vitally needed. Until then, 'How is education possible' remains a challenge for educational theory, as well as does the question of how normativity is proceeding within the social setting of education.

In closing, I would like to avoid a misunderstanding: arguing for theorizing education as a distinctly social phenomenon should not be confused with a pledge for less psychology and more sociology in educational theory. Firstly, even in sociology, there is no consensus on the emergent character of its scientific object of study. Secondly, it is disputable whether the closer relationships of educational theory to the broader field of social sciences that have be established since the 1970s have really brought about a better understanding of education as a social phenomenon. At least in the German discourse of educational theory, the turn to the social sciences most of all brought about a closer attention to the social *context* of education, not to the social quality of education itself. The focus was much more on the level of society and organization than on the level of interaction, and this also holds true also for the romance of educational theory with critical theory. Thus, coming to terms with the social-theoretical deficit in educational theory would involve emancipation from dominant strands both in psychology and sociology. Thirdly, this means that theorizing education as a social phenomenon should not be confused with the application of sociological knowledge to the field of education. Rather, informed by social theory, new perspectives of theorizing might be opened up in the science of education as a discipline of its own. These new perspectives of theorizing would make a difference with regard to both the tradition of educational theory as well as to a scientistic conception of *Bildungswissenschaften* as is widespread in psychology and neuroscience. As a result, the science of education (*Erziehungswissenschaft*) might gain a clearer understanding both of its scientific object of study and of its belonging to the family of social sciences. In any case, these insights are certainly not contradictory.

Notes

1 http://www.gebf-ev.de/
2 For symbolic interactionism in educational studies see, for instance, Jackson (1968) and Hammersley (1990); for ethnomethodology see Mehan (1979) and McHoul (1978).

3 I have probably disregarded some major efforts in that direction, so I will only mention the works of Raf Vanderstraeten and Gert Biesta (2006) as representatives of the English literature and Walter Herzog (2002) and Norbert Ricken (2009) as representatives for the German literature.
4 For an early critique of variable analysis in sociology see Blumer, 1956. For a critique of variable analysis as the dominant methodology in psychology see also Herzog, 2005: 193.
5 Simmel (1908/1968) in particular pointed out three different roles of the third: the impartial arbitrator, the third who benefits (tertius gaudens), and the third who follows the strategy of divide and conquer (*divide et impera*). It is important to note that in Simmel's social theory, the third person singular is not just a 'generalized other' like in Mead's conception, where the social world seems to be an extrapolation of dyadic interaction or, conversely, the social world can be reduced to dyadic interaction (Fischer 2010: 149f.).
6 One of the founders of the social network field states: 'network analysis really begins with triads, for they are the beginnings of a "society" that is independent of the ties between a dyad' (Kadushin 2012: 22).

References

Bedorf, T. (2010) 'Stabilisierung und/oder Irritation. Voraussetzungen und Konsequenzen einer triadischen Sozialphilosophie', in T. Bedorf, J. Fischer and G. Lindemann (eds), *Theorien des Dritten. Innovationen in Soziologie und Sozialphilosophie,* Munich: Fink.

Bellmann, J. (2007) *John Dewey's naturalistische Pädagogik. Argumentationskontexte, Traditionslinien,* Paderborn: Schöningh.

Bellmann, J. and Müller, T. (eds) (2011) *Wissen, was wirkt. Kritik evidenzabasierter Pädagogik.* Wiesbaden: VS Verlag für Sozialwissenschaften.

Bernstein, R. (1979) *The Restructuring of Social and Political Theory*, Oxford: Blackwell.

Biesta, G.J.J. (2010) 'Why 'what works' still won't work: from evidence-based education to value-based education', *Studies in Philosophy and Education,* 29: 491-503.

Biesta, G.J.J. (2011) 'Disciplines and theory in the academic study of education: a comparative analysis of the Anglo-American and Continental construction of the field', *Pedagogy, Culture and Society*, 19: 175-192.

Blumer, H. (1956) 'Sociological analysis and the "variable"', *American Sociological Review*, 21: 683-90.

Breidenstein, G. (2010) 'Überlegungen zu einer Theorie des Unterrichts', *Zeitschrift für Pädagogik* 56: 869-887.

Casale, R., Röhner, C., Schaarschuch, A. and Sünker, H. (2010) 'Entkopplung von Lehrer*Bildung* und *Erziehungs*wissenschaft: Von der *Erziehungs*wissenschaft zur *Bildungs*wissenschaft', *Erziehungswissenschaft. Mitteilungen der Deutschen Gesellschaft für Erziehungswissenschaft (DGfE)*, 21: 43-66.

Dewey, J. and Bentley, A.F. (1989[1949]) 'Knowing and the Known', in J.A. Boydston (ed.), *John Dewey: The Later Works Volume 16*, Carbondale and Edwardsville: Southern Illinois University Press.

Durkheim, E. (1953[1898]) *Sociology and Philosophy,* Glencoe, IL: Free Press.

Elias, N. (2009[1970]) *Was ist Soziologie?,* Weinheim/Munich: Juventa.

Fischer, J. (2010) 'Tertiarität/Der Dritte. Soziologie als Schlüsseldisziplin', in T. Bedorf, J. Fischer and G. Lindemann (eds), *Theorien des Dritten. Innovationen in Soziologie und Sozialphilosophie*, Munich: Fink.

Hammersley, M. (1990) *Classroom ethnography: empirical and methodological essays,* Milton Keynes: Open University Press.

Herzog, W. (2002) *Zeitgemäße Erziehung. Die Konstruktion pädagogischer Wirklichkeit,* Weilerswist: Velbrück Wissenschaft.

Herzog, W. (2005) *Pädagogik und Psychologie. Eine Einführung,* Stuttgart: Kohlhammer.

Hirst, P.H. (1966) 'Educational theory', in J.W. Tibble (ed.), *The Study of Education,* London: Routledge and Keagan Paul.

Illeris, K. (2010) *Lernen verstehen. Bedingungen erfolgreichen Lernens,* Bad Heilbrunn: Klinkhardt.

Jackson, P.W. (1968) *Life in classrooms,* New York: Holt, Rinehart and Winston.

Kadushin, Ch. (2012) *Understanding Social Networks: Theories, Concepts, and Findings,* Ort: Verlag.

Koselleck, R. (2006) *Begriffsgeschichten. Studien zur Semantik und Pragmatik der politischen und sozialen Sprache,* Frankfurt am Main: Suhrkamp Verlag.

Kraft, V. (2007) 'Operative Triangulierung und didaktische Emergenz: Zur Zeigestruktur der *Erziehung*', in J. Aderhold and O. Kranz (eds), *Intention und Funktion. Probleme der Vermittlung psychischer und sozialer Systeme,* Wiesbaden: VS Verlag für Sozialwissenschaften.

Liebau, E. (2002) *Bildungswissenschaft.* Zur Weiterentwicklung der Disziplin', *Vierteljahrsschrift für Pädagogik* 78: 293-299.

Lochner, R. (1969) 'Zur Grundlegung einer selbständigen *Erziehungswissenschaft*', in F. Nicolin (ed.), *Pädagogik als Wissenschaft,* Darmstadt: Wissenschaftliche Buchgesellschaft.

Masschelein, J. (1991) *Kommunikatives Handeln und pädagogisches Handeln. Die Bedeutung der Habermasschen kommunikationstheoretischen Wende für die Pädagogik,* Weinheim: Deutscher Studien Verlag.

McHoul, A.W. (1978) 'The organization of turns in formal talk in the classroom', *Language and Society* 7: 182-213.

Mehan, H. (1979) *Learning Lessons: Social Organization in the Classroom,* Cambridge: Harvard University Press.

Mollenhauer, K. (1972) *Theorien zum Erziehungsprozess. Zur Einführung in Erziehungswissenschaftliche Fragestellungen,* Munich: Juventa Verlag.

OECD (2002) *Understanding the brain. Towards a new learning science,* Paris: OECD.

Osterloh, J. (2004) 'Ethos pädagogischer Verantwortung als Identitätskern der *Erziehungs*wissenschaft. Ein Versuch verantwortungsethischer Grundlegung der Disziplin', in P. Korte (ed.), *Kontinuität, Krise und Zukunft der Bildung. Analysen und Perspektiven.* Münster: Lit Verlag.

Prange, K. (2005) *Die Zeigestruktur der Erziehung. Grundriss der operativen Pädagogik,* Paderborn: Schöningh.

Ricken, N. (2009) 'Über Anerkennung. Spuren einer anderen Subjektivität', in N. Ricken, H. Röhr, J. Ruhloff and K. Schaller (eds), *Umlernen. Festschrift für Käthe Meyer-Drawe,* Paderborn: Fink.

Roth, H. (1966) *Pädagogische Anthropologie. Band I. Bildsamkeit und Bestimmung,* Hannover *et al.*: Schroedel.

Roth, G. (2011) *Bildung braucht Persönlichkeit. Wie Lernen gelingt,* Stuttgart: Klett-Cotta.

Sawyer, R.K. (ed.) (2006) *The Cambridge Handbook of the Learning Sciences,* Cambridge: Cambridge University Press.

Schaller, K. (1987) *Pädagogik der Kommunikation. Annäherungen, Erprobungen,* Sankt Augustin: Richarz.

Schatzki, T.R. (2002) *The Site of the Social: A Philosophical Account of the Constitution of Social Life and Change,* University Park: Pennsylvania State University Press.

Simmel, G. (1968[1908]) *Soziologie. Untersuchungen über die Formen der Vergesellschaftung,* Berlin: Duncker and Humblot.

Spitzer, M. (2010) *Medizin für die Bildung. Ein Weg aus der Krise,* Heidelberg: Spektrum Akademischer Verlag.

Sünkel, W. (1997) 'Generation als pädagogischer Begriff,' in E. Liebau (ed.), *Das Generationenverhältnis. Über das Zusammenleben in Familie und Gesellschaft,* Weinheim: Juventa Verlag.

Tenorth, H.-E. (2011) '*Bildung*' – ein Thema im Dissens der Disziplinen, *Zeitschrift für Erziehungswissenschaft,* 14: 351-62.

Terhart, E. (2012) '*Bildungswissenschaften*': Verlegenheitslösung, Sammelkategorie, Kampfbegriff?' *Zeitschrift für Pädagogik,* 58: 22-39.

Tibble, J.W. (1971) 'The development of the study of education', in J. W. Tibble (ed.), *An introduction to the study of education: An Outline for the Student,* London : Routledge and Kegan Paul.

Tomasello, M. (1999) *Cultural Orgins of Human Cognition,* Cambridge, MA: Harvard University Press.

Tomasello, M. (2009) *Why we Cooperate,* Cambridge MA: The MIT Press.

Vanderstraeten, R. and Biesta, G.J.J. (2006) 'How is education possible? A pragmatist account of communication and the social organisation of education', *British Journal of Educational Studies,* 54: 160-74.

Vogel, P. (1991) 'System – die Antwort der Bildungsphilosophie?', *Pädagogisches Wissen. Zeitschrift für Pädagogik – Beiheft 27:* 333-45.

Wulf, Ch. (1983) *Theorien und Konzepte der Erziehungswissenschaft.* 3rd edition, Munich: Juventa.

Section II

The practice of doing theory

Chapter 5

Theories have consequences, don't they?

On the moral nature of educational theory and research

Deborah Gallagher

Introduction

On a cloudy Friday morning not long ago, the faculty of our academic department convened a meeting of our departmental advisory board that included educators and administrators from the local schools as well as parents and state legislators. The meeting's agenda included small group discussions about pressing educational issues, and we were instructed to join the group of our choice. Not being much interested in the other topics, I chose the group that was to deliberate the 'achievement gap' between impoverished ethnic minority students and their affluent white counterparts. The achievement gap, as it is known in official parlance, has long sustained its centrality as a source of anguish among those sincerely committed to social and educational justice as well as those who have cynically employed it as stalking horse for neo-liberal education 'reform' – reform that runs the gamut from abolishing teachers' unions to privatizing public (state) schools.

The discussion leader opened the session by asking each of us to summarise our interest in the topic. Owing to seating arrangements, I happened to be first in line, and commenced rather inarticulately to frame the problem as having roots in our political, moral, and economic failings as a nation. Heads nodded solemnly all around, but only for an instant before a colleague piped up that the solution most certainly was to be found in shoring up our implementation of evidence-based (meaning 'scientific' based) practices and making sure our new teachers know how to use them effectively. The mood of the group immediately became lively and energetic.

Much agreement ensued as others concurred that, yes, more evidence-based practices were the answer, followed by laments about how we teacher educators were not doing an adequate job of teaching them, how we need ever more data to audit teachers' use of them and so on and so on. Suggestions flew one after the other about how this task could be accomplished. In the process, the solution to the achievement gap problem shifted magically from the moral/political to a superficial, instrumentalism severed from any acknowledgement or consideration of its consequences. Rather than addressing the profound inequalities in power and wealth at the core of the achievement gap, the group seized upon the prospect of enforcing implementation of instructional procedures 'proven' to 'work' by scientific (empiricist) research methods and methodology.

At one point, one of my like-minded young colleagues interrupted by relating a story about one of our very promising graduate students currently in her second year of teaching who is on the verge of quitting the profession because she is being forced to use prescribed evidence-based practices, specifically scripted lessons, with her students. Around the table heads nodded briefly in affirming sympathy, only to be interrupted by another colleague asserting that the answer to the teacher attrition problem lies with better 'resilience training" for new teachers. Resilience training was thus to 'fix' the severe, ongoing shortages of qualified teachers brought on at least in part by the enforcement of the very evidence-based teaching procedures that supposedly made the teachers 'qualified' in the first place. The discussion proceeded with no glimmer of substance beyond procedural fixes and no hope of ever gaining a purchase on the achievement gap or more broadly the crisis that is American public education.

What the foregoing exchange illustrates is not only the allure of scientific (or better said, *scientistic*) educational theory aimed at achieving prediction and control over educational processes, but also the inevitable shunting aside of the moral and political through the persistent denial of the fact that evidence-based practices are not, and never can be, what they're cracked up to be. At the root of all of this is the fundamental problem with mainstream educational research, and by extension, the false promises of *scientific* educational theory. But what scientific theory does indeed offer is an easy way out, as evidenced by the palpable relief of most of the advisory board group members each and every time an instrumentalist solution neatly informed by scientific theory was introduced into the discussion. Despite all – and ongoing – evidence to the contrary, the illusion that every educational problem has an instrumentalist solution draws new breath daily with its promise to assuage what Bernstein (1983: 18) so aptly termed our 'Cartesian anxiety', and perhaps more particularly, to make dispensable the turmoil of having to immerse oneself in moral discourse. Or so it is thought.

In *After Virtue*, MacIntyre (1984) noted that whatever the social sciences are about they are not about instrumentalism, an instrumentalism predicated on the potential for scientific theory to produce prediction and control such that specific educational procedures will directly *cause* a specific educational outcome. He went on to add that what we lack in light of absence of prediction and control is a coherent understanding of the value of social (and educational) inquiry. In this chapter, I attempt to search for such an understanding. I begin with a historical analysis of the rise of social and educational research and its theoretical foundation. Drawing on the work of Dorothy Ross (1992) and Kurt Danziger (1994), whose incisive historical analyses of the rise of the social and educational as sciences in the classic empiricist methodical/methodological sense provide revealing contexts for understanding our present state of affairs, my aim in this chapter is to locate the administrative/political/economic allegiances that sponsored such theorizing.

At the core of this aim is the point that none of these allegiances to administrative efficiency, social control, and free market ideology, can elude the dangers of popular scrutiny absent in the concealing veneer of scientific theory's alleged neutrality. The convenient benefit of this supposed neutrality is that it eclipses the more complexly contentious moral and political concerns at the core of education in the interest of what is thought to be social progress. And because it disqualifies the very essence of what education is about, the eclipsing of the moral and political is itself a fateful consequence of scientific educational theory. Yet one of many consequences of this perspective – of this instrumentalist theorizing – is actually the decoupling of theory and practice. And it should be noted that this separation involves a certain irony in that it obstructs the very goals of its own project. In this section of the chapter I make the case that, along with other fateful consequences of scientific educational theory, the theory/practice divide cannot be overcome until we drop epistemologies (and their theories of justification), competing epistemologies, and all the rest in favour of moral or practical philosophy. The eminently foreseeable responses to such a proposal are questions about the problems of pluralism and relativism. In the final section, I discuss these concerns, and conclude with an alternative understanding of what educational theory, and educational research, are all about.

The rise of the social and educational sciences

Anyone even passingly sceptical about the knowledge claims made by empiricist social scientists will find it difficult to resist being amused by MacIntyre's (1984) forthright assessment of their wildly oversold record of progress – which was to say that there really is no record of success at all. Providing examples from some of the most famous and much vaunted theories from the field of economics along with those of other sub-fields of the social sciences, he noted not only that all of them have turned out to be demonstrably false but also that their predictive failures do not seem to matter. 'One could go on multiplying examples of the predictive ineptitude of economists, and with demography the situation has been even worse, but this would be grossly unfair', he wrote:

> for economists and demographers have at least gone on record with their predictions in systematic fashion. But most sociologists and political scientists keep no systematic records of their predictions and those futurologists who scatter predictions lavishly around rarely, if ever, advert to their predictive failures afterward.
>
> (MacIntyre 1984: 89)

His appraisal obviously applies to educational research, as confirmed by the rare confession supplied by Kaestle (1993) who spoke so candidly about the 'awful reputation' of the education 'sciences.'

So, how did we get to this place that MacIntyre exposed with such force and clarity? No one has given us such a detailed and lucid account as Dorothy Ross (1991) in her acclaimed work, *The Origins of American Social Science*. Her intellectually incisive analysis lends substance to John Kenneth Galbraith's précis that the history of free-market liberalism has been one long 'search for a superior moral justification for selfishness' (Cornwell 2002). The development of the social sciences are intimately bound up in the weaving of such a rationale as in Ross's historical account we see the all too familiar tensions played out through the backdrop of religion versus science, determinism versus indeterminism, and the embrace versus the rejection of historicism – all of which were situated within the economic and racial discord still evident on the contemporary political scene. Most relevant to the present discussion, we see in her work the fundamental divide between two main factions in the fledgling social sciences whose theories were, on the one side, understood to be susceptible to the trial of objective facts and thereby leading to predicting and controlling the social world or, on the other side, understood to be morally and historically contingent interpretations.

Early on, the notion that the social sciences originating in Europe should be modelled after the physical sciences was not a foregone conclusion, but, as Ross illuminated, the ideology of American exceptionalism was the driving force behind just such a modelling. Claiming immunity from Europe's history of class-based inequality, America would set a new ahistorical course by achieving a classless society, founded upon a science of the social world and unmarred by conflict and privation. But with the tumultuous post-Civil War rise of industrialism, the American exceptionalist project fell on distinctly hard times, particularly with the expansion of organized labour. Then, as now, the ranks of academic social scientists debated across the epistemological divides with what Ross referred to as the most 'cosmopolitan' (conservative and hereditarily affluent) among them favouring the positivist version of these new fields that held the greatest potential for restoring social stability.

As she put it, '[t]hey set out to establish their authority and social vision by creating modern universities that would promulgate scientific truth and social science disciplines that would place the old principles of American exceptionalism on unassailable scientific ground' (p. 54). By the end of the first quarter of the twentieth century the social sciences were well on their way to being entrapped by this vision. Ross deftly portrayed the empiricist social scientists' reformist zeal for achieving a social stability animated by a desire for limited democracy, elite rule, and a reassertion of the natural order. 'Control,' she wrote:

> ...was the central theme of the science-oriented social sciences that appeared in the late Progressive period and bloomed during the 1920s. In

> the hands of this cohort the idea of social control took on greater insistence and harder contours, stressing objective, quantitative methods and behaviourist psychology. The principal inventor of American behaviourism, John B. Watson, was a member of this cohort in psychology and his background perfectly epitomized theirs.
>
> (Ross 1991: 311)

This enthusiasm, she further pointed out, was also swayed by the new social scientists' interests in advancing their professions. Not surprisingly, their aspirations inspired generous support from Gilded Age industrialists such as Vanderbilt, Rockefeller, Carnegie, J. P. Morgan, and the like.[1]

World War I, which introduced the horrors of massive death and destruction wrought by new technologies of warfare, shocked people in general, including social scientists looking to the possibilities of their respective professions to engineer a utopian solution through social control. In a very telling passage, Ross quoted anthropologist W. I. Thomas as having stated, "We live in an entirely new world, unique without parallel in history." The only thing that can help us, he said, is a science of social control. 'Then we can establish any attitudes and values whatever' (p. 324). Many if not most readers will also recall that the war gave a significant boost to statisticians in the social sciences as they demonstrated their worth to the military to assist the war effort in many capacities. This dividend provided indispensable sustenance to the least prestigious and most underdeveloped area of the social sciences – scientific psychology with its growing armamentarium of mental tests.

Like the social sciences as a whole, the field of psychology (out of which grew educational psychology) also underwent its philosophical disputes, ones that ultimately resulted in the ascendancy of scientific psychology, most particularly because this field held distinctive promise for an applied science of social control. It is here that Danziger's (1994) discerning history of psychology made apparent the integral role schools played in sponsoring scientific psychology's rise to academic and professional respectability. Conveniently, schools presented psychologists with a captive audience of subjects for applied experimentation. They also supplied a strategic site for the exercise of social control over the lower classes, an acutely felt need during the surges of immigration in early twentieth century America. It was not therefore surprising that the sub-field of school psychology became the engine of scientific psychology's development of what Danziger termed, 'marketable methods.'

It was school psychology that built the consensus between the experimentalist (scientific) faction of psychology and the applied faction. Each needed each other, despite their philosophical differences, much like, as Danziger put it, a bad marriage that nevertheless works. It was the Galtonian version of educational psychology,[2] with its publicly compelling psychological categories, mental testing instruments, and institutional backing that exerted the driving force toward a consensus that ultimately resulted in the experimentalists becoming more like the applied psychologists. To fend off incursions from untrained practitioners, they strove to make their tests more technically sophisticated, not only to improve their 'predictive validity' but also to make them difficult to understand for all but the most 'trained'.

It was also the field of school psychology that developed what is now referred to as the 'gold-standard' of evidence-based educational research, the randomized control group designs used to test educational interventions (Gallagher 2010). To early school psychologists, Danziger explained, these experiments were not simply about how individual students responded to particular types of instruction in a specific context. Instead, they represented 'laws of learning' (p. 115). To draw this conclusion involved a great deal of belief, imagination, and interpretation – as well as a healthy dose of amnesia as they reified their theories about learners and schooling. Thus their theories sanctioned their ideological commitments and not the other way around. As Danzinger put it:

> Only the treatment group could provide a practical construction that was a pure reflection of the kind of theoretical construction that the so-called science of behaviour favoured. As the use of this foundation for knowledge claims became more widespread, the empirical basis for questioning the prevailing shape of psychological theory became narrower. In terms of their overall structure experiments increasingly resembled a practical enactment of what theory presupposed. (p.117)

Invigorated by professional ambition as they assumed the roles of neutral brokers (i.e., free of biases and solely driven by objective evidence) on behalf of administrators and policy makers, they marshalled together a framework of educational theorizing that continues to dominate contemporary education. Its political usefulness ensures the viability of its distinctly eugenic and colonial ideology because the practices and policies it produces contribute not to educational equality but rather to further stigmatising of the students at which it is aimed. And, it is well to restate, the project was one of predicting the results of an action/intervention and thereby attaining mastery of shaping the world to their desires.

Returning to MacIntyre's commentary about the complete lack of predictive success in the scientistic version of the social sciences, it is worth noting that it is impossible to name even one law-like generalisation or causal theory in education. Of course the immediate retort to this indictment is that science-based educational research has never claimed the ability to derive purely law-like generalisations but is nevertheless capable of producing probabilistic ones. This, too, is a hollow claim, as I have explained elsewhere (Gallagher 1998). And of the so-called generalisations and causal theories much vaunted in the teacher effectiveness literature (see Brophy and Good 1986; Wang, *et al.* 1993), not one rises above the level of a truism.[3]

Decoupling of theory and practice

Prediction and control over education not only has failed but will continue to fail, even by its own technical lights. But in another sense it has succeeded in corrupting our understanding of educational theory and education as a whole, most particularly because it has distorted the very act of teaching itself (Kliebard 1993). The failure to pin down a technicist theoretical basis for educational practice is acknowledged by advocates of evidence-based education when they raise the theory/practice gap (Nuthall 2003). However it is clear that this failure is only understood as yet another technical problem to be remedied by more technical fixes rather than a fundamental problem with their methodology. The explanations for this gap are many and varied and include such issues as the existence of too little research, teachers' difficulty in finding the research relevant to their work and lived experiences in classrooms, a lack of communication between researchers and teachers, and so on (see: Broekkamp and van Hout-Wolters 2007, for a discussion of these explanations). Unfortunately, the recommended technical fixes (a more-of-the-same-only-more approach) serve to compound the problems; and, not incidentally, work to mould the classroom to the image of the preferred research methodology and not the other way around (Dudley-Marling 2011; Schwandt 2005).

It is not as if the fundamental problems have not been pointed out and eloquently elaborated upon (see: Biesta 2007; Iano 2004; Kerdeman and Phillips 1993; McDermott and Hall 2007). Rather, it is that the fundamental problems threaten the claim that education can be brought under scientific prediction and control, and this situation represents a crisis that scientistic researchers ignore, oppose with reassertions to the contrary, or simply rationalise away. Because articulation of these difficulties is well-travelled terrain, only a brief reiteration of them is necessary. First, and perhaps foremost, attempts to bring teaching and learning under instrumentalist control invariably lead to prescriptive, decontextualised teaching 'interventions' that once taken out of context are difficult if not impossible to wedge into the real world (Iano 2004). In an attempt to ameliorate this de-contextualisation, researchers have attempted to adjust their research methods or approaches, only to encounter another set of problems that threaten the scientific project. The dilemma here is that the more *scientific* they are the less relevance their research has in real classrooms (Elmore 1993), whereas attempts to be more procedurally flexible with their research procedures undermine the authority of their knowledge claim (see Gallagher 2004 for an extended discussion of this rather comical dilemma).

Second, researchers cannot *get into* the heads of either teachers or students, try as they might. And even if they could they would find that, as is the case for all of us humans, much of what goes on involves tacit knowledge, meaning it is not explicable by the teacher or the students (Polanyi 1962). Third, because much of what goes on in the minds of teachers and students is tacit, it is self-evidently impossible to pin-down all relevant variables that influence teaching and learning; and, even if many other variables can be observed and quantified, along with their influence on each other (Singer 1993), many if most others cannot be. Fourth, if all relevant variables cannot be identified and brought under scientific control, then there can be no scientific generalisations. And, as noted earlier, in the absence of generalisations, there can be no scientific theory-building (Kerdeman and Phillips 1993). Finally, and on a purely non-technical front, the methodological commitment to objectivist assumptions means that the moral consequences of educational practices and policies have become a contingent category of thought (Biesta 2007; Iano 2004; Schwandt 2005). There is something palpably troublesome, as McDermott and Hall (2007: 12) ruefully put it, about turning children into 'eunuchs of analysis'.

Scientific theorizing not only causes but also requires the theory/practice breach that even its advocates find unacceptable. So why doesn't this predicament suggest abandoning this mode of theorizing? Perhaps because something more important is at stake here, something that harkens back to the instrumentalist fantasy of social control. Devotion to this goal means that researchers must persist in misapprehending the quintessence of what they study. The effort to purge the classroom of the moral and political, to make it a pristine world where objective facts impose predictable order, is an attempt to make it what it is not. People are not predictable and cannot be made to be so, not by themselves and certainly not by others. While we can and must be able to *anticipate* others, the ability to do so is a far cry from the power to predict as 'scientific' researchers desire (MacIntyre 1984). And, in passing, I might note that there is a certain irony in a desire to predict the actions of others unless one is also willing to be made predictable.

Toward alternatives

Offering this historical and methodological critique obliges me to offer an alternative, or at least a profile of one. What should educational inquiry look like instead? What should be the purpose or outcome of our research activities? How are we to position ourselves as researchers? In offering this alternative, I draw on the work of Gadamer (1995), Rorty (1979, 1999), and Bernstein (1983; 2005) as well as contemporary voices in education who have put forward conceptually integrated visions centred on transcending the subjective versus objective divide and foundationalist methodology. Although their terminology varies, their ideas present what I consider to be a compelling philosophical framework for educational inquiry and the role of theory.

The need to re-theorize educational inquiry

Educational research can make use of many, indeed an endless array, of methods and approaches. This point does not mean that the use of any particular methods or approaches is beyond critical appraisal of their adequacy, consequences, and so on. What it does mean (and this is a crucial point) is that *methodologically*, all procedures of inquiry can achieve for us is various ways of narrating or telling what we hope are useful, illuminating, and informative accounts about phenomena (practices, arrangements, events, policies) of interest. Further, because all accounts are morally situated and contextually contingent, none can claim the status of neutral fact or truth. As Rorty (1979) put it, all methods are *non-privileged tools* useful in *constructing* knowledge rather than discovering or finding it. And it should be added that these accounts themselves are consequently non-privileged.

Drawing on Putnam (1984), Bernstein (2005: 27) encapsulated three theses that set out the basic outlines of his version of pragmatism – or what Putnam called 'a way of thinking'. And here I want to highlight that these theses share common ground with philosophical hermeneutics and other non-foundational/ non-realist philosophical frameworks. The first thesis centres on the 'fallibilistic' nature of all knowledge, meaning that no knowledge claim or belief is ever beyond the need for revision, and the quest for predictive certainty is pointless as well as destructive. The second holds that, as researchers (as with humans in general) we are obligated to engage in respectful dialogue with each other, and to substantiate or provide reasons both for our beliefs and doubts/disagreements with others. In other words, even though we can never appeal to methodological foundations, it is essential that we provide rational (rhetorically coherent) support for our knowledge claims and for our disbelief in the knowledge claims of others. Third, there is no dichotomy between facts and values, which in turn means that there is no dichotomy between theory and practice. Fallibilism, Bernstein clarified, acknowledges our status as finite human beings, thus raises '...doubt about the very possibility *of absolute incorrigible knowledge*' (p. 29), adding that it:

> ...is not a rarified epistemological doctrine. It consists of a set of virtues – a set of practices – that need to be carefully nurtured in critical communities. A fallibilistic orientation requires a genuine willingness to test one's ideas in public, and to listen carefully to those who criticize them. It requires the imagination to formulate new hypotheses and conjectures, and to subject them to rigorous public testing [intellectual analysis] and critique by the community of inquirers. Fallibilism requires a high tolerance for uncertainty, and the courage to revise, modify and abandon our most cherished beliefs when they have been refuted.
>
> (Bernstein 2005: 279)

Echoing Bernstein, Carr's (2007) description of educational inquiry as a practical science, and Schwandt's (1996) depiction of it as the enactment of practical philosophy, further affirms Gadamer's (1980) practical philosophy model for the social sciences. As described by Schwandt, this model leads to:

> ... social inquiry [that] seeks to examine a dialogical encounter dialogically. It is inquiry as conversation about deliberation, conflicting opinions, and choice of the values or internal aims of a particular practice. These are enduring characteristics of rational behaviour in both social inquiry and the practices that social inquiry examines,
>
> (Schwandt 1996: 64).

So research and theorizing as a practical (and moral) activity carries with it, and in fact requires, the ability to act wisely in the ever mutable conditions that mark human events and interactions – to understand practical situations, deliberate carefully over what to do and choose courses of action that aim for a worthy vision of morally grounded life. In education, our purpose is, or should be, to cultivate each other's and our own facilities for making sense of ourselves within an ever broadening context. In practical philosophy, theory helps the researcher and practitioner, but never replaces practical and often tacit knowledge. It also assists in making more apparent and articulate one's goals and intentions so that their current and possible moral consequences of various practices can be examined deliberately (Gadamer 1975).

Gadamer's philosophical hermeneutics rejected the alienation of means/ends instrumentalist rationality. His rejection stemmed from his conviction that it produces the opposite of reflective practice and is, instead, a kind of mindlessly destructive approach that exerts domination over others. Drawing on Heidegger's (Being and Time) concept of *Dasein*, he described the act of coming to know as one's ongoing encounter with the world and the questioning of it, of others, and of oneself. Just as we cannot separate our consciousness from our interactions with the world and others around us, we cannot separate subjective from objective – thus the collapse and irrelevance of subject/object dualism. Understanding is the ontological given, and for him, as for Rorty, it is a fundamentally social activity – an ongoing and thoroughly unpredictable conversation – an ongoing 'sharing in a common meaning' (Gadamer 1975: 398). '[T]o understand means to come to an understanding with each other' (p. 180). Educational practice and inquiry emerge, according to Gadamer, through the hermeneutical experience, a convergence of tradition (the world of understanding we were all born into), which sets the stage for expectations, beliefs and so on, with the disruption, negation, and clashing of ongoing experiences. We adapt the old and the current to create a new and different understanding. This process cannot be fully conscious and therefore cannot be brought under instrumentalist control. It is always historically and contextually contingent.

Under a non-foundationalist framework, the role of theory and our understanding of it also accedes a vital alteration away from prediction and separation and toward a fundamental unity of practice and theory. Practice and theory are understood to be dialectically inseparable through the reflective process. Educational research should, then, seek to illuminate this process. Application is dialectically interconnected and interdependent with interpretation, and all are historically and culturally contingent. In Gadamer's (1975) words, they are 'one unified process' (p. 308). Elaborating on this point, Misgeld and Nicholson (1992) wrote the following of Gadamer's stance on theory and its irreducible connection to practice (application):

> Only an age of engineering would suppose that the application of a science or a theory would take the results of a theory erected in its own domain, and then impose it somewhere, hoping to produce results useful to human life. Such an understanding also shows up in contemporary discourse about social science and practical politics, on the one hand, or psychology and practical education, on the other hand. By this account, the original science or theory is supposed to be erected without any thought for human welfare. But this is a late and derivative concept, whereas Gadamer himself always understood *applicatio* in an earlier sense that was first generated in antiquity, and which then produced a series of further meanings, articulated well prior to the modern experience of engineering.
>
> (Misgeld and Nicholson 1992: vii)

Put somewhat differently, theory is not and should not be seen to be a tool for reification. Instead, it is a working out of possibilities. And the aim of research in education, as with all of the social sciences, is to bring the consequences of our knowledge and practices under more reflective scrutiny and to weigh more deliberatively the consequences of those actions. By extension, he saw theory as an act of 'true participation, not something active but something passive (pathos), namely being totally involved in and carried away by what one sees' (p. 125).

This theme of complete involvement, of non-separation and openness to others in the context of ongoing events, both educational and otherwise, is echoed in Allan (2008) and Heshusius (1994). By erasing the traditional lines between the researcher and the researched, this alternative framework positions us quite differently – we are not doing research *on* or *about* others, but *with* others (Allan 2008; Schwandt 1996). In her incisive discussion about research on inclusive education, Allan (2008: 148) noted that, '[t]he minimal, and in some cases negative, impact of research on inclusion on its subjects has often been reflected in research relations themselves and the way in which they operate within, and perpetuate, uneven power structures'. What she has affirmed here is that it is only through the intentional act of letting go of concerns about power, status, and control that an opportunity for fruitful understanding emerges.

A very compelling sense of this willingness to 'forget one's own purposes' comes to us from Heshusius's (1994: 16) concept of *participatory consciousness* – 'an inner desire to let go of perceived boundaries that constitute "*self*" and a temporary eclipse of all the perceiver's egocentric thoughts and strivings, of all preoccupations with self and self-esteem'. This letting go of self also includes abandoning concerns about being 'objective' or at the very least 'managing one's subjectivities'. Instead of needing to get rid of or trying to subjugate our 'subjectivities' (as if that were possible), Heshusius further made clear that by attending to them, by noticing them non-judgmentally, access (and hence understanding) is made more rather than less possible. As she deftly clarified, the demise of objectivity (or even a partial version thereof) obviates the viability of its opposite – subjectivity – and lays to rest the outworn dictum that the researcher must find some means, procedural or otherwise, for controlling subjectivity.

> Participatory consciousness, then, does not stand in opposition to the concepts of objectivity and subjectivity: It simply effaces them. Therefore, the possibility and nature of participatory consciousness cannot be evaluated from within the objectivity-subjectivity dualism.
>
> (Heshusius's 1994: 18)

Put another way, subjectivity and its procedural 'management' is merely a prop for the discredited notion of objectivity, one that serves the same purpose as objectivity – to build a fortress around ourselves, effectively constructing an individual self, not only as the centre of the universe but as the entire universe itself. In the willing act of relinquishing we do not risk obscuring what is really there; for as Gadamer explained it, in every act of unconcealment (making evident or illuminated), something is also concealed. Thus, the research act as a representation is better understood as a re-presentation.

Re-theorizing educational research and the question of relativism

Here we are directly confronted with the prospect transcending scientism by dispensing with the need for foundations for our research knowledge, the search for certainty, and all the rest. This is a daunting prospect for many; yet, going beyond the epistemological and ontological is also to realise that being tied to various frameworks of knowledge is not only confounding and stultifying, but also imposes artificial and pointless restrictions on the possibilities of better ways of responding to educational needs. For this transition to occur requires that, as Rorty (1999) advised, we cease asking the question – '[i]s our knowledge of things adequate to the way things really are' and begin asking instead – how do our research descriptions '…fulfil our needs more adequately…?' (Rorty 1999: 72). It also involves realising that theories that supposedly foundationalise inquiry can no longer lead us forward. We have run headlong into the limits of our theories of knowledge and truth, resulting in a confrontation with relativism and therefore the moral nature of our claims to knowledge and truth. The ideal of interdependence rather than those of individualism and detachment signals the way forward.

Rorty's (1979: 24) depiction of research highlights 'the value of cooperative human inquiry' that has 'an ethical base, not an epistemological one' and because it does not have an epistemological base, '…*a fortiori* it does not have a relativistic one'. In other words, cooperative human inquiry does not make a claim on superior knowledge as accurate depiction. In the absence of such a claim, it is non-epistemological and therefore cannot be called relativistic. Gadamer also rejected the notion of naïve (anything goes) relativism, explaining that our history, languages, traditions, and cultural contexts place demands on us, thus making this understanding of relativism a silly idea. To fear relativism is to fear being human. No matter how much we may desire it, we cannot take a godlike stance. We are what we are – finite human beings (Bernstein 1983) – but, without minimizing the difficulty involved, this is not the crisis it is made out to be. Instead, it is an opportunity to re-imagine how we want to be together, both as human beings and as educators.

Theories do have consequences, most of all for those whom we research. But they also have consequences for us as researchers and how we lead our lives. As revealed in the opening scenario of this chapter, the affinity for scientism has given primacy to instrumentalist solutions and consigned moral judgment to a contingent category, a category we avoid as both dangerous and illegitimate grounds for making choices about what is and what is not worth doing in schools and classrooms. But it is an affinity that we have chosen and not one that is imposed upon us. In choosing otherwise, it becomes possible to make better, more edifying decisions not only about what we do, how we inform our educational practices, but also why it matters.

Notes

1 Of further interest is the strange admixture of the social forces recounted above in combination with the vagaries of personal histories that found their way into whether various influential pioneers of the social sciences rationalized their allegiances either toward or away from positivism. For example, John B. Watson's behaviourism emanated from his revolt against the fundamentalist religion in which he was raised, the nervous breakdown resulting from the domestic strife resulting in a broken home, and, as Ross put it, '…his effort to gain rigid control on the strange outer world he encountered and his own conflict-ridden inner world (p. 312). On the other hand, historian Charles Beard hailed from a well-to-do Quaker, abolitionist home. Opposition to his well-known work, *An Economic Interpretation of the Constitution of the United States* (an interpretive work revealing how the economic interests of the members of the Constitutional Convention influenced their votes), led, in part, to his resignation/dismissal from Columbia University

and his initiative to found The New School for Social Research dedicated to open inquiry and allied to social democratic philosophy. Because The New School was not, therefore, a recipient of large conservative foundations, it remained chronically underfunded in its reliance less lucrative gifts from individual donors.

2 We should note here that Edward L. Thorndike, widely known as the 'father of school psychology', was himself an avid supporter and active participant in the American Eugenics movement (see: Aldrich, Carruth, and Davenport 1914).

3 Consider the claims of progress toward a scientific theoretical framework for a knowledge base of teaching that emerged out of the 1980s and is still cited as 'the knowledge base' (Brophy and Good 1987; Wang, Haertel, and Walberg 1993). For example, in the category of *Quality of Instruction*, we are told that the amount of time teachers and students spend actually involved in teaching and learning (time on task) determines educational outcomes and is an important research finding. Under the category *of Classroom Management*, we are told that a high degree of teacher attentiveness to the events in the classroom (teacher 'with-itness') is an important scientific discovery. A close examination of this knowledge base will assure readers that the above examples are prototypes of all others.

Note that the authors call these a 'list of characteristics of effective schools' just as MacIntyre pointed out – a list of instances is not a law-like prediction.

References

Aldrich, M. A., Carruth, W. H., and Davenport, C. B. (eds) (1914) *Eugenics: Twelve University Lectures*, New York: Dodd, Mead, and Company.

Bernstein, R. J. (1983) *Beyond Objectivism and Relativism*, Philadelphia: University of Pennsylvania Press.

Bernstein, R. J. (2005) *The Abuse of Evil: The Corruption of Politics and Religion Since 9/11*, Cambridge, UK: Polity Press.

Biesta, G. (2007) 'Why "what works" won't work: Evidence-based practice and the democratic deficit in educational research', *Educational Theory,* 57: 1-22.

Broekkamp, H., and van Hout-Wolters, B. (2007) 'The gap between educational research and practice: A literature review, symposium, and questionnaire', *Educational Research and Evaluation,* 13: 203-220.

Brophy, J. E., and Good, T. L. (1986) 'Teacher behavior and student achievement', in M. C. Wittrock (ed.) *Handbook of Research on Teaching* (3rd ed., pp. 328-375), New York: Macmillan.

Carr, W. (2007) 'Education research a practical science', *International Journal of Research and Method in Education,* 30: 271-286.

Cornwell, R. (July 6, 2002) 'Interview with John Kenneth Galbraith', *Toronto Globe and Mail.*

Danziger, K. (1994) '*Constructing the subject: Historical origins of psychological research*', Cambridge: Cambridge University Press.

Dudley-Marling, C. (2011) 'Researching in classrooms: Getting beyond "what works"', *Learning Disability Quarterly,* 34: 141-149.

Elmore, R. E. (1993) 'What knowledge base?', *Review of Educational Research,* 63: 314-318.

Gadamer, H.-G. (1975) '*Truth and Method*', Translated and edited by Garrett Barden and John Cumming. New York: Seabury Press.

Gadamer, H.-G. (1980) 'Practical philosophy as a model of the human sciences', *Research in Phenomenology,* I: 74-85.

Gallagher, D. J. (1998) 'The scientific knowledge base of special education: Do we know what we think we know?' *Exceptional Children,* 64: 493-502.

Gallagher, D. J. (2004b) 'Educational research, philosophical orthodoxy and unfulfilled promises: The quandary of traditional research in US special education', in G. Thomas and R. Pring (eds), *Evidence-based practice in education* (pp. 119-130), Berkshire, UK: Open University Press.

Gallagher, D. J. (2010) 'Educational researchers and the making of normal people', In C. Dudley-Marling and A. Gurn, (eds) *Deconstructing the normal curve and reconstructing education for students with disabilities* (pp. 25-38), New York: Peter Lang.

Iano, R. P. (2004) 'The study and development of teaching: With implications for the advancement of special education', in D. J. Gallagher, L. Heshusius, R. P. Iano, and T. M. Skrtic (eds) *Challenging orthodoxy in special education: Dissenting voices,* Denver, CO: Love Publishing.

Kaestle, C. (1993) 'The awful reputation of education research', *Educational Researcher,* 22: 23-31.

Keredeman, D., and Phillips, D. C. (1993) 'Empiricism and the knowledge base of educational practice. *Review of Educational* Research' 63: 305-313.

Kliebard, H. M. (1993) 'What is a knowledge base, and who would use it if we had one?' *Review of Educational Research,* 63: 295-303.

McDermott, R., and Hall, K. D. (2007) Scientifically debased research on learning, 1854 – 2006. *Anthropology and Education Quarterly,* 38: 9-15.

Misgeld, D., and Nicholson, G. (1992) *Hans-Georg Gadamer on education, poetry, and history: Applied hermeneutics,* Albany, NY: State University of New York Press.

Nuthall, G. (2004) 'Relating classroom teaching to student learning: A critical analysis of why research has failed to bridge the theory-practice gap', *Harvard Educational Review,* 74: 273-306.

Polanyi, M. (1962) *Personal Knowledge,* Chicago: University of Chicago Press.

Putnam, H. (1994) *Words and Life.* James Conant (ed.), Cambridge, MA: Harvard University Press.

Rorty, R.(1979) *Objectivity, Relativism, and Truth,* Cambridge: Cambridge University Press.

Rorty, R. (1999) *Philosophy and Social Hope,* London: Penguin Books.

Ross, D. (1992) *The Origins of American Social Science.* Cambridge: Cambridge University Press.

Singer, J. D. (1993) 'On faith and microscopes: Methodological lenses for learning about learning', *Review of Educational Research,* 63: 353-364.

Schwandt, T. A. (1996) 'Farewell to criteriology', *Qualitative Inquiry,* 2: 58-72.

Schwandt, T. A. (2005) 'A diagnostic reading of scientifically based research for education', *Educational Theory,* 55: 285-305.

Wang, M. C., Haertel, G. D., and Walberg, H. (1993) 'Toward a knowledge base for school learning', *Review of Educational Research,* 63: 249-294.

Chapter 6

Bildung and educational language

Talking of 'the self' in Anglo-American education

Norm Friesen

Introduction

The language used to frame and discuss educational issues, both in scholarly publication and in everyday talk, shapes broader possibilities for theory and practice. It both enables and limits ways of defining and addressing pedagogical concerns, from general policy to the minutiae of practice. For example, to speak of education as 'a process of living and not [as] a preparation for future living' (Dewey 1897: 7) has rather different implications than conceiving of it as a form of 'human control' exercised through 'fundamental laws of change' (Thorndike 1912: 95, 97). Over the past century or more, the language associated with educational scholarship has changed considerably. In this chapter I present an overview of some of these changes, focusing on the field of educational psychology, beginning with the work of Dewey and Mead on the one hand, and Thorndike on the other. I conclude with an examination of the vocabulary of the 'Learning Sciences' and of other contemporary contributions that bring with them rather different possibilities for theory and practice.

I focus specifically on the use of the term 'the self' in educational psychology, beginning with the late 19th century, when a vocabulary and frame of reference was prevalent in North American education that is markedly different from the familiar assumptions of contemporary scientific psychology. This terminology and its philosophical grounding are associated with the term *Bildung*. Variously translated as edification, formation or growth, *Bildung* is notoriously difficult to define. It refers on the one hand to the 'developmental formation of an individual's unique potential through participation in the social practices and institutions of culture' (Good and Garrison 2007: 44). On the other hand, it includes the "cultivation of inner life," the development of subjectivity as a kind of "quality of selfhood," and also as a manifestation of the self's freedom or agency. In *Bildung*, this formation and cultivation is seen as occurring both inside and outside of educational institutions. As a result, the remarks of Hegel, Mead or Dewey, who were markedly influenced by theories of *Bildung* should be seen as denoting both formal and informal, institutional and extra-institutional contexts.

I then examine how these possibilities of speaking of the self were extinguished (but for a few exceptions) by behaviorism in the educational mainstream. The self was only gradually re-introduced in relatively recent developments in cognitive psychology – specifically in the form of 'self-processes' or 'self-referent phenomena' such as 'self-regulation' and 'self-efficacy' (Bandura 1993). Despite the increasing integration of references to the self in the cognitivist discourses of educational psychology, I argue that the vocabulary provided by this and related paradigms is inadequate as a resource for educational theorizing and practice.

Rather than trying to anticipate scientific progress and discovery, I make a case for the need to recover language and theoretical connections that have been long been forgotten. In his book *Forgotten Connections: On Culture and Upbringing* (1983) Klaus Mollenhauer[1] speaks of this task of recovery and recuperation as one of paramount importance for pedagogy: 'Pedagogy must work at the task of cultural and biographical recollection; it must find through this recollection those principles which are of lasting value; pedagogy has to find a precise and suitable language for this task.' (Mollenhauer forthcoming)

Mollenhauer goes on to say that education must look to its past to find the '*elementaria*' of its theory and practice. He frames the task of recovery as linguistic in nature, asking whether 'terms such as learning, education, *Bildung* or teaching' are sometimes not more of a hindrance than a help. Mollenhauer raised these questions nearly three decades ago, but the timescales that he is invoking, which I also wish to take into account, are expansive, stretching multiple decades if not centuries. Like Mollenhauer, I also wish to inquire into the language of teaching, learning, education and pedagogy. Ultimately I do so in order to make the case that more integrative ways of speaking of the self, reflective of the vocabulary of *Bildung*, need to be re-introduced, radicalized and extended, not so much in the direction of any romantic idealist past, but in responsiveness to present cultural and historical circumstances.

Dewey's new psychology

As foreshadowed in its opening, this chapter uses as its reference points the 'new psychology' of John Dewey (and the closely related symbolic interactionism of Mead), and the 'connectionist' or proto-behaviorist psychology of Edward L. Thorndike. Despite Dewey and Thorndike's shared patriarchal status in America, the legacies of these two figures could not be more different. Whereas Thorndike's career began with the study of animal behavior, and the articulation of an 'animal method of learning,' Dewey's (as well as Mead's) early work is steeped in German idealism and related theories of individual and collective formation or *Bildung*. Dewey himself famously observed that the philosophy of the German idealist, G.W.F. Hegel 'left a permanent deposit' in his thinking, and this influence has recently been well-documented in Dewey scholarship (e.g., Good and Garrison, 2007; Good 2006). Hegel's dialectical theory of the formation or *Bildung* of the self through processes of contradiction and reconciliation, alienation and activity forms a general framework that structures a large part of Dewey's theorizing: 'the most significant Hegelian deposit in Dewey's... thought,' as Good concludes in his book-length study, 'is the *Bildung* model of philosophy' (2006: xx). The influence of the German tradition of Bildung on Dewey is not limited to Hegel. As this chapter shows, it also extends to educational theorists concerned specifically with schooling and upbringing, particularly Friedrich Fröbel. Both philosophical and educational areas of influence will first be considered briefly in the work of Dewey and Mead before this chapter turns to Thorndike and subsequent developments in educational theorizing.

Self and its formation in Hegelianism above all concerns the consciousness of the self, a quality that does not simply refer to mere sensory cognizance, but to a capacity for attentiveness, feeling and volition. This awareness encompasses both the self and the world around it and is shaped by experience and purpose. Hegel conceives of the self as undergoing constant development, gradually maturing through a transition from an immediate consciousness or sensory awareness to a more mediated *self*-consciousness via engagement with the world and with others. In the prepositional language of German idealism, the self changes from an existence that is *an sich* (potential being-in-itself) to one that is *für sich* (actual being-for-itself). Formation or development for Hegel is the process of moving from 'being in itself' to being that is 'for itself.' The self in this sense can be said to be manifest as a *development occurring through activity*, to paraphrase Dewey's comments, below.

Hegel's emphasis on consciousness and action, and on their combined significance for development is also central to Dewey's educational philosophy, and is reflected in Mead's social interactionism from the same time-period. In one of his earliest books (1887), Dewey defines psychology as 'the Science of the Facts or Phenomena of the Self [sic]' and identifies as the fundamental characteristic of the self as the simple 'fact of consciousness,' the reality that it is aware of itself and the world around it:

> The self not only exists, but may know that it exists...A stick, a stone, exists and undergoes changes...But it is aware neither of its existence nor of these changes. It does not, in short, exist *for itself*. It exists only *for* some consciousness. Consequently the stone has no self. But the [self as mind and body]...knows that it is, and what [the] experiences are which it passes through. *It exists for itself*. That is to say, it is a self.
>
> (Dewey 1887: 7-8; emphases in original)

Dewey is asserting that the self, through its awareness and experience, is qualitatively distinct from the passive or reactive objects around it. Whereas these objects are fully determined through laws of physical and causal necessity, the self is able to know and act for itself. It is in this sense something 'for' itself, rather than simply for another.

Dewey goes on to describe the ways in which the self develops through and as a result of conscious activity. 'The individual is not born a realized self,' he says, 'but his psychical existence is the process of realization' (ibid.: 157). It is an active consciousness. It is through its feeling and volition, that the self's essence, its selfhood, is realized. But for Dewey, as for Mead and Hegel, this is not a solitary activity. It occurs in and through engagement with others:

> The self which is the object of intuition is not an object existing ready made, and needing only to have consciousness turned to it, as towards other objects, to be known like them as a separate object...The self is [instead] a connecting, relating activity, and hence is a real unity, one which unites into a whole all the various elements and members of our knowledge.
>
> (Dewey 1887: 210)

Among the elements that Dewey sees as making up this unified whole, of course, are those that 'arise from the relations of self-conscious beings to each other' (ibid.: 281). The self is a type of awareness and activity that is not isolated or solipsistic, but social and communal. Hegel's emphasis on action, and the (at first) paradoxical idea of simultaneous self-realization and social integration as being interdependent are essential to *Bildung*. The ontogenetic growth of the individual self, in other words, is seen as resonant with the phylogenetic development of society (or humankind), and vice versa.

Mead provides an important contribution in the way that he describes the social and communal nature of the self. Like Hegel and Dewey, Mead starts by explaining that the self develops in consciousness through a dynamic that takes place between self and other, part and whole:

> It is only through the response that consciousness of meaning appears, a response which involves the consciousness of another self as the presupposition of the meaning in one's own attitude. Other selves in a social environment logically antedate the consciousness of self which introspection analyzes.
>
> (Dewey 1910: 135)

In other words: Social reality antedates self-awareness and is ultimately constitutive of the self. This is exemplified for Mead in communication and language. Mead explains that the self is able to be an object to itself or to be "for itself" *not* simply because of the active, reflective power of its consciousness, but because of its participation in *language*:

> The self arises in conduct, when the individual becomes a social object in experience to himself. This takes place when the individual assumes the attitude or uses the gesture which another individual would use and responds to it himself...Especially [if this self] talks to himself as he talks to others and in keeping up this conversation in the inner forum constitutes the field which is called that of mind. Then those objects and experiences which belong to his own body, those images which belong to his own past, become part of this self.
>
> (Mead 1922: 160)

Communication and talk form the means and the medium through which the self becomes a self. In relating to ourselves through language, we achieve selfhood *through* the other, and through participation in society in general. Language after all is used both for one's self and for others. In making ourselves into an object of our own awareness through language, we are realized socially – a reality captured in the brevity of Mead's wit: 'A person who is saying something is saying to himself what he says to others; otherwise he does not know what he is talking about' (Mead 1934: 142). Of course, as selves, we *do* know what we are talking about (at least some of the time). If we communicate with ourselves in a way that is substantially different from the way we communicate with others, we fall into solipsism. According to Mead, we are *for* ourselves (*an sich*) because, in a sense, we *are* language and relation: 'Mind is then a field that is not confined to the individual much less located in a brain. Significance belongs to things in their relations to individuals' (Mead 1922: 163).

As his thinking and work progresses, Dewey brings his broadly Hegelian frame of reference to bear on a number of questions related to education and at this point registers the influence of Fröbel and other *educational* theorists of *Bildung*. It is in this context that the potential of *Bildung* for framing the self – and for connecting educational theory with educational practice – is specifically and clearly illustrated. The approach to *Bildung* developed by Fröbel enjoyed considerable popularity in America early in Dewey's career. Translations and interpretations of Fröbel published in the late 19th century and the first dozen years of the 20th century were used by Dewey and are also referenced here. One notion appearing in Dewey that is central to Fröbel's philosophy and to his conception of self and its development is captured in the term 'self-activity.' Referencing Hegel's notion of the mirroring or the maturation of self in larger social and cultural development, Fröbel explains:

> (E)ach successive individual human being, inasmuch as he would understand the past and present, must pass through all preceding phases of human development and culture, and this should not be done in the way of dead imitation or mere copying, but in the way of living, spontaneous

> *self-activity*. Every human being should represent these phases spontaneously and freely as a type for himself and others.
>
> (Fröbel, as quoted in Hughes 1910: 261; emphasis added)

The correspondence between ontogenetic and phylogenetic development, while very important, is not slavish. The self always retains its distinction from others, and pedagogy has as one of its principle tasks to encourage and cultivate this distinctiveness, individuality and subjectivity is expressed through independent activity. Writing approvingly of 'Fröbel's Educational Principles' in *School and Society* (Dewey 1907), Dewey describes self-activity as nothing less than 'the primary root of all educative activity,' which:

> is in the instinctive, impulsive attitudes and activities of the child, and not in the presentation and application of external material, whether through the ideas of others or through the senses; and that, accordingly, numberless spontaneous activities of children, plays, games, mimic efforts, even the apparently meaningless motions of infants –exhibitions previously ignored as trivial, futile, or even condemned as positively evil – are capable of educational use; nay, are the foundation-stones of educational method.
>
> (Dewey 1907: 112)

Dewey makes the notion of self-activity concrete. For him, it refers not only abstractly to self-initiated activity, but also to the concrete movements, exhibitions, and attitudes of children. A self-initiated activity such as interest in a sport or a musical instrument can provide the basis for the individual's participation in a range of social practices and institutions. At the same time, this "interest" acts as an expression and development of the individual's unique, personal potential. This very concrete way of understanding self-activity is framed in slightly different terms some 15 years later in the pages of Dewey's *Democracy and Education* (Dewey 1916). The passage begins with a critique of the conventionalized understanding of self-activity as being 'too frequently…restricted to something merely internal – something excluding the free use of sensory and motor organs' (Dewey 1916: 302). Dewey then expands the notion of self-activity by connecting it with what he refers to as 'interest,' saying that the latter is centrally constitutive of the self in its active formation.

> (T)he self is not something ready-made, but something in continuous formation through choice of action…In fact, self and interest are two names for the same fact; the kind and amount of interest actively taken in a thing reveals and measures the quality of selfhood which exists. Bear in mind that interest means the active or moving identity of the self with a certain object...
>
> (Ibid.: 34)

The self is an ever-developing and purposeful activity that is in constant and active engagement with the world and its objects. And this action, significantly, is inseparable from the self's interest and its very identity.

The fate of the self in the 20th century: behaviorist precedents

By the time Dewey's words appeared in *Democracy and Education* his conception of the self was very much in competition with a rather different view of psychology and its proper object of study. The early twentieth century was a time when a paradigm of comparative, connectivist psychology emerged and established an important precedent for educational theorizing to follow. Ellen Lagemann has observed of this period that:

> one cannot understand the history of education in the United States... unless one realizes that Edward L. Thorndike won and John Dewey lost. The statement is too simple, of course, but nevertheless more true than untrue...If Dewey has been revered among some educators and his thought has had influence across a greater range of scholarly domains – philosophy, sociology, politics, and social psychology, among them – Thorndike's thought has been more influential within education. It helped to shape public school practice as well as scholarship about education.
>
> (Lagemann 1989: 185)

As I argue, Thorndike's approach to education not only 'helped to shape scholarship about education,' it also set the terms for a century of educational psychology as a positivistic enterprise. The 'foundation-stones' of educational practice are no longer spontaneous or self-directed activity – much less the awareness of self, posited by Dewey and Mead as psychology's starting point. The goal of educational psychology became instead the definition of verifiable regularities or 'laws' of learning, as measured in both human and animal physiology. Psychology, as Thorndike himself declares, 'is the science of the intellects, characters and behavior of animals, including man' (1910: 5). Both the object and objective of education and psychology are reconfigured in terms radically opposed to those of Dewey and Mead. The objective of psychology is no longer the cultivation of active selfhood, but the modification of these regularities in accordance with the causal laws.

In his groundbreaking dissertation research on animal intelligence, Thorndike experimented with cats, dogs and other caged animals, timing their repeated attempts to access food by pressing on a lever or pulling on rope. Based on these investigations, he established a series of 'laws of acquired behavior or learning' (Thorndike 1911: 244), based on the relationship between factors of 'situation,' 'repetition' and 'satisfaction.' It is not so much the proto-behaviorist character of these laws that prefigures subsequent educational psychologies, but the concern with learning as an isolatable, naturalized set of responses to a situation or environment, subject to rules of causality, and thus also subject to calculation and manipulation. Individually, the causal regularities or 'laws' laws identified by Thorndike are simple. But together, he maintained, they could explain the most subtle and complex behaviors. 'Any problem of education' he asserts, 'may be put in the form: "Given a certain desired change in a man, what situation shall we create to produce it, either directly or by the response which it provokes from him?"' (Thorndike 1912: 55-56). More complex notions, such as knowledge, character and personality, are similarly reducible to situation and recurrent response: 'What we call intellect, character and skill [is] in the case of any man, the sum of the man's tendencies to respond to situations and elements of situations' (Thorndike 1912: 102). In a broader social context, the goal of education is one of human control, specifically for the purpose 'matching individuals to existing social and economic roles' (Thorndike as quoted in Lagemann 1989: 212).

Terms normally attributable to persons in everyday language like character, interest or skill can be accounted for using the rather different terminology of behavioral responses, situations, and the connections between them. The everyday language of personal intention, volition and agency is consequently, eliminated in this account. Apparently taking aim at Dewey's own language of consciousness and volitional action, Thorndike put this as follows:

> In the case of the so-called action-consciousness the neglect of the connections becomes preposterous. The adventitious scraps of consciousness called "willing" which may intervene between a situation productive of a given act and the act itself are hopelessly uninstructive in comparison with the bonds of instinct and habit which cause the situation to produce the act.
>
> (Thorndike 1911: 18)

Thorndike leaves little doubt that a self that is constituted through factors such as will, activity and consciousness is superfluous for scientific studies of behavior and learning. Such terminology is extrinsic, epiphenomenal, and 'hopelessly uninstructive' when compared to the ineluctable connections of instinct and habit.

Behaviorism and its interdictions against 'adventitious' phenomena such as volition or "willing" far outlasted Thorndike's long and prolific career. They extend all the way to the 1960s and 1970s in the form of the radical behaviorism of B.F. Skinner – albiet with some modifications: Situations came to be known as 'environments;' environments, in turn, presented various 'contingencies' or 'stimuli.' The creation of responses, connections or bonds through these situations came to be known as 'conditioning' or 'reinforcement.' This vocabulary allowed Skinner to be very explicit about the fundamentally technical, instrumental character of education, framing teaching specifically as a 'technology' which could operate through the precise arrangement of 'contingencies of reinforcement under which behavior changes" (Skinner 1968: 9). In this way, the role of the teacher is effectively reduced to a relatively simple set of operations that can, in theory, just as easily be undertaken by human as by a machine. In fact, Skinner fully expected such machines to replace the teacher as a 'mechanism' for the provision of instructionally effective reinforcement. 'We have every reason to expect that the most effective control of human learning will require instrumental aid. The simple fact is that, as a mere reinforcing mechanism, the teacher is out of date.' (Skinner 1968: 22)

One such mechanism was Skinner's 'teaching machine.' Placed on a student's desk, this wooden box provided stimuli in the form of small units of information or questions, and offered an immediate, programmemed reinforcement according to a student's scoring of his or her own response. Teaching complex subjects – or 'programme[ming] complex forms of behaviour' according to Skinner – consequently became a question simply of 'effective sequencing.' Here is an example of one such sequence to teach the spelling and meaning of a single word:

1 MANUFACTURE means to make or build. Chair factories manufacture chairs. Copy the word here: ___ ___ ___ ___ ___ ___ ___ ___ ___ ___ ___
2 Part of the word is like part of the word FACTORY. Both parts come from an old word meaning make or build. M A N U ___ ___ ___ ___ U R E
3 Part of the word is like part of the word MANUAL. Both parts come from an old word for hand. Many things are made by hand. ___ ___ ___ ___ F A C T U R E
4 The same letter goes in both spaces. M ___ N U F ___ C T U R E
5 The same letter goes in both spaces. M A N ___ F A C T ___ R E
6 Chair factories ___ ___ ___ ___ ___ ___ ___ ___ ___ ___ ___ chairs.

(Skinner 1958: 973)

The mechanical, combinatory nature of Skinner's conception of learning could not be clearer. Each instance of behavior is isolated in an individual letter or sequence of the same, and this behavior is repeatedly reinforced in a highly programmed manner.

Significantly, Skinner integrated a notion of the 'self' in his psychology of control, conditioning and response, and the manner in which he does so is significant. The self for Skinner is 'simply a device for representing *a functionally unified system of responses*.' It is, in other words, a label for something that is able to react to stimuli in a systematically consistent way. By this definition, of course, many organisms, not just humans or their close mammalian relatives, possess 'selves.' Skinner also combined his conception of the self as a functional system with the experimental, scientific sense of the word 'control' – referring to the experimental isolation and variation of one or more causal factors. As

Skinner defines it, the phrase 'self-control,' thus refers to exercising this type of control over oneself, 'precisely as [one] would control the behavior of anyone else – through the manipulation of variables of which behavior is a function.' In this way, Skinner posits a self that is responsive, functionally coordinated, and is also able to manipulate variables to impact its own behavior as a scientist would manipulate controls in an experiment. Skinner is not particularly clear, though, about the source or location of the intelligence or agency that would determine such control.

However, in reintroducing the self to psychology in this way, Skinner sets an important precedent for its further treatment in education: The self is gradually reintegrated as a term in psychology by making one of the key causal terms or processes in the given psychological lexicon (in this case, 'control') into one that is specifically *reflexive*. Experimental control of different variables is reflexively turned into one's own control over factors impacting one's self or rather, one's behavior. This additional monitoring function, however, cannot itself be readily accounted for in the few terms originally used to describe the self in behaviorism (i.e. as a "functionally unified set of responses").

The fate of the self to the present: cognitivism and the learning sciences

Starting in the late 1960s, psychology moved relatively rapidly from a paradigm or set of metaphors based on stimulus and (reflexive) response to ones founded computation and processing. This new, *cognitive* psychology develops from the hypothesis that the processing and representational capabilities of the computer can serve as a model for understanding the mind. In the 1970s and 1980s, cognitive psychology focused primarily on modeling basic logical and perceptual processes, leaving little room for considerations of a "self." Writing in the early 1990s, educational psychologist Alfred Bandura critiqued this state of affairs as presenting an unnecessarily 'austere cognitivism' – one that 'neglected self-regulatory processes that govern human development and adaption.' The multiple 'self-processes' or 'self-referent phenomena' that Bandura wished to highlight at this point include most prominently 'self-regulation,' 'self-efficacy' and 'self-concept:'

> Effective intellectual functioning requires much more than simply understanding the factual knowledge and reasoning operations for given activities...Self influences affect the selection and construction of environments. The impact of most environmental influences on human motivation, affect, and action is heavily mediated through self processes. They give meaning and valence to external events. Self influences thus operate as important proximal determinants at the very heart of causal processes.
>
> (Bandura 1992: 117–118)

Given their view of the mind as fundamentally computational, cognitive psychologists posited that self-processes like self-regulation function as the reflexive application of computational procedures and representational structures onto these procedures and structures themselves. This is most clearly suggested by the term 'metacognition,' which refers to an active monitoring of one's cognitive processes, an attempt to regulate one's cognitive processes in relationship to further learning, and an application of a set of heuristics as an effective device for helping people organize their methods of attack on problems in general. (Hennessey, as quoted in Lai, 2011)

A similar construction is identified in the phrase "self-regulated learning," which refers to the control and optimization of information processing operations not dissimilar to the kind of control exercised by basic cybernetic systems (of which the steam engine governor and thermostat are early examples). It is expressed also in terms of self-efficacy and self-concept, as organized sets of assessments, perceptions or representational structures formed by the self about itself. (See Figure 6.1, below, for a diagram showing how these self-representations or concepts are ordered hierarchically by Bandura in his 1993 article).

Self-efficacy refers to 'people's beliefs about their capabilities to produce designated levels of performance.' Bandura underscores the importance of this self-phenomenon as follows: 'People make causal contributions to their own functioning through mechanisms of personal agency. Among the mechanisms of agency, none is more central or pervasive than people's beliefs about their capabilities to exercise control over their own level of functioning and over events that affect their lives.' (Bandura 1993: 118)

It is important to note that the concept of agency is made a part of this less 'austere' incarnation of cognitive educational psychology. Agency, a notoriously vague term, has been defined as 'the capacity for willed (voluntary) action,' but in many cases, often serves as 'no more than a synonym for action' in general (Agency 1994:7). In the specific case of Bandura and psychologists in his wake, this capacity to act voluntarily is articulated using a rather restricted vocabulary – one referencing beliefs or assessments regarding the self's (largely cognitive) performance, and the regulation and maximization of this performance. In other words, cognitive psychology provides the vocabulary and conceptual means to describe the self as an entity that is able to accomplish tasks by optimizing its perceptions, evaluations and through them, cognitive processes themselves.

This less austere cognitive framework, which affirms precisely circumscribed 'self-phenomena' while keeping cognitivist metaphors of information and computation in place, has persisted in educational psychology to the present. This is particularly evident in the interdisciplinary efforts that have come to be known as the 'Learning Sciences.' For example, a content analysis of *The Journal of the Learning Sciences*, published since 1991 and ranked as the most influential periodical in education overall, shows that the term 'self' occurs in the title or

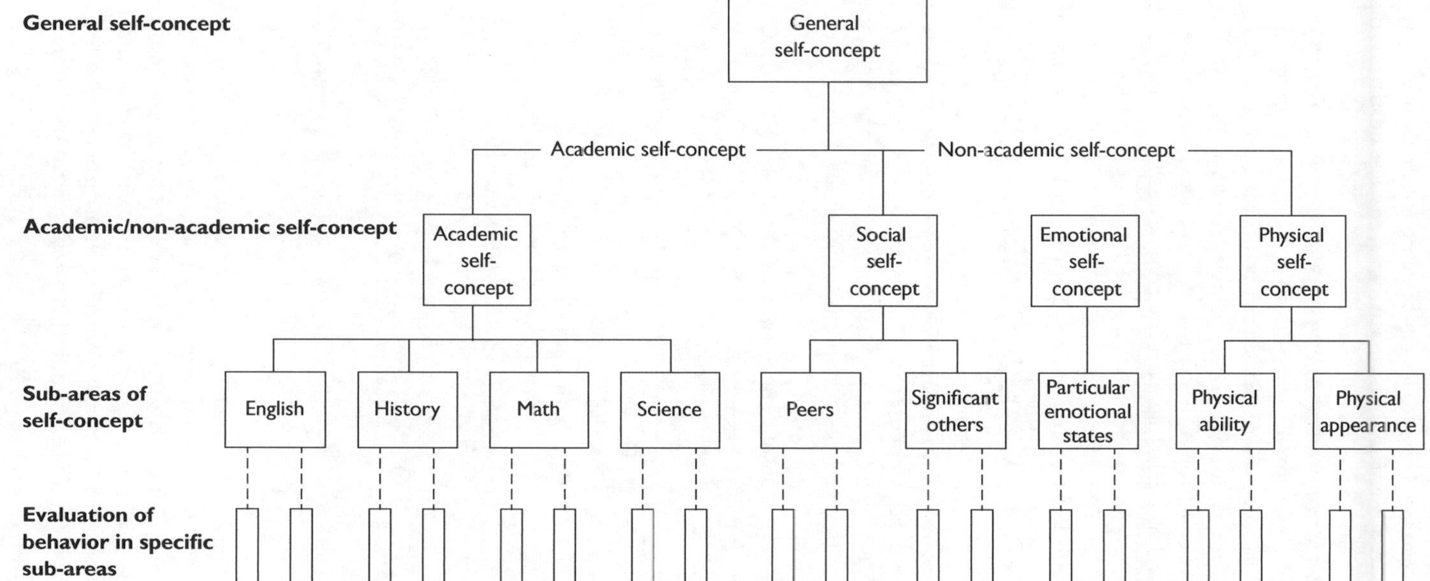

Figure 6.1 Self-concept as a hierarchical organization of evaluations of behavior in various sub-areas and situations (diagram based on illustration in Bandura: 1993).

abstract of no fewer than 183 articles. Its appearance in theoretically systematic uses in these contexts is entirely consistent with the less austere and marginally agentic cognitivism of Bandura. The psychologically-significant 'self-process' that appears by far the most frequently – twice as often as runners up 'self-regulation' and 'self-assessment' – is *self-explanation*. Coined by Chi *et al.*, in a 1989 article in *Cognitive Science*, self-explanation refers to the 'generat[ion] of explanations to oneself…to make sense of new information.' Findings showing that this particular self-process is positively associated with student ability to solve clearly defined problems have produced what is known as 'self-explanation effect' (Van Lehn, Jones and Chi, 1992): 'We find that 'Good' students learn with understanding: They generate many explanations …[and] these self-explanations are guided by accurate monitoring of their own understanding and misunderstanding. Such learning results in example-independent knowledge and in a better understanding.' (Chi *et al.* 1989: 145)

Chi and her co-authors provide an example of such a "good" student – whose monitoring, "self-explanations" and readings are all carefully elicited and recorded by an experimenter – in a table like the one below. The right column records the content of experimenter elicitations and student self-phenomena, while the left classifies their cognitive function:

Table 6.1 Self-explanation study protocol from Chi et al. 1989, p. 159.

	Idea Statements	*Protocol lines*
	Read line 6:	*Fa, Fb, and Fe are all the forces acting on the body.* (pause)
I.	Monitoring:	1) Okay.
	Read line 7.	*Since the …* (pause)
	Experimenter:	(Okay. what are you thinking about?)
II.	Monitoring:	2) I'm trying to think where Forces Fb and Fa
		3) are going to get the thing.
III.	Explanation:	4) They'd just be the force, the rest mass of
		5) the thing holding it up would be the force.
		6) It could, well, actually it'd be the force of weight.

Comparing this example with similar evidence gathered from students identified as 'Poor,' the authors explain:

> the problem solver is saying what he is thinking about or dumping the content of his or her working memory. Thus, longer protocols simply refer to a greater degree of processing…the Good students often dwell quite a bit on a single idea either because they realize that they do not understand it, or they want to provide a more complete explanation…the Good students generate a significantly greater number of ideas than the Poor…
>
> (Chi *et al.*: 160-161)

In this and other formulations concerning the self and self-reflexive processes, the particular psychological entity of the self is construed in a way that is not too different from Skinner's behaviorist conceptions. It is 'a functionally unified system' that is capable, in some instances, of exercising agency by applying its own functions (e.g., behavior, control, monitoring or explanation) reflexively to itself or its performance. The conception of self mobilized in studies like that of Chi *et al.*, moreover, leaves the meaning of the terms 'good' or 'poor' almost devoid of normative significance: What constitutes a "good" student in this scenario is simply the quantity of self-monitoring and self-explaining actions generated – a criterion rather distant from what might otherwise or informally be understood in referring to a student who is "good."

Recovering a deeper sense of self

However, to be able to address a student's activities or performance as either good or poor – or as corresponding with perhaps more nuanced normative categories – requires a broader vocabulary and frame of reference. To be able to acquire such a vocabulary and framework, it is not advisable or even possible to go back and adopt, *tout court*, the vocabulary of the early Dewey or of idealist dialectics. At the same time, though, this does not mean that some of the connections and meanings from Fröbel via Dewey – and even of the broader tradition of *Bildung* relevant to them – are not utterly irretrievable or unusable. The task of integrating a more meaningful conception of self into theoretically-grounded educational vocabularies, however, is more a process of recovery than of *sui generis* invention. This chapter now briefly illustrates what might be recuperated from *Bildung* for a language of the self in education. It begins with a relatively concrete discussion of self-activity from Mollenhauer's *Forgotten Connections*, and proceeds to a more general consideration of the current relevance of an idealist dialectics of individuality and society overall.

One of the lengthier chapters in Mollenhauer's text is titled 'Self-Activity: Children's own plans and projects,' and in it, Mollenhauer almost seems to pick up from where Dewey left off in developing this dialectical notion:

> In a pedagogical context, self-activity does not simply refer to an activity of one form or another; nor is it a natural biological phenomenon or some kind of random action; for self-activity is an activity that brings into play *potential powers* that are activated not by 'spontaneous generation' but rather by 'encouragement' via *social interaction*. Hence in a pedagogic context, the teacher or parent's responsibility is to nurture and call forth these potential powers...The skills and abilities thus acquired or "appropriated" then become the drivers of *personalization*, i.e. the productive forces that pave the way for the child to be brought up.
>
> (Mollenhaur 1983: 141, my translation)

Self-activity for Mollenhauer arises from within the self; but it is not entirely spontaneous, random and certainly not solitary in nature (as some of Dewey's examples might suggest). Instead, as Mollenhauer sees it, it is called forth in engagement or relation with another, generally an adult. (This may be seen as Dewey's 'certain object' or as Mead's 'other' or 'society' through which the mind itself is constituted.) At the same time, for Mollenhauer, the self's activity is not predetermined by being thus called upon or encouraged; its emergence is coeval with the emergence of the self in its autonomy and personality.[2]

Despite the somewhat abstract flavor of his description, above, the remainder of Mollenhauer's chapter on self-activity illustrates the notion in the most plain and concrete manner: in terms of learning to walk, to speak, to draw and to do arithmetic. Although these are clearly generic learning tasks and activities, Mollenhauer provides very specific illustrations of how children engage with them in terms of their own autonomous individual interests. He describes, for example, a mother assisting her child to walk while simultaneously appearing to be holding the child back. He also describes a shy, developmentally-challenged eight-year-old child being taught mathematics while at the same time learning to become more self-assertive. This last example illustrates Mollenhauer's understanding of self-activity, and may also provide a helpful contrast with the behaviorist and cognitivist protocols cited above. In this exchange the child, Didier, is being tutored by his teacher:[3]

Teacher: How many fingers do you have?
Didier: Just a sec. Hmmm...one, two three four. Four.
Teacher: And how many do I have?
Didier: *(Didier counts)* Five
Teacher: Does everyone have the same number of fingers?
Didier: Yup.
Teacher: So how many fingers does Charles have?
Didier: Five.
Teacher: And you?
Didier: I just told you.
Teacher: But how many was that?
Didier: Oh come on, four!
Teacher: But I have five, right?
Didier: Yeah, but I've still got fewer.

The teacher's interpretation of this rather odd interchange is as follows: 'Didier cannot abstract from what is [emotionally] concrete, and this is what gets in the way of his activity or efforts.' Thus, Didier's feelings of inadequacy and the cognitive tasks before him are seen to be competing for validity, preventing him from dealing with his own situation (i.e. the number of fingers on his hand) in simple mathematical terms. The teacher is gently and patiently challenging Didier to see this contradiction and to move towards the possibilities offered by the exercise of abstraction. Eventually, this teacher describes Didier's personal success (and also his own, pedagogical accomplishment) as follows:

> Didier has since made some progress – in fact he's made quite a bit of progress. He's completely different from the way he was in September. He's much less scattered and has totally stopped being such a tame and unadventurous kid. He's become lively and even a bit mischievous, and has learned how to stand up for himself.

This description is conspicuously different from the characterizations of "good" and "poor" students produced by research into self-explanation or that might be extended to the contingencies of reinforcement of Skinner's behaviorism. It makes no reference to Didier's progress in terms of his efficiency in solving math problems. Instead, this progress is measured in terms of ethical and social dimensions, and in the "calling forth" of potentiality in a general sense – indeed, in terms that are actually opposed to the stereotype of a "good" student. These are characteristics that are forcefully expressive of self-activity, and that are understood in a manner largely congruent with Dewey's descriptions, above. Although this realization of his "self" as active presumably also makes Didier a less behaviorally compliant boy, and probably decreases the efficiency of his academic or monitorial "self-processes," it also expresses the development of his self or selfhood.

At the same time – and arguably unlike Dewey's and Mead's earlier accounts of the self and its activity – this relatively simple story of Didier points to something well beyond the externally observable words and actions of student and teacher. The story foregrounds the *subjective* dimension of self-activity, as Mollenhauer has developed it from the Hegelian and idealist tradition. Mathematics and counting, for Didier, are not just a matter of external acts or facts, but of a crippling sense of inadequacy that Didier clearly carries with him. Subjectivity in this sense is notably different from Bandura's self-efficacy in that it is not about an (accurate or inaccurate) assessment of one's aggregate abilities. Instead, it refers to "how" Didier is (or might be) as a person and a subject, rather than his identity, or what he is or could become.[4]

The self's possible future: punctual or integral?

Having outlined three general constructions of the self in education – behaviorist, cognitivist-rationalist, and that of a recovered conception of *Bildung* – this chapter concludes by locating these constructions in the most basic philosophical and practical terms. Following the philosopher Charles Taylor, educational psychologist Jack Martin indicates that the self of cognitivism or of Bandura's cognitivism – as a nexus of reflexive regulation, assessment or control – represents a '*punctual self*.' Such a self, as Martin explains, is the expression of a combination of philosophical influences, primarily traceable to René Descartes and John Locke. Descartes famously defined self-certainty as achievable in terms of the self's rational power ('I think therefore I am'), and he further believed that 'clear and distinct perception' of what is true is best attained through contemplative disengagement, rather than active involvement. The 'disengagement and rational control' implied in Descartes' epistemology is combined with John Locke's assumption that the self can be 'turn[ed] inward' and its attention directed at the disengaged observation of its 'own activity and of the processes which form' it (Taylor 1992: 174). Locke, in other words, rejected Descartes' famous distinction between *res cogitans* (the thinking or cogitating spirit or substance) and *res extensa* (the physical reality of the body and the world around it), and spoke of thoughts and ideas as arising from 'globules' or 'insensible particles.' The mind, in short, could be described using the same terms as those used for the external, physical world, and therefore, it could be known and also manipulated like any other part of this world. As a result, thoughts and experiences, consequently, are not as much our own, private possessions as they are material effects that are ultimately indifferent and interchangeable. Referencing Descartes' initial emphasis on disengagement, Taylor explains the further implications of these developments.

> The disengagement is carried further in being turned towards the subject himself...It involves taking a stance to ourselves which takes us out of the normal way of experiencing the world and ourselves...What [it] calls on us to do is to stop living "in" or "through" the experience, to treat it itself as an object, or what is the same thing, as an experience which could just as well have been someone else's.
>
> (Taylor 1992: 161-162)

The 'self' that thus arises from Descartes' rational disengagement and Locke's material disenchantment of the spirit or mind is *punctual* precisely in the sense that its reason and control is detached and disengaged from those phenomena that are usually considered to be aspects of selfhood, such as relation, experience or interest. Such a tightly circumscribed self – one that is reduced to a point of detached rationality subsisting outside of even its own thoughts and experiences – is at once the origin and object of processes disengaged reasoning, evaluation, and control. Employing the terminology of the cognitive sciences, Martin explains that such a self,

> is constituted by specifically focused sets of executive skills and strategies attuned instrumentally to the accomplishment of specific academic and life tasks. The central concern [in this view of the self] is the development and promotion of a self-confident individual agent capable of simultaneous action and reflection on this action.
>
> (Martin 2004: 192)

There is no particular way in which this self is related to another or a larger whole – except as it might serve its performance in specific academic and life tasks. Its own self-controls, self-assessments and self-regulation might, for example, benefit from information made available by another. Conceivably having another as an addressee might also serve as a pretext for its self-explanations and this self's leveraging of the 'self-explanation effect.' However, this human other and its conceivable contributions to this punctual self and its optimal self-regulation is certainly not a necessary part of these processes. Indeed, in the literature of educational technology, this source of regulative, managerial feedback has just as often been described as a computational device as it has been identified as a teacher or any other 'person' (e.g., Friesen, 2010) Since the tasks of learning as well as the development of the self are all calculative and computational in this account, as one educational technologist observed, 'an information processor could hardly be better suited' for their support and advancement (Kozma 1987: 22).

But what type of person would such a punctual self actually be? He or she is someone who, as Martin describes, simply engages in processes that are in his or her own best interests at a given moment: 'Cut off from wider, historical and contemporary traditions of life with others, and unencumbered by political and ethical considerations that attend communal living…[this punctual] self simply does what it wills itself to do in its own best interests of the moment.' (Martin 2004: 200). Going further, Martin concludes: 'there is nothing in [this] self that would distinguish between Mother Theresa and Tony Soprano, so long as it can be assumed that both have a plan and feel reasonably good about themselves.'

Of course, what distinguishes Mother Theresa from Tony Soprano is their social roles and the moral and personal implications integral to them. The saint and the gangster are stereotypes occupying relatively opposed locations in a larger social field, and their positionality is defined according to normative judgments, according to the social value or esteem granted or withheld. The panoply of existing and possible social roles and types lying between these two extremes are, of course, of central interest to education. And any student's progress or devolution towards any one of these roles and types is often how the overall value of their education and development is evaluated. The question 'What do you want to be when you grow up?' asked of a child by adults, by her peers, and also of herself, is a common everyday way in which development, selfhood and the larger societal context are engaged. But these must remain outside of the theoretical sanction of educational psychology as it has been discussed above.[5] The best that this psychology is able to do in this regard is to consider the optimization of various self-processes, and on this basis to identify them approvingly as 'Good students' or label them simply as 'Poor.'

With a vocabulary bequeathed by behaviorism and subsequent paradigms of educational psychology, education is trading on terms that are supposed to carry the everyday weight of intention, interest, morality, and value. However, it is clear that these same terms are by definition unable to sustain these multiple meanings and associations: The self of self-control, self-regulation and self-efficacy is not one of spontaneous activity – one that might follow an interest through to a career, or that can even be accounted for as living "in" or "through" its own everyday experience. It is not about the integration or constitution of self in or through the other, or the pursuit of interests in the context of a child's growing consciousness of both self and other. Instead, this self of 20th or 21st century educational psychology is one that is presumably preoccupied with disengaged calculations of instrumental manipulation and control.

Consider as a concluding point of contrast this more integral description of the self or person by Clifford Geertz:

> The Western conception of the person as a bounded, unique, more or less integrated motivational and cognitive universe, a dynamic center of awareness, emotion, judgment, and action organized into a distinctive whole and set contrastively both against other such wholes and against its social and natural background.
>
> (Geertz 1979: 176)

The notion of the self as a centre of awareness, set off contrastively against its social and natural background, resonates richly with the language of Fröbel and Hegel with which this chapter began. Like Dewey, Mead, or Mollenhauer, this chapter is not alone in its engagement with and critique of this Hegelian legacy. It is consistent with a much broader engagement with Hegel that is central to continental philosophy and theory, that is indispensable in many studies of society, culture and politics, but that (particularly in the terms discussed above) is strangely absent from educational discourse. As Foucault declared, 'whether through logic or epistemology...Marx or Nietzsche[,] our entire epoch struggles to disengage itself from Hegel' (Foucault, as cited in Descombes 1981: 12), and as Adorno has more cryptically (and dialectically) observed of Hegel's thought, 'The world-Spirit is, but it is no such thing' (1980: 298). We would do well to both recall and engage with this heritage, if only to have the chance to retrieve and revise a notion of the self that is worthy of its remit and responsibility.

Notes

1 The translation of *Forgotten Connections* cited here is forthcoming from Routledge, edited and translated by the author of this article, and in the same series as this edited collection. The full text of Mollenhauer's introduction to *Forgotten Connections* and other associated material is currently available at: http://www.culture-and-upbringing.com.

2 Mollenhauer describes this in the simplest terms as: 'A parent or educator who encourages a child to achieve self-activity need not come across as a highly active person themselves, or engage in pursuits that aim to achieve a particular effect. All the parent/educator need do is be reasonably attentive to the difference between the possible and the real. Hence

the cardinal virtues in such settings are attentiveness, being a good listener, and patient observation.'

3 This narrative is taken by Mollenhauer from Manoni, M. (1978) *Ein Ort zum Leben. Die von Kinder von Bonneuil*, Frankfurt: Syndikat.

4 I owe this insight to the advice and feedback of Gert Biesta.

5 Of course, this question is addressed on an instrumental and literal level through devices such as the Brainard occupational preference inventory test. However, these tests do little negotiate the appropriateness and social value (nor the changing practical value) of an occupation in relation to a child's developing interest and activity.

References

Adorno, T.W. (1980) *Negative Dialectics*, London: Continuum Publishing.

'Agency' (1994) *The Concise Oxford dictionary of sociology*, Oxford: Oxford UP.

Bandura, A. (1993) 'Perceived Self-Efficacy in Cognitive Development and Functioning,' *Educational Psychologist,* 28:117-148.

Chi, M.T.H., Bassok, M., Lewis, M., Reimann, P., and Glasser, R. (1989) 'Self-explanations: How students study and use examples in learning to solve problems,' *Cognitive Science*, 13: 145-182.

Chi, M.T.H. (2000) 'Self-explaining expository texts: The dual processes of generating inferences and repairing mental models,' in R. Glaser (ed.), *Advances in Instructional Psychology,* Mahwah, NJ: Erlbaum, pp. 161-238.

Dewey, J. (1887) *Psychology*, New York: Harper.

——(1897) My 'Pedagogic Creed,' *School Journal*, January, 54: 77-80.

——(1907) *School and Society*, Chicago: University of Chicago Press.

——(1916) *Democracy and education: an introduction to the philosophy of education*, New York: Macmillan.

Flavell, J. (1976) 'Metacognitive aspects of problem-solving,' in L. Resnick (ed.), *The Nature of Intelligence*, Hillsdale, NJ: Erlbaum.

Friesen, N. (2010) 'Mind and Machine: Ethical and Epistemological Implications for Applied Research,' *AI & Society* 25(1) 83-92.

Geertz, C. (1979) 'From the native's point of view: on the nature of anthropological understanding,' in P. Rabinow and W.M. Sullivan (eds), *Interpretive Social Science: A Reader*, Berkeley: University of California Press.

Good, J.A. (2006) *A Search for unity in diversity: The 'Permanent Hegelian Deposit' in the philosophy of John Dewey*, Lanham, MD: Lexington Books.

Good, J. A. and Garrison, J. (2007) 'Traces of Hegelian *Bildung* in Dewey's philosophy,' in P. Fairfield (ed.), *John Dewey and Continental Philosophy*. Carbondale: SIU Press.

Hughes, J.L. (1910) *Froebel's educational laws for all teachers*, New York: D. Appleton and Company.

Kozma, R.B. (1987) 'The implications of cognitive psychology for computer-based learning tools,' *Educational Technology* 27: 20–25.

Lagemann, E.C. (1989) 'The plural worlds of educational research,' *History of Education Quarterly* 29: 185-214.

Martin, J. (2004) 'The educational inadequacy of conceptions of self in educational psychology,' *Interchange 35*: 185-208.

Mead, G.H. (1910) 'What Social Objects Must Psychology Presuppose?,' *Journal of Philosophy, Psychology and Scientific Methods* 7: 174-180. Available at: <http://www.brocku.ca/MeadProject/Mead/pubs/Mead_1910d.html>.

——(1922) 'A Behaviouristic Account of the Significant Symbol,' *Journal of Philosophy* 19: 157-163. Available at: <http://www.brocku.ca/MeadProject/Mead/pubs/Mead_1922.html>.

——(1934) *Mind, Self, and Society*, C. W. Morris (ed.), Chicago: University of Chicago Press.

Mollenhauer, K. (forthcoming) *Forgotten Connections: On Culture and Upbringing*, London: Routledge.

Skinner, B.F. (1953) *Science and human behavior*, New York: Free Press.

——(1968) *The technology of teaching*, New York: Appleton-Century Crofts.

Taylor, C. (1992) *Sources of the Self. The Making of the Modern Identity*, Cambridge, MA: Harvard University Press.

Thorndike, E.L. (1910) 'The contribution of psychology to education,' *The Journal of Educational Psychology* 1: 5-12.

——(1911) *Animal intelligence*, New York: Macmillan.

——(1912) *Education: A first book*, New York: MacMillan.

Van Lehn, K. Jones R.M. and Chi, M.T.H. (1992) 'A Model of the self-explanation effect,' *The Journal of the Learning Sciences* 2: 1-59.

Chapter 7

On the theoretical limits of education

Alexander M. Sidorkin

Introduction

What is education? The issue that seems to be fundamental to our field is very far from being resolved. Both the practical field and the theory can exist without answering this fundamental question, both can run on intuitive assumptions. However, we are entering a period of change that is likely to shake such assumptions. Our collective fundamental beliefs would have been disputed if they were explicit, but as assumptions, they held up enough coherence for us to operate. But now the relationships between humans, and their information, knowledge, and learning have been shifting. The very basic questions can no longer be answered with the silent omission. What is learning? What is teaching? What is education and how is it related to schooling? This chapter is an attempt to squarely face the issue of the nature of education. While it is does not purport to resolve it, it does show that such conversations are both possible and necessary.

The notion of a theoretical limit

In 1824 Sadi Carnot calculated the theoretical efficiency limit of any heat engine (Carnot 1824). The efficiency limit has to do with the highest possible and the lowest possible temperature inside and outside the engine. The theoretical limit for an engine operating in the ambient temperature is about 63%, and modern coal-fired power stations reach about 42%. For power engineers, this is a very useful knowledge. There is room for improvement, but the limit is fairly close and inching towards it becomes increasingly difficult. Instead, we may design engines that are not based on heat exchange involving water and steel, and are therefore not subject to the limit established by Carnot's theorem. They will still be subject to the second law of thermodynamics, which is a different, much more distant, but also useful limit to know about. The distinction between the far limits and the near limits is important; the former apply to a broader set of phenomena, and the latter – to the specific version of the phenomenon we are used to dealing with.

The notion of a theoretical limit is widely used in sciences. Google Scholar returns 56,600 hits on the search. For no obvious reason, it is almost never used in social sciences. It is perhaps more difficult to locate the limits of social institutions, but intuitively, the notion makes sense. In fact, it is used implicitly in many social sciences, for no social arrangement can be changed (improved) indefinitely. For example, within a market economy, considerations of private initiative limit the extent to which social equality can be achieved. Milton Friedman's (1968) theory of the natural unemployment rate is another example of a theoretical limit. Many more can be found.

Knowledge of limits is another expression of the philosophical notion of essence – something an entity possesses by necessity, and not by accident. The limit is a pragmatist expression of essence; it helps to answer one important question: how much can we push a certain thing; how much can we change it without destroying or turning it into something completely different and no longer useful. Another way of describing a limit is as something that prevents our agency from turning against our own intentions. When the agency is ignorant of limits, we start destroying something in an effort to improve it. This is not to suggest a Platonist understanding of essences; the 'nature' of things is a function of our ways of dealing with them. For example, a pile of sand and a slab of granite in many respects have the same essence. However, in our dealing with sand and granite, the two materials pose very different sets of challenges, and therefore appear to us to be essentially different. As soon as we engage in another practice where those differences do not matter, sand and granite may look the same, and therefore acquire different essences. Therefore the limits of sand and granite as materials depend on the context of human practice with them.

Does improvement of education and schooling have limits? The question may appear to be trivial. Of course, everything has limits. However, the international school reforming scene may create an impression that it does not. Or, rather, the reformers seem to hold an assumption that the limits are very far, and that the educational outcomes can be improved dramatically. In truth, we simply do not know how close the limits are, nor do we have a clear understanding of the nature of such limits. The purpose of this chapter is to at least begin a conversation on how much can education – and schools – be improved.

Why do reforms falter?

In the United States, the pace of school reform is perceived to be frustratingly slow. The gains in academic achievement are disproportional to the increases in public expenditures. Between 1995 and 2009, per-student expenditures rose 37% (OECD, 2012:232), which is lower than average OECD growth. However, the US spends about $16,000 per student, much more than the OECD average, but it does not measure particularly well on international comparison tests. The country has been engaged in a continuous reform effort for at least a quarter of century. Its main strategies stay the same: use high-stakes assessments and other accountability measures to improve the overall quality of education, to increase high school graduation rate, and reduce the achievement gap among racial and socio-economic groups. The results have been positive, but modest (NAEP, 2012): mathematics scores rose somewhat, while reading, history, and science scores remained mostly flat. Geography scores for 12th graders declined. Why is that?

Many seem to believe it is because the reforms were not pursued with sufficient rigour. Therefore the huge Race to the Top (RttT) programme has been created to pour new money into the old wineskins of accountability reform. However, the failure of previous reforms may be a case of approaching a limit which we do not know exists. If that is the case, the 4.35 billion dollars invested in the RttT will move the dial on the National Assessment of Educational Progress only slightly or not at all. Of course, if the RttT programme is very successful, and brings about significant improvements, the premise of this chapter is incorrect, and we indeed do not need to worry about the proximity of limits, at least for a while. It seems unlikely though, and we need to come to grips with the persistent failure of educational reform to meet the reasonable expectations. We cannot simply pretend that there was another implementation failure, or that someone sabotaged the effort. One will have to admit that the very essence of education – as we know it in the context of schooling – resists our efforts. This is an uncomfortable thought, and I wish it was not true. It is easier to be an optimist, to convey hope rather than warn of more disappointments. Yet in the absence of plausible alternative theories, it is difficult to ignore the very real possibility that this is true.

There is a more common explanation of the educational reform's failure: the problems with American education lie outside of the educational system. It is the social challenges outside the system – poverty, unemployment, poor early care, lack of healthcare, poor nutrition, dangerous neighbourhoods, chronic absenteeism – that prevent many children from learning at schools. Richard Rothstein (2010), for example reminds us that 'teacher quality is not the most important factor determining student success; it is the most important *in-school* factor'. Parents' socio-economic status has a larger influence. While I am very sympathetic to this line of reasoning, it does not negate the need for understanding of the theoretical limits of educational improvement. Even in the most egalitarian and affluent societies, schooling cannot be improved indefinitely. My life and career began in the Soviet Union which was not only one of the more egalitarian societies, but which also had a decent preschool system and good public schooling. The Soviets were very careful about mixing more educated and less educated classes in the same neighbourhoods. Still, the Soviet schools performance on international comparisons was fairly good, but never spectacular. Even now, the academic achievement differences between more and less egalitarian countries are not that great. There does not seem to be strong evidence of a causal relation between the level of social inequality and overall educational achievement. At least one study actually finds a small negative effect of redistributive government activities on student performance (Falch and Fisher, 2008). The equality of educational achievement is an important ethical goal in itself, but achieving it does not affect the overall effectiveness of schooling in a significant way.

I have no doubt that Rothstein and the entire post-Coleman Study (1966) line of thought are correct to some extent. However what they call out-of-school factors is just another way of describing for the theoretical limits of the educational systems itself. The assumption is often that we need to address the out-of-school factors to make education more effective and more equal. But of course, this creates a catch-22 situation: to improve schools, we need to address social factors, but to do this we almost always have to improve education. When one particular institution cannot be improved without reshaping the entire society, it amounts to saying that the institution is not improvable.

Yet another criticism of the school reform is that the strategy itself is misguided. For example, Supovitz (2009) argues that the use of tests is a weak intervention by design, because testing only reveals possible problems without addressing their causes. Brodsky (2009) shows that 'shining the light' on underperforming schools may have a very small positive effect on future performance, but nowhere near of what is needed to address the achievement gap. Fullan (2009) examines the history of large scale educational reform and shows that very little purposeful reforming was actually going on before 1997, and in United States still no real reform is being implemented. Instead, we have a 'policy without a strategy,' the Race to the Top being a case in point. He cites Finland, Singapore, Canada, Hong Kong, and South Korea as examples of an effective reform, which engages at least three levels: school, district, and government. Fullan and many others believe the significant school improvement can be done, if it is done correctly.

Again, I do not doubt Fullan is right. It is the extent of the possible improvements that I question. Even a cursory look at any of the big international comparison datasets (PISA, TIMMS, PEARLS) shows gradual and relatively mild differences among countries, not the qualitative jumps one would expect from Fullan's notion of the 'right' kind of reform. We can and should work at the margins improving the institution of schooling. Some economists claim that even the incremental improvements in academic achievement bring about huge economic returns over the life of a generation. For example, they estimate that bringing every European nation to the level of Finland's performance will result in economic gains equal 785% of current GDP (Hanushek and Woessmann 2012: 101). This chapter does not critique the theoretical assumptions of these exuberant estimates. Suffice it to say they are still based on correlational analysis, and extrapolate the current rates of economic growth to 2090. I will show later how the Finnish example is inadequate. As long as the institution of mass schooling remains intact, we can only extract so much learning from students.

The most common explanations of the low effectiveness of school reform are somewhat unsatisfactory. They do not explain why countries with different reform policies and with different levels of social support and inequality get somewhat similar results. Something more fundamental is going on. To understand the limits of schooling, let us first consider the far limits of education as such. As the reader shall see, the near limits are not independent of far limits. The former are particular expressions of the latter.

The bio-economic limits

The most fundamental set of limits has to do with human bio-economics. There is a limit to human ability to learn. It is easy for us to see clear limits of other animals' learning. For example, we readily concede that dogs will never be able to talk or to drive a car. It is very difficult to apply the same logic to ourselves. But we will never be able to maintain several conversations at the same time, or drive our cars safely at 300 miles per hour. We will never remember the contents of the *Encyclopedia Britannica*, nor will we be a perfect employee who never makes a mistake. Indeed, there is only so much a human being can learn. The myth about vast unused resources in our brains is evolutionarily indefensible (Radford 1999). It probably originates from observations of savants' extraordinary abilities to perform calculations. The myth ignores the fact that their exceptional abilities come at the expense of other functions of the brains being severely compromised. The inability to keep track of human relationships frees up significant brain resources. If we just assume human brain to be a data storage device, its volume as well as the speed of uploading must be limited.

We also differ from one another. As Wulczyn (2009: 3) noted, 'Growth in human capital slows, at least theoretically, as the limits of innate ability are reached'. It would be safe to assume that most children, especially those from disadvantaged backgrounds, never reach the limits of their innate ability to learn. The human society would be fundamentally transformed if all children learned to their full potential. But this does not negate the great variety of abilities that exist in any human population. And we cannot use the exceptional brains as benchmarks of what is achievable for everyone.

This is not all; there are other far limits. The length of human life is one of them. As the time spent on learning lengthens, the productive life of an individual shortens. The advanced training for occupations such as scientific research already stretches into mid- to late-30s; more and more people are required to participate in the occupations which require more training. This situation is very different from that of just a hundred years ago. Only very few people needed the extended training then, while the large majority needed only basic literacy or no schooling at all. Now occupations that do not need at least a high school diploma are scarce. The length of training required for a doctor or for a bricklayer may not have changed that dramatically. However, fewer bricklayers and more doctors are needed. Collectively, the workforce now spends significantly more time in training, which reduces the time spent in production. The aggregate time dedicated to training cannot be extended indefinitely, even though until now productivity gains outpaced the relative shortening of work lives. It is not difficult to imagine a time when increased schooling will reach the point of diminishing returns. In other words, learning lives may become too long and productive lives too short to sustain the economy. Add to this equation the increasing non-productive lifespans of retired persons. The ration of learning life to productive life may not only be a limit of education, but also a limit of technological progress. We will eventually experience a more and more acute global shortage of qualified workers.

The bio-economic limit to the ability to learn is further narrowed by the sensitivity age. The capacity to learn is not evenly distributed throughout the lifespan. For example, the ability to learn first languages has a relatively narrow window, the so-called critical period (Mayberry and Lock, 2003). A similar, but broader concept of sensitivity periods describes ages when particular kinds of learning are particularly effective. While these notions remain somewhat controversial, there is significant evidence to support them (Thompson-Schill *et al.* 2009).

It is reasonable to assume that critical and/or sensitivity periods affect not only the capacity for learning, but also the desire to learn. Between ages 10 and 13, most human minds switch from the omnivorous interest in the world to a focused interest in friendship, relationships, and eventually to interest in reproduction. Children's eyes shift their focus from the world onto each other. Some children also develop an interest in a particular school subject, such as history or music or science. Others acquire interest in other subjects outside of school – sports, fashion, dating, entertainment, cars, etc. However, it seems highly implausible that all children will remain interested in all subjects that secondary school requires. The very notion of an interest is exclusive to other interests. While children are still eager to learn, they no longer want to learn the things that adults want them to learn. The concept of curriculum describes the conflict between what the society needs children to learn and what they would rather learn if left to their own devices. The conflict deepens as the need for more learning arises.

It is especially difficult to maintain interest in disciplines that are in most demand on the labour market, such as mathematics and science. We witness the gradual change of elementary and secondary school curriculum towards serving the technological needs of our civilisation and away from serving its social needs. We need more engineers, doctors, and scientists, and fewer priests and clerks. Not only do we need more learning per capita, we also need more of *less interesting* learning. The dream of the knowledge economy cherished by formerly industrialised nations may be limited by something as trivial as lack of interest among their school children. I will not consider here what curriculum should be in schools. As long as there is curriculum, the tension between it and children's interest remains.

Indeed, the relative scarcity of math and science skills may be better described as the scarcity of interest, not as scarcity of good teaching. Many educators still hope to find a trick that would make learning these subjects interesting to all children. The critique of such a hope is outside the scope of this chapter (see Sidorkin 2009a). Suffice it to say, the idea of organically linking children's own interests with school curriculum have not found an empirical confirmation in over a century of trying. Interstellar travel is a staple of science fiction, and most non-scientists probably think it is inevitable. However, most scientists agree it is in principle impossible, because infinite speeds require infinite energy (Lemos 2008). The hopes of engaging all students in STEM-centred school curricula strike me as a similar fallacy: we want it so badly that we confuse the strength of our desire with the feasibility of attaining the goal.

Pushing against learning motivation

The adolescent shift in interest means that we must deal with learning motivation rather than with learning potential. If the elementary school is about simply reaping the fruits of children's abundant curiosity, then middle and high school are about a much more difficult task of *creating* learning motivation. Relatively recently, our civilisation crossed an important border: we now need all children (not just some) to go on learning well beyond their biologically allotted time for learning, in the subject areas to which they have little natural interest.

Here is where we make a shift from far limits to near limits of education. The relative scarcity of children's interest in learning school curriculum is a far limit. The way in which we have been able to make children learn is a particular historical form of addressing the problem. As such it has a set of much more narrowly constrained conditions that we call the institution of mass compulsory schooling. Compulsory schooling is to education what steam engine is to the second law of thermodynamics.

The limit of learning motivation can be understood as a very simple question: 'How do we compel children to learn things we want them to learn?' This question is very different from 'How much can a typical human being learn?' The former question is fundamentally related to a labour arrangement, for learning is primarily a result of student's own work. The distinction between the two questions is central to my argument here. Any time we try to compel people to do something they would rather not do on their own, it is work. One may be forced, paid, or pressured into working – these methods refer to different labour arrangements; all are means of achieving the same goal. But there is a fundamental difference between what a human being can do and what she will agree to do. We never confuse those matters with adults, therefore in the market economy most kinds of labour are compensated. We do not assume that our doctor is sufficiently intrinsically motivated to help us. What children do for work – their school labour – is not compensated, and is, in effect, an obligation. And yet we tend to assume the productivity of that labour can be as intense as that of an adult worker.

Here we must deal with the compulsory mass school; a unique and in a certain sense bizarre labour arrangement that came to dominate the educational landscape in the last century or so. It is worth noting that the institution has truly become universal only within the last 40 years or so, and only within the advanced societies. Our thinking of it as natural has to do more with our own life experiences than with historical accuracy. There are no reasons to believe it is the last and the best institution of learning.

The notion of mass schooling is difficult to understand for another reason: it emerged from a very different and still co-existing institution of elite schooling. The two may look very similar, but produce vastly different results from very similar sets of genetic material. This fact makes us ignore the fundamental difference between the two, and creates a persistent myth that mass schooling can be refashioned into elite schooling. Additionally, many policymakers have themselves gone through elite schooling, and have little understanding of mass schooling; they simply assume that mass schools are bad versions of the elite schools they attended as children. Yet the two institutions are no more similar to each other than a Formula 1 racetrack is similar to my neighbourhood street. Yes, people drive cars on both, but no, they cannot produce similar speeds, or safe outcomes. The two groups of people drive cars for different reasons and they follow different sets of rules.

The simple comparison between the elite and the mass schools can be useful in discovering the essence of the latter, and therefore in finding the limits of its improvements. The limits of improving mass schooling are the theoretical near limits of education.

1 Compensation. Students at elite schools are handsomely compensated. They are sure that every effort will count towards obtaining a college degree, often from a prestigious college, and lead to a good job and high standards of living. Students at mass school, to the contrary, have very little certainly about the economic rewards on their school labour. They are aware that there is a certain possibility of them individually breaking away from the condition of their neighbourhood. However, that possibility is perceived to be low. Objectively speaking, they are right; even if one manages to graduate from a high school, obtaining a full college degree remains elusive. The total graduation rate for American freshmen entering college in 2003 was 55.5%; however it was only 37.7% and 46.2% for African-Americans and Hispanics, respectively (Knapp *et al.* 2012: 15). Converting a degree into a well-paid job is not guaranteed either. According to a recent AP story, '53.6 percent, of bachelor's degree-holders under the age of 25 last year were jobless or underemployed' (Yen, 2012).

In other words, students in mass schools are compensated not only at a much lower average rate, but the rates of compensation are highly variable, and are not clarified before the engagement.

2 Enforcement mechanisms. The elite schools are often run in a more democratic and freer manner than the mass schools. Yet underneath all the niceties there lies a simple and well-understood fact: anyone who does not accept the school rules can and will be expelled. Mass schools, in contrast, have little ability to select. This creates a vacuum of power for school authorities, and plentiful opportunities for disruptive behaviour to occur. The elite schools receive plentiful learning motivation; mass schools are faced with a very difficult task of *generating* this critical resource first. The direct link between learning motivation and power may strike someone as ill-conceived. But those are the same if we consider the school's function: to extract the labour of learning from children.

3 Support. Elite school students typically have access to significant learning resources to supplement school learning. This includes both the social capital – attitudes toward schooling, parents' knowledge of the conventions and norms in the world of education, and the actual information resources – books, high speed internet access, early exposure to complex language patterns, rich afterschool and summer learning opportunities, family trips, access to museums, libraries, and quality TV channels. An elite school student with a learning disability typically receives earlier diagnostics and better compensatory help. The combination of these resources makes school learning significantly more effective. Teachers can afford to concentrate on advanced skills, because they trust the small informational gaps will be filled through the support system.

4 Methods. The elite schools tend to use more progressive, authentic teaching methods, because they are less pressured to comply with accountability measures. The mass schools are increasingly under pressure to demonstrate growth as measured by high stakes standardized testing. Therefore, they are forced into less creative, more routine instructional modes, which tend to be less effective in the long run, and diminish students' motivation even further.

The comparison above is not to demonstrate the superiority of the elite schools over the mass schools. I just want to make a point that despite superficial similarities, we deal with two different social institutions, based on two very different *labour arrangements*. Efficiency and intensity of labour are functions of the social arrangement as much as a function of technology. The purposes and the technologies of learning labour are very similar in both institutions. However, the social conditions of labour are very different. The key difference is that mass schools must *produce* learning motivation, while the elite schools operate with an abundance of this critical resource. To expect both to demonstrate similar productivity would be unwise.

The scarcity of incentives for students to learn represents the key limit for the improvement of mass schooling. Because the arrangement relies on the unpaid compulsory work of students with very uncertain promises of rewards, it is simply not clear where the learning motivation will come from. Mass schools rely on the power of administrative, extra-economic compulsion to make students attend schools and to learn the subjects they need as employees. In more traditional patriarchal countries, like Finland (Simola 2005), schools can still draw on family-derived power but this option is more limited in more diverse and heterogeneous societies like the United States. As more societies around the world become more heterogeneous, the traditional patriarchal values play a smaller and smaller role in compelling children to learn at schools. I find social conservatives' dreams of going back in time to be utterly unrealistic.

In order to increase the productivity of school labour, mass schools should be able to generate huge volumes of student motivation. This critical need is either completely ignored, or answers are brought from the land of fantasy. One fantastic answer is to assume that all children are naturally curious and we only need to tap that magic source of energy. This myth of children's abundant, hidden curiosity neither makes much evolutionary sense, nor does it have any kind of empirical support. Another fantastic answer is the myth of a great teacher. It goes like this: a great teacher can infect students with love for any subject through the sheer force of his or her personality. Hanushek (2010) acknowledges that we know little about training effective teachers. His proposal is simply to remove the least effective teachers from classrooms, once we identify them. The hope is to create learning motivation from a substance that we neither understand nor are able to replicate.

Yes, it is fairly obvious that many children do not learn as much as they could in schools. But from that premise it does not follow that the institution of schooling is capable of producing more effort and more efficient learning. The limit of improving mass schooling is the immediate *near* theoretical limit of education. And it is my contention that we are very close to that near limit, which explains the disappointing pace of school reform. Mass schooling simply will not improve much more, because it is pushing up against the theoretical limits of the institution.

Even though it increasingly looks like beating the dead horse, the entire accountability reform should not be simply abandoned. Some of its aspects are worthy of continuing: the improvement of standards and especially of testing instruments and procedures, the creation of state and national databases on student performance, the development of teacher evaluation systems, training teachers to use data in instruction, and the teacher professional development and induction programmes. We do have to lower our expectations, however, and generally curb our enthusiasm. The excessive belief in the efficacy of a very meek reform brings distortions and disappointments. An example of such a distortion would be undue emphasis on teacher evaluation systems at the expense of meaningful professional development. Such programmes take time and financial resources from what can plausibly make teaching more effective. Another common distortion is putting all resources into one particular system of canned curriculum. These systems are based on little research evidence, but they also emphasize fidelity of implementation over independent thinking of teachers, and often degrade teacher skills.

The next reform

While we are salvaging the sound elements of the current reform, a much broader, and a much more radical conversation must begin. It has to start with the acknowledgment that the contemporary institution of mass schooling is nearing its theoretical limit. It simply cannot be improved much more and must be replaced or at least augmented by one or more other institution of learning.

In education, we are in the situation of trying to build steam aircraft. It is simply difficult to do, because the power to weight ratio of a steam engine is insufficient. The idea is very much alive among the Steampunk artists, but not among the engineers. Similarly, the hope of reforming mass schooling into providing high quality secondary and tertiary education to all children belongs to the world of fiction, not to the world of educational policy. The institution's labour arrangements will never deliver sufficient motivation among sufficient portion of students. The dreams of a knowledge economy will remain dreams as long as the compulsory schooling as we know it is charged with delivering the educated workforce and the educated consumer. The engine does not create enough lift to do the job. And the job is very ambitious: sending the entire population through some form of post-secondary education amounts to a radical transformation of society. It has never been accomplished at any point in history, in any corner of the world. It can be done well within the far limits of human learning, just not within the near limits presented by the compulsory mass schooling system.

The institution or institutions can supplement or replace mass schooling is not yet clear. It is certain though that the new educational world order must effectively address the problem of learning motivation, and do it in a non-utopian sort of way. Thus far, I can only see two possibilities here; there are perhaps others I fail to imagine. One is to pay students to go to school. There exists early evidence that monetary incentives do not significantly affect student performance (Fryer 2012). However, in my opinion, the incentives used in the trial were insufficient in size. Instead of small incentives, we should try to estimate the actual economic value of student labour and fair compensation. It is also possible, as Fryer speculates, that incentives are more effective if 'tailored to appropriate inputs to the educational production function' (Fryer 2010: 1791). The lessons from Fryer's pioneering study are invaluable, however.

The other route to new schooling is to transform schools into institutions that provide students with enough services they want so that in return, students will demonstrate significantly more effort in academic learning. These are actually not that difficult to implement; I have written about both before (Sidorkin 2002, 2009b) and will not repeat the arguments for or against both of these approaches.

One consequence of both approaches is that education will become more and more expensive. Paying students to learn or providing massive social services to all children requires increased (although not astronomical) investments. No one has yet figured out a technology that would make teaching and learning less labour-intensive. And not one country has yet mustered the political will to spend more than 7% of its GDP on education. The irony is that simply increasing investment into the reforming of mass schooling will reach a point of diminishing returns fairly soon. However, to invest public funds into untried and unproven alternative educational institutions seem to be politically risky. These limitations suggest other possibilities for resolving the near limits of education.

One plausible possibility is to ignore the theoretical limit of mass schooling and maintain the status quo. This sort of educational reforming may continue indefinitely, with insignificant or non-existent results. Politicians will blame each other for failures, and continue with yet another version of the same accountability reforming. Countries will continue to eek small advantages over each other in what Novoa and Yariv-Mashal (2003) aptly described as 'international spectacle and the politics of mutual accountability.' Developed countries will have to ease our race towards the knowledge-based economies, and ultimately slow the rate of global economic growth. In this scenario, all industrialised countries will experience shortages of engineers and doctors and increased structural unemployment. Ignoring the theoretical limits of schooling is not without its own risks.

Another possibility is that progress in automatics and artificial intelligence will eventually diminish our need in educated workers. The current trend is the opposite: most jobs now require post-secondary training. But eventually we may be able to learn to enjoy greater productivity with a smaller proportion of population educated for work. This scenario still leaves wide open the question of structural unemployment. It is simply not clear how the underclass will participate in the economy. The contemporary post-industrial societies have developed a sharp divide between the overworked employed and the unemployed. If this divide is not addressed, the entire premise of mass schooling is undermined and it will lose its credibility. For certain groups this is already a reality. The chances of getting a good job are perceived as so remote that any investment into schooling seems to be unreasonably risky. Under this scenario, the advanced societies would have to regress back into the model of the elite schooling, where only a minority of population receive meaningful education. The technological advances can help us to back away from the limits of schooling, yet that will push us against the limits of inequality that a democratic society cannot afford to bear.

Conclusion

The argument above does not prove that the near limits of education aka the limits of schooling are very near. I was simply hoping to convince the reader that they *may* be much closer than we assume, and that schools just may not be improvable much more. I would be happy to achieve only the recognition that the limits of improvability exist.

My aim was not as much to expose the limits of education and the limits of schooling, as to demonstrate the possibilities of a particular kind of thinking about social phenomena. Focusing on limits does not equal pessimism, or passivity. On the contrary, a clear understanding of how much we can push a particular social institution opens up possibilities for imagining other institutions that do not have the same sets of intrinsic limits. And reversely, ignoring the existence of hard limits invites doing more of the same even after it becomes unproductive. This is especially true about social problems that seem to be intractable, such as the inequality of academic achievement.

In the end, the issue remains unresolved; we do not know what education is; we do not know which classes of phenomena can be reliably grouped to be called education. There can be a number of ways of addressing the issue, other than trying to understand the pragmatic limits of education improvement. However, without understanding of the essence of education, our analysis of practices and our recommendations will remain imprecise and ineffective. Why? Simply because we will always deal with a partial and contaminated set of phenomena brought together by convention rather than through understanding. Educational theory as a field cannot mature and take the next step without defining its central concept.

References

Bourdieu, P. (1998) *Practical Reason,* Stanford, CA: Stanford University Press.

Brodsky, A. (2009) *Accountability Reform and Student Achievement in Colorado Public Schools,* unpublished thesis, University of Colorado at Boulder. Available at: <http://gradworks.umi.com/33/37/3337065.html>.

Carnot, S. (1824) *Réflexions sur la Puissance Motrice du Feu et sur les Machines Propres à Développer cette Puissance,* Paris: Bachelier.

Coleman, J. (1966) *Equality of Educational Opportunity,* Washington: U.S. Dept. of Health Education and Welfare Office of Education.

Commander, S., Kangasniemi, M. and Winters, L.A. (2004) 'The brain drain: curse or boon? A survey of the literature', in R.E. Baldwin and L.A. Winters (eds), *Challenges to Globalization: Analyzing the Economics,* Chicago: University of Chicago Press.

Falch, T. and Fischer, J.A.V. (2008)'Does a Generous Welfare State Crowd Out Student Achievement? Panel Data Evidence from International Student Tests', CESifo Working Paper Series No. 2383. Available at: <http://ssrn.com/abstract=1264915>.

Friedman, M. (1968) 'The role of monetary policy', *American Economic Review,* 58: 1-15.

Fryer R.G. (2010) *Financial Incentives and Student Achievement: Evidence from Randomized Trials,* The National Bureau of economic research, NBER Working Paper No. 15898. Available at: <http://www.nber.org/papers/w15898>.

Fullan, M. (2009) 'Large-scale reform comes of age', *Journal of Educational Change* 10: 101-113.

Hanushek, E.A. (2010) *The Economic Value of Higher Teacher Quality,* Urban Institute Brief. Available at <http://www.urban.org/publications/1001507.html>.

Hanushek, E.A. and Woessmann, L. (2012) 'The Economic Benefit of Educational Reform in the European Union', *CESifo Economic Studies* 58: 73–109.

Knapp, L.G., Kelly-Reid, J.E., and Ginder, S.A. (2011) *Enrollment in Postsecondary Institutions, Fall 2009; Graduation Rates, 2003 & 2006 Cohorts; and Financial Statistics, Fiscal Year 2009,* Institute of Education Sciences. Available at: <http://nces.ed.gov/pubs2011/2011230.pdf>

Lemos, R. (2008) 'Rocket Scientists Say We'll Never Reach the Stars', *Wired* 08/19/2008. Available at: <http://www.wired.com/science/space/news/2008/08/space_limits#>.

Malinowski, B. (1922) *Argonauts of the western Pacific; an account of native enterprise and adventure in the archipelagoes of Melanesian New Guinea,* London: Routledge.

Mayberry, R.I. and Lock, E. (2003) 'Age constraints on first versus second language acquisition: evidence for linguistic plasticity and epigenesis', *Brain and Language* 87: 369-84.

NAEP (2012) *National Asessment of Educational Progress,* National Center for Educational Statistics. Available at: <http://nces.ed.gov/nationsreportcard/>.

Novoa, A and Yariv-Mashal, T. (2003) 'Comparative research in education: a mode of governance or a historical journey?' *Comparative Education* 39: 423-38.

OECD (2012) *Education at a Glance 2012,* Paris: IECD.

Radford, B. (1999) 'The ten-percent myth', *Sceptical Inquirer,* 23. Available at: <http://www.csicop.org/SI/show/the_ten-percent_myth/>.

Rothstein, R. (2010) 'How to fix our schools', *Economic Policy Institute,* Issue Brief #286. Available at: <http://secure.epi.org/page/-/pdf/ib286.pdf>.

Sidorkin, A.M. (2002) *Learning Relations: Impure Education, Deschooled Schools, and Dialogue with Evil,* New York: Peter Lang.

Sidorkin, A.M. (2009a) 'John Dewey: a case of educational utopianism', *Philosophy of Education,* Urbana, Illinois: Philosophy of Education Society.

Sidorkin, A.M. (2009b) *Labor of Learning: Market and the Next Generation of Educational Reform,* Rotterdam: Sense Publishers.

Simola, H. (2005) 'The Finnish miracle of PISA: historical and sociological remarks on teaching and teacher education', *Comparative Education* 41: 455-70.

Supovitz, J. (2009) 'Can high stakes testing leverage educational improvement? Prospects from the last decade of testing and accountability reform', *Journal of Educational Change* 10: 211-27.

Thompson-Schill, S. L., Ramscar, M. and Chrysikou, E.G. (2009) 'Cognition without control: when a little frontal lobe goes a long way', *Current Directions In Psychological Science,* 18: 259-63.

Wulczyn, F. (2008) *Child Well-Being as Human Capital,* Chicago: Chapin Hall Center for Children at the University of Chicago. Available at: <http://www.chapinhall.org/sites/default/files/old_reports/439.pdf>.

Yen, H. (2012) '1 in 2 new graduates are jobless or underemployed', Associated Press – Mon, Apr 23, 2012. Available at: <http://news.yahoo.com/1-2-graduates-jobless-underemployed-140300522.html>.

Section III

Refractions on and agendas for theory

Chapter 8

Educational theory and the practice of critique

Robin Usher and Anna Anderson

On theory and theorizing

'Theory' has many connotations. In origin, it signified contemplation as against action, a species of thought, neutral, disinterested and removed from the quotidian. In contemporary everyday usage, a theory is commonly understood as something akin to speculation as against the practical. All of this of course is far removed from theory as understood in the natural sciences. Here theory refers to a comprehensive explanation of some natural feature supported by empirical phenomena gathered in a way consistent with scientific method and which enables generalisation and prediction about as yet unobserved phenomena. Whilst there have been trends in the social sciences which have sought to import the hypothetico-deductive model, developments over time have shown that an inductive model deploying ethnographic/ethnomethodological approaches to theory-building is more congenial and appropriate in the domain of the social sciences.

When we consider educational theory, we find that it has been understood in each and all these various ways. Clearly, there is no one education theory. At least, it is possible to say this without doubt and equally to claim that there are probably as many educational theories as there are disciplines that have relevance to the practice of education. If that is the case, then it could be argued that a particular educational theory is an artefact of a particular discipline or related disciplines. Despite the variety, there is one common feature that some theories in education have; they seek to interpret or explain educational phenomena as an *application* of theory to educational practice. Thus in much educational theorizing we find deployed a generalising/predictive model, such as constructivism in learning, or culture in schooling, whose purpose is to be applied to practice. As such, practice has generally been considered a *consequence* of theorizing with the implication that theory was the opposite of practice – thinking as against doing, with thinking being cognitively and temporally prior to doing.

There are a number of issues here that we want to briefly consider as they relate to our concern with the notion and practice of critique in relation to educational theorizing. The first is that of generalizability, a contentious issue commonly found not only in educational theorizing but in most theorizing in the social sciences. The issue here is not so much the generalizability per se of theory but any claim made by theorizing of *universality*. Indeed, one could say this is not only an issue in the social sciences but also a major problem because theory in those domains, including in education, is ineluctably specific and particular. It is a problem because generalizability and universality are not the same, even though they are invariably treated as such. Generality is not synonymous with universality since the former can take specificity and particularity on board in a way which the latter cannot.

Unfortunately, there is a drive to universality, taken for granted in the natural sciences but found even in many sectors of the social sciences, that occludes specificity and particularity. For Foucault, even though phenomena need to be studied in their specificity, this can accommodate generalisation but not universality. His genealogical methodology, which we will say more about later, requires that things be understood on their own terms, which means paying close attention to particularities. His treatment of this issue, drawing a sharp distinction between generalizability and universality, is congenial to the argument we are trying to make.

The second issue is that of the relationship between theory and practice. As Deleuze in his conversation with Foucault put it:

> The relationships between theory and practice are far more partial and fragmentary. On one side, a theory is always local and related to a limited field, and it is applied in another sphere, more or less distant from it. The relationship which holds in the application of a theory is never one of resemblance...Practice is a set of relays from one theoretical point to another, and theory is a relay from one practice to another.
>
> (1977a: 205-206)

Referring to Foucault's work with prisoners in the GIP, Deleuze characterises this practice as creating conditions for them to speak – 'it would be false to say...that in moving to this practice you were applying your theories...this was not an application' (ibid). Following this position, we argue that theory is itself a practice, a theoretical practice, and practice is always imbued with theory. Further, using Foucault's formulation, this theoretical practice is 'a power-knowledge' formation; it is not abstract, transcendental, removed from the world and its actions but on the contrary it is grounded in the material, very much in and of the world but also specific and partial.

In this chapter we will argue that although there is no one single educational theory, nonetheless, critical theory and its educational cognate critical pedagogy have probably been most influential in educational circles. It offers a way of doing critique in the cause of social justice that has proved to be very attractive to educators. However, in our view, the limitations of critical theory make it necessary to consider a different approach to critique, that of genealogy, which we will argue is worthy of consideration by educators. We will present genealogy as a particular conception and method of practising critique that can be useful to producing critical studies of education but without the limitations imposed by the theory and practice of critical pedagogy.

Critical theory

It is always difficult to do full justice to the range of approaches that could be subsumed under the term 'critical'. Indeed, that is part of the problem for the term itself has a complex and confusing range of connotations and applications. This means that there is a great deal of disagreement as to what constitutes a critical approach. Critical theory is seen as 'critical' because its aim is emancipation. Thus it is critical in the sense that it does not simply seek to generate knowledge of the world as it is, but to detect and unmask beliefs and practices that limit human freedom, justice and democracy and to deploy this knowledge or theory in actions that brings these things about. The task of educational theorizing and practice then is to become transformative both in relation to individuals and the social world – it itself needs to be part of the process of establishing the conditions for a rational conduct of social life free of the oppressive effects of ideology.

Critical theory argues that knowledge and truth can exist only where power relations are suspended or neutralised. The pursuit of knowledge is imagined as an emancipatory interested search for truth which power impedes, corrupts and distorts. From this perspective, knowledge that is linked with power is not 'true' knowledge but ideology. If true knowledge can exist only where power is absent, this leads to '…a longing for a space of knowledge simultaneously outside of formulations of power and yet capable of undermining them all' (Rabinow 1997: xvii). Theorizing, research and praxis become inseparable. The theorizer, the teacher, the researcher and the activist cannot simply stand aside and adopt a passive disinterested stance. On the contrary, they have to be very much in, and part of, their world. Furthermore, they should be one and the same.

Critical theory and the approach it offers has resonated with both educational theorizers and practitioners. Its discourse of basic social needs, of distortions and false consciousness, its foregrounding of critical dialogue and praxis, provides an appealing basis for theory and practice, particularly for educators committed to social action and change. Its refusal to separate research and knowledge (theory) from action (practice) demolishes the debilitating tension between theory and practice. An approach informed by critical theory provides one possible answer to both the epistemological question – what is valid knowledge? – and the ethical question – how can it best be used? Its aim of empowerment in the cause of emancipation provides a purposive goal and a moral dimension for educational research and practice. Above all, critical theory provides a standard by which the present can be evaluated and, in the sense that the empirically existing world is never going to match up to the standard set by critical theory, it provides an endless resource for research and action.

However, critical theory is not unproblematic. Although it seeks to unmask distortions and constraints, it itself offers a very partial and limited view of human experience and social interaction. It speaks a very modernist and rationalistic discourse, redefining rather than challenging categories and hierarchies. It privileges the place of a particular kind of rationality and, although this is not positivism's narrow version, it is nonetheless a totalising and excluding rationality, which in its own way is equally oppressive. Related to this are problems arising from the commitment to an emancipatory project construed in a naturalistic and universalising way – that is, in terms of concepts of basic needs and emancipatory goals, suitable for all. The assumption is that as universals these are invariant in their meaning and interpretation across cultural contexts, readily discernible by a rational mind purged of ideology. As we have noted earlier, there are problems with a theorizing that claims such universality.

The most well-known and influential application of critical theory to education is critical pedagogy, which is characterised by the unity of theory, research and practice demanded by critical theory. For critical pedagogues, all education is not only about learning but also unlearning and relearning, reflection and evaluation leading to more learning, etc. This process, it is claimed, is prevented by traditional education, particularly schooling and by educational theory that does not recognise the unity of theory and practice and the place of education and learning in the furtherance of human emancipation and social justice.

In a sense, we are now too much influenced by the critique of critical theory articulated by scholars such as Foucault and Derrida of invariant essences, originating presences, and universalising emancipatory discourses. We have become aware that there is too much indignity in speaking for others, no matter how well-intentioned. Furthermore, we now recognise that such discourses do not always have the effect intended – in fact, very often quite the opposite. Gore (1993: 61) argues that 'critical theory has its own power-knowledge nexus which in particular contexts and particular historical moments will operate in ways that are oppressive and repressive to people within and/or outside'.

It is not too difficult to see how critical theory itself can so easily become a 'masterful' discourse. The universalising thrust of theorizing in the critical theory mode can become a will to know which is also a will to govern. It could be argued that although critical theory enjoins the unity of theory and practice it is still theory that is privileged because practice requires the *right* and therefore prior theoretical perspective in the struggle for emancipation.

The possibility that critical theory can easily become a masterful discourse is heightened by its failure to foreground reflexivity. A significant place is allocated to reflection but critical theorists are not required to be *reflexive*, they are not required to submit their own position to critical scrutiny and examine the nature and effects of the power relations, operating 'behind their backs' but still nonetheless present, in their emancipatory project. On the other hand, as we shall see later, reflexivity is an explicit feature of genealogy.

Foucault and education

Since generally this is not always made explicit, we can only speculate that the limitations of any educational theory informed by critical theory and its interests, among other things, are what has driven many in theoretical studies in education to take up some of Foucault's concepts and instruments of analysis. In some cases however, this is made explicit and there are examples of this take-up in education. All have proved productive in different and varied ways (e.g. Biesta 2005; Fejes and Nicoll 2008; Peters 2005; Rabinow 2009). Rather than enumerate the take-up we will consider the more interesting issue of why the take-up of Foucault's concepts and methods was first resisted in education and still is by some.

Critical theory and its offshoot critical pedagogy held sway in education for a long time because there seemed to be no radical alternative. Foucault was always a possibility but for a while his work seemed too disturbing for a number of reasons. First, because it seemed to provide no plan, no programme, no 'curriculum', for what educators could and should do. Foucault certainly disturbed educators' modernist presuppositions but seemed to have nothing to put in its place. Second, this was exacerbated by Foucault's apparent determinism. If we are enveloped by power which shapes our very subjectivity, then what can we do other than submit? If all 'progress' is no more than the development of more sophisticated forms of regulation, then what indeed is the point of the educational enterprise other than as another means of actualising regulation. What was ignored here was Foucault's argument that power could have positive as well as negative effects and that his methods make it possible to distinguish between different forms of regulation. Holding onto the Enlightenment dream of an education without regulation, educators generally were plunged into anxiety about what the role of education might be in contemporary times. Any smack of determinism has a tendency to make educators fear that they will fall victim to a paranoid fantasy of helplessness in the face of overwhelming power. A state, one could say, of no answers, no hope.

This of course has now changed dramatically since it has been recognised by leading scholars that education is fundamental in shaping modern western society and in its effects on subjects. The rules of modern culture, particularly given the emphasis on liberal governance through knowledge rather than coercion, have been such that people have had to be considered free, they have had to contract to work, and not live according to imposed rules. They have had to be taught to organise their lives in particular ways, 'trained' to be self-governing. Hence, modernity's interest in teaching people, the emphasis on knowledge and education and therefore, the influence of pedagogy as the preferred means of governance in a culture whose values prohibit force in the micro-practices of government. Modernity must use knowledge to discipline and discipline is an exercise of power that works through the 'gentle' means of teaching.

When Foucault refers to education, he does so invariably in the context of other issues, in particular, the exercise of disciplinary techniques in relation to crime, madness, and sexuality. Yet, despite the relative lack of interest in education, what he has to say about the prison and the asylum is equally applicable to institutional education. In both the prison and the school, power is inscribed on the bodies of subjects to create a particular sort of subjectivity, which at the same time produces knowledge about those subjects. Surveillance is not something that was simply added on to older models of educational practice, but rather forms an integral part of the educational practices of modernity.

Despite this lack of an explicit focus on education, a whole library of books and articles has emerged devoted to arguing why Foucault's concepts and methods ought to be taken up in pursuing new directions in educational research and theory. The discussion and application of Foucault's concepts and methods has therefore now become a more common feature in educational research and theory. However, an exception to this is the concept and practice of critique articulated through Foucault's concept and method of genealogy. While genealogy has received some attention, this has most often been confined to methodological discussions, including attempts to reconcile genealogy with critical theory approaches (e.g. Tamboukou and Ball 2003), or passing references in relation to Foucault's other concepts and methods, or commentaries on Foucault's own work (e.g. Peters and Besley 2007). Rarely, however, does one see genealogies actually being done in educational research, despite the critical effectiveness of the few genealogies that have been undertaken (e.g. Hunter 1994; Jones 1990; Meredyth and Tyler 1993). Even rarer in education is to come across a discussion and application of the concept of critique articulated through genealogy. It is to a discussion of this that we turn to in the next section.

Genealogy as concept and method of critique

The advantage of genealogy as a method of critique is that it produces strategic knowledge, so that we can ask the question: do we want to govern, or want to be governed, like that? It has a strategic usefulness in providing historical analyses into the mechanisms of power, forms of rationality and discourse that dominate the present field of education. The political usefulness of a genealogical analysis derives from its capacity to disrupt or discomfort and destabilise the fixedness, inevitability and necessity of these contemporary ways of thinking and acting by showing their fragility and contingency. When Foucault deployed the term 'genealogy' he had in mind Nietzsche's genealogy of morals where history is characterised as both complex and mundane. One of the points of a genealogical analysis is to show that theories are the contingent turns of history rather than the outcome of rationally inevitable trends. History is a matter of complex processes which can only be understood in their specificity and their potential to have been otherwise.

Genealogy is however, not simply a method but a particular way of conceptualising and approaching the practice of critique. Through the concept of genealogy, the practice of critique is re-defined as '...the movement by which the subject gives himself the right to question truth on its effects of power and question power on its discourses of truth.' (Foucault 1997: 47) Genealogies are thus characterised by an attitude of scepticism with respect to what is held most revered, questioning all scientific and humanitarian motives for reform as well as notions of progress (Oksala 2007) and unitary origins. As such, genealogy uses history to show that many of the things we take for granted or conceive as 'natural' or 'true' have a history, a genealogy or lineage, and therefore are artefacts of previous events, discourses, rationalities and practices (Dean 1998).

One of the features of genealogy which makes it into the opposite of critical theory's critique of ideology is the central concern with analysing the intrinsic and historically specific links between knowledge and power. This transforms the task of critique '...from that of the practice of a legislating subject passing judgement on a deficient reality to an analysis of the assumptions on which taken-for-granted practice rests' (Dean 1994: 119). The concept of power-knowledge functions to make visible and intelligible how the knowledges (theories) of the human sciences make possible and play a role in the practices (relations of power) used in the regulation, including the education, of people. The object is to study the different and historically specific relations between forms by which subjects are known and technologies of power (the acting upon of subjects), so that it is possible to understand how technologies of power constitute a field of truth and the types of subjectivities formed and re-formed on the basis of these knowledge-power relations. This makes it possible to analyse how we have come to govern both ourselves and others through the truths produced about what we are, and then how these practices of governing change with changes in what is accepted as truth and vice versa. Genealogy is thus a form of critique carried out within a framework that pays attention to the positive, productive effects of modern forms of power and contends that their effectiveness rests on the installation of a discourse or regime of truth (Gordon 1980).

Thus, as an approach to critique, genealogy confounds critical theory's assumptions about the role of critique and the relationship between theory and practice. From the perspective of genealogy, a critique is not a matter of saying what is bad or deficient. It is a matter of identifying and problematizing the assumptions, familiar notions, unexamined ways of thinking on which the practices we accept rest (Foucault 2000). Genealogy, through the concept of knowledge-power, enables the researcher to evade all problems concerned with the privileging of theory over practice, and the reverse. Theory (forms of knowledge) and practice (relations of power) are not seen as opposed, but as interdependent and as such '...theory does not express, translate or serve to apply practice: it is practice' (Foucault 1977a: 207) – both a problematizing practice and a practice of constituting knowledge. To practice criticism using genealogy is an intellectual activity that makes visible what is taken for granted through the action of theory.

Through the concept of genealogy, a certain attitude towards the present is introduced where what is presented as natural, timeless, self-evident, true or necessary ways of seeing, ways of knowing and ways of acting at present are approached as something to be problematized through historical investigation. Whilst the present emerges from the past, it does not do so in a fixed form and it is part of a process that continues into the future. Problematization here refers both to the way in which specific historical practices give rise to or provide the conditions necessary for the emergence of forms of knowledge and practice, as well as to the ways in which genealogies are able to turn a 'given' into a question (Deacon 2000). This problematization shows the fragility and contingency of the present in relation to the past (Barry *et al.* 1996). Genealogical analyses do not aim to show that our contemporary ways of thinking and acting are only habits of a particular time and place but '[r]ather than relativise the present, these perspectival studies hope to destabilise it...', in order to bring into view the 'historically sedimented underpinnings' of particular ways of thinking and acting that dominate our contemporary experience (Barry *et al.* 1996: 5). In so doing, these dominant and present ways of thinking and acting require rethinking, as their accepted necessity is challenged. Thus, as a particular way of conceptualising, using and doing history, genealogy has come to be known as a 'history of the present'. As Deleuze argued, 'Foucault's work is a strange machine, it actually makes it impossible to think of history as other than present history' (Foucault 1972: 102).

Furthermore, genealogy is not only a way of approaching questions of the present and using history as a tool of critique, but also a way of approaching the *doing* of history. Historical analysis becomes an action of critique and tracing the past becomes a genealogy. The genealogical approach to doing history differs from those approaches that start from a theory of the subject. In so doing, genealogy offers a critical approach that permits an analysis of the self-determining subject, ever present in educational theorizing, as itself something to be *explained* rather than as a taken-for-granted or *a priori* truth upon which an analysis of knowledge and power can be based. Genealogy also places itself against the various conventional approaches of 'teleologization', 'totalisation', synthesis, reconciliation and promise (Dean 1992) of conventional history. The contrast between conventional and genealogical history hinges on conventional history's totalising or synthesising priorities where, believing in ahistorical absolutes, it attempts to assimilate individual events into progressions and totalities, counting as significant only those events that can be so assimilated (Prado 1995). This approach to doing history is evident in critical education studies. Individual historical events are assimilated into, and used to tell, a totalising history of education in terms of the progressive repression or liberation of people's true human capacity for agency. In contrast, genealogy is concerned with continuity and discontinuity, with 'subjugated knowledges' and practices, with those knowledges and practices that do not fit the totalising story, and by this means the flow of a totalising historical narrative is disrupted (Foucault 1998).

Genealogy stands against the critical use of history to judge and condemn the past in the name of present truths – a critical use of history that is also employed in critical studies of education. Instead the historical knowledge established by genealogical research is used strategically to show how things have come to be constituted at present and therefore that they could have been, or could still be, constituted in a different manner. As such, genealogies produce critical historical discourses, but these do not form part of a plan or programme for what we should do. Rather than prescribe explicit political programmes, genealogies open up a politicised space that makes it possible to challenge accepted necessities, which is utterly indispensable for any transformation (Oksala 2007). They do not eschew emancipation but, unlike critical theory, they do not make it a telos or totalising goal. Genealogical studies produce theories without producing totalising theory, as their objective is not to produce truth but to grasp the conditions within which human beings have been and are being made into known and knowing, governed and governing, moralised and moralising subjects (Deacon 2000).

History is therefore used as a privileged instrument of genealogical analysis, but it is a special sort of 'effective history' that is done (Foucault 1994: 381). A key aspect of this historical method is what Foucault (1991: 79) terms 'eventalisation'. It involves defining and attempting to understand an event in its singularity instead of seeing and analysing it as the result, or expression, of an underlying historical necessity, in order to bring about a breach of self-evidence and a suspension of commonplace assumptions (Mahon 1992). It defines a method that aims to identify instances of practices and forms of knowledge or discourses that are an exception to totalising narratives and breach them by so doing. History is thus used by genealogy not to reassure us of the virtue and necessity of present thinking, policy and practice but as a tool to disrupt and undermine it (Dean 1991). The delineation of the event serves as a marker of change and persistence as well as a means of breaching those self-evidences on which present knowledge and practice rests. As the objective is to define and analyse events in their singularity or specificity, eventalisation as a method of historical analysis proceeds by case-histories or case-studies. This then avoids the temptation of posing or imposing a general theory of the relations between knowledge/theories (regimes of truth and rationality) and power (modes of government or regimes of practices for directing conduct). In this sense, if we return to the issue of universality and generalizability explored in the introduction, we can say that while genealogy sets itself against, and seeks to problematize universalising theory, the specific studies it makes possible provide historical material that can have general effects and implications. These are general in the sense that the disruptive effects of a genealogy can extend to all those discourses and practices which rely on the taken for granted premises that have been problematized.

Genealogy has a strategic usefulness in providing historical analyses that problematize the mechanisms of power, forms of rationality and discourses that dominate the present field of education. Understanding and practising critique in this way exposes new possibilities of thinking, perceiving and acting. By showing how things that we take for granted and assume to be necessities have in fact emerged out of a network of contingent practices, genealogy makes possible not only thought experiments and idle speculations, but also concrete change that can transform ways of life, power relations and identities (Oksala 2007). In this sense, genealogy can work not in the service of a universal emancipatory project, but rather as a more local form of resistance and practice of freedom. It is not a matter of offering prescriptions for resistance. Instead genealogy is *itself* a practice of resistance which opens up possibilities for the practice of freedom. The effect of genealogy is not then to produce universalising theory but to critique and mount a constructive challenge though producing studies of the intrinsic and historically specific links between theory and practice in particular contexts.

The advantages of genealogy

At this point, let us explore briefly the advantages and critical capacity of genealogy using one recent example of the application of the genealogical concept and method of critique. This research critically analysed the significance of youth participation policies and programmes recently introduced in Australia and across Europe designed to reform the way young people are governed (Anderson 2011). The reform was a response to the perceived problem of what are identified as 'traditional' ways of treating and governing young people, repressive ways that deny their agency and silence their voices.

This problem is defined by a critical youth studies discourse, driven by a critical theory perspective, which draws heavily from a critical educational discourse interested in promoting 'student voice' and with challenging the persistence of traditional practices of schooling that systematically deny agency and voice. This discourse defines the problem as a legacy of repressive nineteenth century institutional regimes sustained and advanced by a false, yet still dominant, knowledge of youth that misrepresents young people as being incapable of agency. It argues the need to rethink the concept of youth in a way that recognises young people's true capacity and right to exercise agency, and for policies and programmes of youth participation which empower and enhance their autonomy and voice. This, in turn, is understood to be linked to and part of a larger emancipatory project, concerned with democratising traditional oppressive hierarchies of power within educational and other social institutions as well as recognising and empowering young people as active citizens.

Taking up genealogy as a concept and method of critique enabled an understanding and critical analysis of the connection between the contemporary critical discourse of youth and youth participation programmes introduced to reform the government of youth as a relation of knowledge-power. It thereby enabled taking as an object of critical and historical analysis, the mutual relations between this way of knowing and governing youth and problematizing these through producing a genealogy. In so doing, the universal nature of the self-determining youth subject is problematized and the corresponding totalizing historical narrative of repression questioned. It enables instead a consideration that this way of knowing and governing youth, precisely like those ways of knowing and governing youth they are seemingly opposed to, also has a history.

In this study the event is the emergence of a liberal mode of governmental power that takes as its target young people defined and demarcated as certain kinds of social subjects with a capacity for agency and that governs through inciting participation in practices of self-government. The object was not then to examine all instances in the nineteenth century of the constitution of a knowledge and liberal mode of governing young people as subjects with a capacity for agency and through inciting practices in self-government. Rather, following the method of eventalisation, the objective was to define and analyse the event in its singularity by using exemplifying case studies.

Two historical case studies were presented. The first traced one line of the genealogy of this knowledge and mode of governing youth to the nineteenth century debates about, and new practices introduced to, reform the system of disciplining boys in the public schools of England and later the Australian Colony of Victoria. The second traces another line of this genealogy to the nineteenth century debates about, and new methods introduced to, reform the system of disciplining juvenile criminals in the prison system of the Australian Colony of Victoria – a debate and project of prison reform that largely followed those already undertaken in France and England. What emerged clearly from both cases was that among the methods of exercising power introduced to reform both the public school and prison system were those that presupposed and required a subject and social group with a capacity for agency. They worked not by repressing or excluding individual and collective autonomy but rather by inciting and directing it – a positive way of conceptualising and exercising power and an example of 'governmentality'. This historical material breaches the self-evidence and seeming necessity of those ways of knowing and governing youth that are presented and accepted today as representing a total reversal of nineteenth-century discourses and practices and a counter to power. In doing so, it makes it difficult to think about youth or student participation in the way that it is dominantly thought about and therefore new ways of thinking about it, and acting in relation to it, become urgent and entirely possible.

What emerges from doing genealogy and how does this relate to educational theorizing?

Through reconceiving our notion of critique in terms of genealogy and by doing genealogy we have learned a number of things useful to educational theorizing. First, there is an understanding of the importance and strategic usefulness of history to the practice of critique and theorizing. In the absence of history, critique is in danger of being superficial, grounded in the same assumptions as that which it seeks to critique and therefore neglecting to disturb the very assumptions on which it rests. Second, general principles or universalising theories are neither essential to motivate the practice of critique nor essential for critique to be effective. Nor does critical research need to produce theories which are 'universalizable' to be valuable and to have a critical and general effect. Third, a concept and practice of critique need not ground itself in truth or a theory of the subject, but can take truth and the subject as its object of analysis. Lastly, that the relationship between critique and freedom need not be seen solely in terms of emancipation, as a production of knowledge that can free us from the authoritative effects of power and thus realise our inherent freedom. Rather, it can be conceived in terms of a production of knowledge that shows how our thought and action is always variously constrained, but also how we can stretch these limits, opening up possibilities for the practice of freedom by exposing new possibilities of thinking, perceiving and acting.

If this learning is related to educational theorizing, then it can have a number of productive effects. This is particularly so if we understand the importance and role of theory as helping us to think differently and to ask different, new and critical questions, as well as informing and guiding the conduct of empirical research. Genealogy offers educational theorizing a way of using history as a tool of critical analysis rather than to make claims to have discovered essences or truth or to unmask ideology. It can also free educational theorizing from the prejudice that theory is only as good or valuable as its ability to be universal. In so doing, it can inspire an educational theorizing of the particular and the specific rather than of the general and the universal.

Genealogy also provides educational theorizing a constant reminder of the potentially subjectifying and normalising practices and effects of theorizing by the reflexivity that it demands as a consequence of its way of understanding knowledge-power relations. It provides an opportunity to reconceptualise the role of the critical educational researcher and practitioner from one who battles on behalf of truth, to one who questions educational truths as to their effects of power and questions power on its educational discourses of truth. We see critical educational theorizing as primarily a matter of making the certain uncertain, the familiar that is also unfamiliar, the given that is also contingent. Not simply to be disruptive, but rather to open up possibilities for changing the ways we conventionally think about and practice education.

Concluding comments

Taking up genealogy as a concept and method of critique in order to consider what it can offer educational theorizing means that we can no longer think of issues of truth, power and subjectivity in a naive way. The belief that there are truths about human beings that hold in all cultures and at all times must be subjected to radical, historical questioning. Genealogy insists that we must work without absolutes and this implies a systematic scepticism towards all universalising truths. It also demands a reflexivity that continually asks – what is educational theory? What are the assumptions and pre-suppositions that inform, animate and validate educational theory and practice? A genealogical approach demands that any educational theory and practice must itself be understood as having a history and, moreover, a contested and contingent one. In return, genealogy offers a concept and method of critique which avoids the limitations of a critical theory approach.

References

Anderson, A. (2011) *The Constitution of Youth: Toward a Genealogy of the Discourse and Government of Youth*, unpublished PhD thesis, RMIT University.

Ball, S. (ed.) (1990) *Foucault and Education: Disciplines and Knowledge*, London: Routledge.

Barry, A., Osborne, T. and Rose, N. (1996) 'Introduction', in A. Barry, T. Osborne and N. Rose (eds) *Foucault and Political Reason: Liberalism, Neo-liberalism and Rationalities of Government*, Chicago: The University of Chicago Press.

Biesta, G. (2005) 'What can critical pedagogy learn from postmodernism: further reflections on the impossible future of critical pedagogy', in I. Gur Ze-ev (ed.), *Critical Theory and Critical Pedagogy Today: Towards a New Language in Education,* Haifa: The University of Haifa Press.

Deacon, R. (2000) 'Theory and practice: Foucault's concept of problematisation', *Telos*, 2000, 118: 127-142.

Dean, M. (1991) *The Constitution of Poverty: Toward a Genealogy of Liberal Governance*, London: Routledge.

Dean, M. (1992) 'A genealogy of the government of poverty', *Economy and Society*, 21, 3: 215-251.

Dean, M. (1994) *Critical and Effective Histories: Foucault's Methods and Historical Sociology*, London: Routledge.

Dean, M. (1998) 'Questions of method', in I. Velody and R. Williams (eds) *The Politics of Constructionism*, London: Sage Publications.

Fejes, A and Nicoll, K. (eds) (2008) *Foucault and Lifelong Learning: Governing the Subject*, Oxan: Routledge.

Foucault, M. (1977a) 'Intellectuals and power', in D. Bouchard (ed.) *Language, Counter-memory, Practice*, New York: Cornell University Press. Online. Available at: <http://www.libcom.org.htm>. (Accessed 6 February 2012).

Foucault, M. (1977b) *Discipline and Punish: the Birth of the Prison*, trans. A. Sheridan, London: Penguin Books.

Foucault, M. (1980) 'Truth and power', in C. Gordon (ed.) *Power/Knowledge: Selected Interviews and Other Writings 1972 - 1977*, New York: Pantheon Books.

Foucault, M. (1989) 'The order of things', in S. Lotringer (ed.) *Foucault Live*, trans. L.

Foucault, M. (1991) 'A question of method', in G. Burchell, C. Gorden and P. Miller (eds) *The Foucault Effect: Studies in Governmentality*, Chicago: University of Chicago Press.

Foucault, M. (1997) 'What is critique?', in S. Lotringer (ed.) *The Politics of Truth*, trans. L. Hochroth and C. Porter, Los Angeles: Semiotext.

Foucault, M. (1994) 'Nietzsche, genealogy, history', in J. D. Fabion (ed.) *Aesthetics: Essential Works of Foucault 1954-1984*, vol. 2, tans. R. Hurley, London: Penguin Books.

Foucault, M. (2000) 'So is it important to think?', in J. D. Fabion (ed.) *Aesthetics: Essential Works of Foucault 1954-1984*, vol. 3, trans. R. Hurley, New York: The New Press.

Gordon, C. (1980) 'Afterword', in C. Gorden (ed.) *Power/Knowledge: Selected Interviews and Other Writings 1972 - 1977*, New York: Pantheon Books.

Gore, J. (1998) 'Disciplining bodies: on the continuity of power relations in pedagogy', in T. Popkewitz and M. Brennan (eds), *Foucault's Challenge: Discourse, Knowledge, and Power in Education*, New York: Teachers College.

Hunter, I. (1994) *Rethinking the School: Subjectivity, Bureaucracy, Criticism*, Australian Cultural Studies: A Reader Series, St Leonards: Allen & Unwin.

Jones, D. (1990) 'The genealogy of the urban schoolteacher', in S. Ball (ed.) *Foucault and Education: Disciplines and Knowledge*, London: Routledge.

Mahon, M. (1992) *Foucault's Nietzschean Genealogy: Truth, Power and the Subject*, Albany: Suny Press.

Meredyth, D. and Tyler, D. (1993) *Child and Citizen: Genealogies of Schooling and Subjectivity*, Brisbane: Institute for Cultural Policy Studies.

Oksala, J. (2007) *How to Read Foucault*, London: Granta.

Peters, M. (2005) 'Critical pedagogy and the futures of critical theory', in I. Gur Ze-ev (ed), *Critical Theory and Critical Pedagogy Today: Towards a New Language in Education*, Haifa: The University of Haifa Press.

Peters, M. and Besley, T. (eds) (2007) *Why Foucault? New Directions in Educational Research*, New York: Peter Lang.

Prado, C. G. (1995) *Starting with Foucault: an Introduction to Genealogy*, 2nd edn., Colorado: Westview Press.

Rabinow, P. (1997) 'Introduction: the history of systems of thought', in P. Rabinow (ed.) *The Essential Works 1954-1984*, vol. 1, *Ethics*, New York: The New Press.

Rabinow, P. (2009) 'Foucault's untimely struggle: toward a form of spirituality', in *Theory, Culture and Society*, 26, 6, 25-44.

Tamboukou, M. and Ball, S. (eds) (2003) *Dangerous Encounters: Genealogy and Ethnography*, New York: Peter Lang.

Tyler, D. and McCallum, D. (1997) 'History of the human sciences special feature: introduction', *Economy and Society*, 26, 2: 159-160.

Chapter 9

The excess of theory

On the functions of educational theory in apparent reality

Tomasz Szkudlarek

Introduction

As the title of this chapter suggests, I argue that there is something 'excessive' in theoretical thinking about education, something that supposedly is a 'surplus' to its normally perceived operations. I also consider the possibility that this excess, too, is somehow functional, that it is utilised in the power/knowledge relations of modern societies.

I start with a brief outline of the functions of educational theory based on Habermas's typology of interests that constitute cognition. By placing them in a processual framework, as momentums in theory/practice relations, I expose a 'place' where those excessive functions can be identified. This place is *apparent reality* (in Hegel's terms), which is a product of our failure to construct the world on conceptual premises. Apart from the need to give such reality a new conceptualisation, of which Hegel speaks, there are 'excessive' functions of theory that are pertinent and intrinsic to the domain of the apparent. In education, they are related to postulational rhetoric, the plurality and inconsistency of theoretical ideas, and the impossibility of precisely defining their basic concepts. I interpret such phenomena in terms of discursive practices related to the construction of society in power relations. My suggestion is that educational theory contributes to the economy of power, in particular to making its structures 'invisible', disguised in pedagogical rather than political attire. Educational rhetoric becomes here an important part of the 'ontological' rhetoric that constitutes political identities in Ernesto Laclau's understanding (Laclau 2005).

Functions of theory

What functions can we ascribe to theory in education? A fairly commonplace implies a technological understanding of the relation between theory and practice; that is, it claims that theory has the task of designing pedagogies and procedures of assessing their efficiency. Another answer refers to the hermeneutic tradition and claims that the need for theory can be understood through the notion of understanding. This implies that the ways we educate are not necessarily derived from prior theoretical statements. Education is a practical thing performed by people who do not have to design their actions before they act. Theory, in this perspective, provides us with languages for reflection, and languages through which we can share those reflections with others, contributing to mutual understanding. A third, perhaps less common answer, is that theory questions the realities we live in. Its abstract language creates distance to the experiential domain. The access to theory makes the world relative, less familiar, and creates a space in which different ways of living and learning are imaginable.

These three uses of theory paraphrase Jürgen Habermas's formulation of the 'interests' that constitute human cognition (Habermas 1972). Management (or technology in a broader sense), reflective understanding and critique that brings emancipation, form an epistemological framework largely consistent with the array of modern political and educational ideologies. However, those modalities can be understood not only in terms of competing ideological positions that pit their power one against another, but as momentums in the cycle of human actions as well. We may see them as partial epistemological tools, applicable sequentially: when we do things according to our knowledges; when we realize that what we have done is different from what had been planned and that we need another language to understand it; and when – as a result – the legitimacy of what has been done is questioned. Then we open space for a new design. To sum up, theoretical languages (technological, hermeneutical and critical) may be seen as functional in relation to different momentums of social practice in modern societies. Such circular, or spiral, movement revokes the Hegelian tradition.

One of the interesting applications of Hegel's dialectics in contemporary political theory, which can help to fine-tune the question of the functions of theory, is Jadwiga Staniszkis' reconstruction of the ontology of socialism based on Hegel's dialectic of reality and appearance. According to Staniszkis, socialist Poland before 1989, with its political system imposed by the USSR, was an apparent state that could not be understood in terms of the foundational logic (ideology and theories) that preceded its creation. As she says (following Hegel), such foundational languages are based on abstract concepts that are believed to capture the essence of things. But everything, in its immediacy, is characterized not only by its essence, but also by accidental features not covered by the concept. As a result, when we act according to conceptual blueprints our practices produce numerous accidental effects that have nothing to do with the essences that those concepts claim to capture, and that, therefore, cannot be understood in terms of the language that we used to plan our action. From the perspective of its foundational logic, the effect of our action is appearance (Hegel 1990), something 'unreal' and incomprehensible, deprived of rationality. It is a 'fake' reality that lacks its constitutive elements. An important task, as Staniszkis claims, is to overcome the intuitive understanding of appearances in negative terms, through what they 'lack' and what is 'absurd' in them, because such an approach only reflects the failure of the theoretical/foundational language to capture what it has produced. We need a language that captures this reality in positive ontological dimensions, that grasps what 'there is' rather than what 'is not'. Staniszkis identified several areas where such a linguistic shift was necessary to understand socialist Poland of the 1980s. 'Economy without property', 'power without politics' and 'political crises without conflicts of interests' that were, instead, 'an expression of the efforts of atomized societies to form themselves as collective subjects' (Staniszkis 2006: 11) formed the framework of the apparent reality that demanded a new language to make it comprehensible in its own ontological terms.

In my understanding, Staniszkis' reconstruction applies not only to one historical formation, but – because of her reliance on Hegel – presents a more universal logic of social practices informed by conceptual premises. In a book written shortly after the publication of Staniszkis' text (Szkudlarek 1990), I used this analysis to question of the role of educational theory. Public education in its modern shape shares its roots with the ideas of political modernization, of which socialism is an important part. Knowledge seems to play two functions here. The first is that of providing for systematically organised ideas that precede human action. It can be understood as 'technical' knowledge in Habermas, but it is a lame technology, one that always fails, or – in other words – always produces things that are different from those intended. In this respect, political and pedagogical theories are very similar. If we educate in a planned manner, which is typical of institutional education, we create artefacts that cannot be understood in the language used to design those practices. Here, both in education and politics, the second function of knowledge comes to the fore: We need to invent new languages so that apparent realities can find their foundational logic.[1] In a similar way, Henry Giroux (1983) spoke of the difference between technically understood 'theory *for* practice', and 'theory *of* practice' the aim of which is to understand diverse practices of education, including subversive ones. Those two functions repeat the Hegelian instances of conceptualisation in his dialectic of reality and appearance.

However, there seems to be a yet another aspect of theoretical thinking, which I would like to consider here. It becomes visible when we confront historical examples of educational theories with what we otherwise know about the societies in which they were proposed (see the next section). It can also be derived from the very nature of appearance, providing that we detach this notion from Hegel's idea of *Aufhebung* – from the idea that oppositions (including that between reality and appearance) are logically overcome to form new syntheses. If we assume that apparent reality is, in fact, 'all there is', and that we can never accomplish the process of conceptualisation in a way that would overcome the recurrent work of 'designing' practices and 'explaining' them conceptually, then we should delineate the functions of theory *within* apparent reality – as different from those that precede its construction and those that aim at finding its foundational logic. The first possible function of educational theories within the ontology of appearance is that they build an *epistemology of evasion* (Szkudlarek 1990, 1995). They help to render the apparent status of reality – its ontological fault, or incompleteness – *invisible.* This idea was first proposed in the analysis of the discourse of socialist pedagogy in Poland (Szkudlarek 1990). Educational theory was, obviously, in the imposed socialist system, part of the ideological apparatus of the state. Apart from creating a body of utopian ideas that designed and legitimized the political system, it was also marked by a *refusal to know* the social reality, by an almost systematic evasion of data, problems and regularities that could make the apparent *visible as apparent* and problematic, and thus contribute to the creation of a new conceptualisation of the system. In a way, educational theory was then a device that domesticated educationists in an 'absurd' political system.

Treating an epistemology of evasion as pertinent in other historical contexts requires broadening the scope of analysis both in historical and theoretical terms. For this purpose, I have to move beyond the Hegelian perspective toward ontologies that refuse his insistence on the logical nature of social reality. First, however, I focus on a historical case that, while being a powerful intellectual construction, can be interpreted as an example of the epistemology of evasion.

Herbart and Foucault

As I said before, Staniszkis's ontological analysis of appearance extends beyond the nature of socialism. The same should apply to its supplementary element – epistemological evasion. It is possible to grasp its significance for understanding the 'excessive' functions of educational theory by juxtaposing Michel Foucault's genealogies of modernity (especially in his *Discipline and Punish,* 1995) with theoretical texts about education written in the epoch that is the subject of his analysis. The foundational pedagogical texts of modernity, like those by Rousseau or Herbart, were created in the time when, according to Foucault, modern regimes of power/knowledge and disciplinary surveillance were gaining a dominant role in shaping modern societies. In Rousseau, but especially in Herbart, we can find numerous and detailed theoretical descriptions of how disciplinary power and instruction *should* operate in education. In Herbart's *Allgemeine Pädagogik* (Herbart 1806, 1908 for the American edition), those postulates are presented within a conceptual framework almost perfectly reflected in Foucault's theory.[2] When we read Herbart *after* having read Foucault, it seems almost odd that the French genealogist did not analyse the foundations of educational science, that he missed the theory that explicitly conveys the message he tries to decipher in the archives: that the subject is shaped through *instruction* that creates his *will.* The condition for such an operation of knowledge is *discipline* – an internalised *government* over children. Herbart's cognitivistic psychology makes instruction the ultimate instance in the process of the formation of character. It is through knowledge that the will of the subject is created and that moral character – as the structure that frees the subject from the fate of accidental and uncontrolled movements – is established. This work of knowledge cannot be done without that of government and discipline. The difference between these latter instances lies with the locus of control. Government is external. The child must obey the tutor, following imposed rules and restrictions. Discipline must be internalised. It has to work tacitly, almost unnoticed, only occasionally resorting to rewards and punishments, as if to recall the existence of the energy that brings order to the world. Also, discipline works deeper and involves instances that are not visible to external viewers. 'Government only takes into account the results of actions, later on discipline must look to unexecuted intentions' (Herbart 1908: 233). An interesting passage in Herbart's text speaks of discipline as a kind of medium, a scarcely visible, liquid environment in which the growing subject has to be submerged:

> In order that character may take a moral direction, individuality must be dipped, as it were, in fluid element, which according to circumstances either resists or favors it, but for the most part it is hardly perceptible to it. This element is *discipline* which is mainly operative on the arbitrary will (*Willkür*), but also partly on the judgment.
>
> (Herbart 1908: 120)

We have to imagine Herbart's child as growing from the chaotic to the orderly; from being reactional to external incentives (not only those imparted in government, but, first of all, to spontaneous excitations and scattered attractions) to possessing the ability to follow his/her own interests and will.

> So much is certain, that a man whose will does not, like ideas held in his memory, spontaneously re-appear as the same as often as occasion recurs – a man who is obliged to carry himself back by reflection to his former resolution – will have great trouble in building up his character. And it is because natural constancy of will is not so often found in children, that discipline has so much to do.
>
> (Herbart 1908: 202--203).

This may be read very simply: Foucault was right, and Herbart's text is a proof of his accuracy. It definitely represents the discourse that lies behind the new mode of power relations in modern Europe. It is one of many, including legal, medical or religious discourses, that proclaims discipline and internal control based on knowledge as the ways of creating moral subjects. I call this new regime of power, resorting to the means that we usually identify with education, *pedagogism*.[3] It is the complex relation between pedagogism as a mode of control and pedagogy, and its rationalised variety that emerges as the science of education, that needs more detailed scrutiny here. If Foucault is right in his recognition of the proliferation of disciplinary power permeating all institutions of modern Europe, which – by the year of publication of Herbart's treatise – must have been a mature process, why is Herbart *inventing* his pedagogy? Why is he using a persuasive, rather than a descriptive language? It seems that such rhetoric is not accidental and that it can point to an important aspect of educational theory. Dealing with this question in terms of the theory itself, we have an easy answer: 'the science of education', as the American editors called Herbart's *Allgemeine Pädagogik*, rests on two pillars - ethics and psychology. The goals of education are defined in ethical terms, while the role of psychology is to invent the means to achieve them. Consequently, the rhetoric of invention and of postulating a particular pedagogy is simply a derivate of the ethical foundation of the theory itself. This is less obvious when we ask – in line with Foucault – the question of the possible uses of educational theory in the circulation of power/knowledge. What does it 'do' to society? How does it work as discursive practice? As I have noted above, according to Foucault, the mechanisms postulated by Herbart *must have already been in operation* for some time before the theory was formulated. This may point to a peculiar feature of educational theory, and possibly to one that is not confined to the peculiarity of that historical moment. In technical terms, educational theory is *excessive*, and it is so in several dimensions. It repeats and reformulates things which permeate the whole fabric of social life. As a 'technology of the self', or as biopolitical rationality, it arrives late, when other disciplines and knowledge regimes have already defined their concepts and structured their relations.[4] It seems that its function in designing modern technologies of control is secondary in relation to legal or medical discourse. For its use to educational practices, the knowledge of education could have probably remained in its 'natural' shape, without turning into an academic discipline. What keeps it alive?

Education and pedagogism

In contemporary societies we may see a similarly uneasy relation between certain educational theories and the regimes of governmentality, in Foucault's understanding (Foucault 1979). A trait of contemporary literature is that of the pedagogization or educationalization of social problems. This usually refers to the phenomenon described as an excessive burden of social issues that schools are supposed (or forced) to address, with the simultaneous withdrawal of the state from policies that could responsibly solve those problems. This brings up the question of justified and unjustified expectations *vis-à-vis* education, with an observation that many such practices are inappropriate (Bridges 2008). A paradigmatic example is that of unemployment. Instead of being addressed as a structural phenomenon that results from the concentration of capital in global economies, it is presented, and institutionally dealt with, as that of 'miseducation', of the lack of an adequacy between the outputs of schooling and the demands of the job market. The unemployed are perceived not as those who need income, but rather as those who need 'additional learning' (Simons and Masschelein 2008: 405). In a broader sense (and similar to the meaning of pedagogism of which I spoke above) educationalization is seen as intrinsically linked to modernization processes in general. As Marc Depaepe and Paul Smeyers (2008) note, the category of *Pädagogisierung* has been used in Germany since the 1950s, but current references usually refer to Foucault's notion of governmentality (Foucault 1979; Simons and Masschelein 2008). In some articulations (e.g. Sarnowski 1993), this phenomenon is linked to even deeper layers of European civilisation, that is to its dependence on philosophy and Christianity that established the instances of idealism and the incompleteness of the human, thus demanding constant improvement by morality and education. The history of the proliferation of pedagogical reason finds its peak with the Enlightenment and its later incarnations. In this light, modern society, in general, is seen as resorting to disciplinary and, even more generally, pedagogical means as dominant instruments of government. It means that people are taught to internalise power relations by acquiring certain knowledge and by being subjected to disciplinary regimes that position them within certain architectures of social structure, and, thus, they learn to act 'rationally' in given circumstances.

In a very interesting account on the link between modernization and educationalization, Simons and Massechlein (2008) speak of 'the assemblage of the learning apparatus' as part of the process of 'governmentalization of learning', that is, of constructing a 'strategic linkage between the "grammar of education", the "grammar of societal order" and the "grammar of governing"' in the twentieth century' (Simons and Masschelein 2008: 395). In current 'advanced liberal' societies we have become, as a result, self-governing subjects. This is more than the governmerntalization of education in its institutional shape: the new regime addresses learning as personal experience. Individuals should be managers of their own learning, or 'entrepreneurs', 'employed' in the business of their own life, and responsible for 'the preservation, reproduction and reconstruction of one's own human capital' (Collin Gordon, quoted in Simons and Masschelein 2008: 407). Learning thus becomes the core of the whole political apparatus of government:

> [T]he point of departure for governmental reflection is no longer social [in]equality and "post-factum redistribution" (as was the case for a lot of public policies developed within the social regime of governing), but inclusion and exclusion. And inclusion and exclusion are thus problematized not in "social" terms, but in terms of "learning".
>
> (Simons and Masschelein 2008: 405).

In their concluding remarks, Simons and Masschelein point to the paradoxical construction of freedom:

> [L]ooking at learning and the liberation of our learning (from the state, from institutions, from the dominance of the teacher, from the impact of economy, and so on) as a condition of our freedom and autonomy implies that we *forget* that this learning and the way in which we conceive it are from the very beginning both effect and instrument of the current governmental regime
>
> (Ibid: 414, italics added).

Further, referring to Foucault, they argue that 'what is familiar (our current experience of learning) [...] is often *invisible due to this familiarity*' (415, italics added).

Invisibility, ontology and rhetorics

The issue of invisibility in power relations is a classic theme, criss-crossing numerous philosophical traditions. To name just a few such traditions from our recent history, it is present in Rousseau and Herbart, in Nietzsche, Marx, Freud, Foucault and Rancière. Power works best when unnoticed, and its invisibility is often, simply, the result of the internalisation of its mechanisms, or its aesthetics in Rancière's terms (Rancière 2007). What I present here is just one of the ways of securing such invisibility – by a certain rhetoric which is characteristic of the language of education. My thesis is that educational rhetoric involves a large dose of postulates, appeals and demands. I call it postulational language. Its functions are manifold, but one of them is that of turning the world-as-it-is into a provisional, 'less existent' entity. This rhetoric is particularly interesting when what is postulated already exists. Here, I am referring again to the case of Herbart's theory *vis-à-vis* Foucault's history, but it can be illustrated by more trivial examples. 'You should work hard', 'Parents should devote time to their children', or 'Teachers should respect cultural diversity in the classroom' are double-edged utterances. They obviously call for certain action, but those calls are grounded in an act of *denial*: they presuppose that the postulated state of things does not exist. In cases where such a presupposition is problematic, they may deprive the reality of conceptual representations, make it incomprehensive and elusive, one that is fictional by virtue of its allegedly incomplete incarnation of what is desired. They operate in a peculiar 'present imperfect tense', in a suspended temporality of the not-yet. Returning to Hegel's language, we can argue that they *stabilize the apparent*, delaying the recognition of its ontological features.[5]

I believe that we can recognize such utterances as fairly typical of educational discourse. As I have noted in relation to Herbart's theory, it is ethics that demands the use of language that tells us what we should do, and, thus, implies what we do not do. It is not the case that Herbart invented this language. It is merely a translation (into the scientific genre) of the ancient tradition, continued in the discourse of Christianity, which implies that education is achieved by rhetorical means, while rhetoric itself is understood as the art of persuasion. In other words, the foundations of educational theory, as proposed by Herbart, *maintain the inscription of education in the domain of rhetorics.*

This, of course, is a broader issue that does not pertain to education alone. But education, especially in its modern form, is especially prone to this kind of normativity. This is often perceived as the fundamental deficit that makes its scientific status problematic (an old debate on facts and values in science). Still, it seems to be an intrinsic, inevitable aspect of theorizing education. The moment when education became an academic discipline (in continental Europe, rather than in the Anglo-American context, see Biesta 2011) was the moment when the social world was being re-invented along the ideas of the Enlightenment, ideas of rationality and liberty, and when 'a new man' was *postulated* as the condition of that modernization. No wonder, then, that the language of education is persuasive, saturated with terms of obligation, and filled with postulates and condemnations.

A particularly interesting situation occurs when the language of educational theory (or of the professional discourse of education in any conceivable form, scientific, legal or religious) interacts with *pedagogism* (the dispersed and proliferated pedagogical regime of political control). This is exactly the case, among others, with regard to Herbart's theory and to the contemporary discourse of learning. What happens then may produce an effect of *duplicating reality with its abstract idealization*, and – in a culture like ours, well accustomed to the idea that ideas *precede* reality – it is *the real* that becomes a duplicate, or caricaturization, of the ideal, a mockery of truth, a simulacrum.

In summary, I have so far addressed two instances of invisibility that are involved in the 'excessive' work of theory in education. First, the very reliance on ideas that precede practice (such as ethical ones) creates appearances that make educational practice incomprehensible in terms of those ideas. This is the Hegelian trope. Second, within the domain of the apparent, the postulational language of educational theory hides the operations of power, which form the provisional identity of the social, especially in cases when educationists postulate things that are part of those power regimes. In this way such a language stabilizes the apparent in its inability to find a more appropriate conceptualization.

Education in the apparent reality: for good

An epistemology of evasion and the creation of invisibility supplement the functions of educational theory that I have written about in the first section of the paper, but in so doing, they challenge the simplicity of the ontological premises on which the preceding analysis is based. As I remarked previously, appearance is more than just a dialectic momentum in the process of reality's gaining its conceptual form. It takes time. It is persistent and it is, in fact, 'all there is' for us as temporally limited beings. In other words, we will never live in a world that is *not* apparent or fictional, in a reality that has its fully conceptual representation. On the other hand, living in the apparent world, we need to see it as structured. We need to construe its identity, but we cannot achieve this by conceptual means. These premises inform the theory of identity proposed by Ernesto Laclau (2005). Laclau's is one of the most comprehensive ontologies that can offer a starting point for a new understanding of the political contexts and functions of education.[6] This theory uses certain Hegelian inventions,[7] but transcends this heritage toward a new ontology of the social, based on the assumption of its radical heterogeneity. Laclau's heterogeneity is another way of expressing the idea of appearance: it speaks of a world deprived of conceptual representation, and does so in a radical way: this deprivation is permanent. This means that identity can only be achieved by *rhetorical* (rather than logical) means. As Laclau argues, society will never gain conceptual representation; it will never constitute itself as totality or a fully reconciled society (Laclau 2005) – neither in a Hegelian way (through self-awareness) nor in a Habermasian one (through rational consensus). It can only achieve identity when one of its heterogeneous elements assumes the role of representing the missing whole, which Laclau calls hegemony. This is only possible when such a representation 'transcends' its particular content and becomes an *empty signifier*. As such, it can give a name to a whole chain of otherwise unstructured demands and desires, which are only connected by their equivalence in relation to what they exclude.[8] To put it succinctly, identity is construed *within* the heterogeneous, or within the apparent and 'fake' reality we inhabit. Hegemony, through its reliance on empty signifiers, is our lame, human, inevitably rhetorical, and fundamentally political way of creating a semblance of transcendence, in the name of which our social worlds gain epistemic and normative coherence.

Education plays an important role in the construction of hegemony. As a *rhetorical* enterprise, educational discourse helps to maintain a world that has no conceptual form and cannot be grasped in logical terms. The apparent, as I have called it following Hegel, or the heterogeneous in Laclau's terms (both speak of the lack of conceptual identification), can only find its identity by means of rhetorics. Rhetorics, as Laclau convincingly claims, are an *ontological* issue here. We are close to drawing the conclusion. The theory of education – and the discourse of education in general, as rhetorical practice – are at the centre of the rhetorical construction of the world. Their technical efficiency is dubious, but they 'do other things' that are essential in the political construction of society, and they do those in a way that is difficult to replace by other languages. Education as rhetorical practice, and educational theory as its rationalized and postulational discourse, gain an *ontological* status in this perspective.

This conclusion can be illustrated by David Labaree's (2008) remarks on educationalization. Labaree does not refer to Laclau's theory (which would be perfect for his argument), but his findings support my idea despite this. Speaking of a surprising persistence in charging education with goals it keeps failing to achieve, he declares that 'education may not be doing what we ask, but it is doing what we want' (448). The mix of goals imposed on education is simply impossible to achieve, first of all because they are contradictory, and this contradiction reflects the tension between liberalism and democracy (which has been called a 'democratic paradox' by Chantal Mouffe 2005).

> With this mix of goals imposed on it, education in liberal democracies has come to look like an institution at odds with itself. After all, it is being asked simultaneously to serve politics and markets, promote equality and inequality, construct itself as public good and private good. Politically, its structure should be flat, its curriculum common, and enrollment universal; economically, its structure should be hierarchical, its curriculum stratified, and enrollment scaled by high rates of attrition. [...] In this sense, then, these educational goals represent the contradictions embedded in any liberal democracy. Contradictions that cannot be resolved without removing either the society's liberalism or its democracy. Therefore when we project our liberal democratic goals on schools, we want them to take each of those goals seriously but not to implement any of them beyond modest limits, since to do so would be to put the other equally valued goals in significant jeopardy [...]. As a result, the educational system is an abject failure in its ability to achieve any one of its primary social goals.
>
> (Labaree 2008: 456)

What we learn from this is that it is not just socialism that produces apparent realities that cannot find conceptual form. Any social form is a conflict-ridden and 'impossible' structure. What is noteworthy here is that educational practice is an instrument of *maintaining* that apparent reality in its impossible shape, preventing a slippage towards a more clear form, towards one more 'rational' (and totalizing) in terms of its possible conceptual representations.

> The educationalization of society integrates society around a set of common experiences, processes, and curricular languages. It stabilizes and legitimizes a social structure of inequality that otherwise may drive us into an open conflict. It stabilizes and legitimizes government by providing an institution that can be assigned difficult social problems and that can be blamed when these problems are not solved. It provides orderly and credible processes for people to run their lives [...]. Most of all, it gives us a mechanism for expressing serious concern about social problems without actually doing anything to solve those problems.
>
> (Labaree 2008: 459)

All that work would be impossible without a body of theories that *appeal* to us, calling us to act for the implementation of important values. This refers to a yet another 'excessive' function of education, but before I describe it, I will sum up the previously identified ones. The first one is grounded in the normative character of theory that maintains the rhetorical, postulational narrative, in spite of translating education into an academic genre. The second one relates to inconsistency. Educational theories reside side by side without substantial collisions; in fact, they ignore one another. The way Labaree describes their work suggests that they voice conflictual positions within the ontology of the present. In the first passage quoted above, he speaks about two competing paradigms, each of which is theoretically coherent both in political and pedagogical terms, which jointly form the ideology of liberal democracy. However, this is still a simplified picture, if we account for what Roland Paulston (1993) once identified as paradigmatic heterogeneity, which is evidently congruent with a diagnosis of social heterogeneity as an ontological condition. Going back to Labaree's observations, I would say that this inconsistency (and indifference to inconsistency) are 'metatheoretically true', in the sense that they represent the antagonistic and heterogeneous nature of the social. Under such circumstances, the practice of education appears conceptually over-determined rather than determined, and its actors gain freedom to move within this complex field, and are – in consequence – fully responsible for their decisions. This is still more important in the light of the complex functions embedded in the practice of education, which simultaneously has to cater for the socialisation, qualification and subjectification of its subjects (Biesta 2010). Third, and this is the dimension of education I want to point to now, if we deal with *important* values and do *nothing* effectively to implement them (and rightly so, as Labaree argues), we are probably engaged in yet another rhetorical practice, and a very important one in terms of the ontology of the social – in the *pedagogical production of empty signifiers.* These are terms capable of integrating popular demands which – in spite of being partial and representing conflictual prospective identifications – can be invested with the meaning of 'the whole' and become identifiers of social identity. Education is very important rhetorical machinery that produces the repertoires of terms that can work as such empty signifiers, terms that are 'important' but impossible to define, even in a pragmatic sense (Szkudlarek 2003; 2007; 2010; 2011).

Conclusion and discussion

I have focused on understanding educational theory as a particular rhetorical practice applicable not only in work with children and otherwise dependent persons, but also in socio-ontological processes in general. Educational theories may be conceived in the world of ideas and they may be concerned with conceptual clarity and coherence, but they 'live' in the apparent, the heterogeneous and the incomprehensible; their incomplete structures and lame incarnations play complex roles in this world. They are linguistic tools that sustain the world and help us act within its limits with a sense of relative rationality, but they also challenge this world and turn it into a provisional, unnecessary entity. They contribute to making its parts visible or invisible (we may say that they contribute to the production of the *police* in Jacques Rancière's terms; Rancière 2007), and they contribute to the production of empty signifiers that constitute *the* fundamental resources in a process of construing political identities (Laclau 1997; 2005).

The focus on the rhetorical functions of theories in education diverts one from the question of their 'truth value'. Saying that theories are rhetorics, I do not address or challenge the issue of their cognitive validity or reliability, conceptual coherence or innovative potential. My intention lies elsewhere. I want to point to a possibility that the features we usually find problematic in theoretical work in education (like the impossibility of adequately describing educational practices, postulational language that makes education vulnerable to accusations of its weak academic status, or the heterogeneity of incommensurable theoretical conceptions) are *functional* in the discursive production of society. We are accustomed to seeing this functionality on the 'ontic' level, where given theories and practices are adequate to particular interests and ideological positions, like in the debate on hidden curricula. What I argue here speaks to the 'ontological' level,[9] where we have to acknowledge the fundamental impossibility of finding the ultimate conceptual representation of the social world, and where rhetorics – as linguistic tools that support our 'radical investments' (in Laclau's terms) that provisionally establish the political identity of the social – remain the most accessible cognitive resources we have at our disposal. My chief argument is that the discourse of education, and theory of education as its most rationalized part, plays an important role in the very process of the *ontological construction of the world*, and it also does this in ways that are difficult to control within its own rationality. We could speak here of 'hidden epistemologies' functional to the ontology of heterogeneity.

This is a highly entangled ontology. Even if we *could* eventually formulate 'the theory' of education in a fully conceptualized and coherent way, this would not lead us to a world free of such ambiguities. In line with Hegel, the moment of application of such a theory would produce (or reproduce) appearance; it would create another instance of the incomprehensible. When we abandon Hegelian eschatological optimism (a faith in the final *Aufhebung* that will form the ultimate synthesis of a self-conscious culture), we have to include this incomprehensibility (appearance, heterogeneity) within our horizon of understanding of theory. Hence the reference to rhetorics, because it is rhetorical tropes that work where concepts fail, and that make it possible to construe our provisional identities.

There are ethical questions here, though. The 'bridging' of the rhetoric dimensions of theory and practice in their rhetorical aspects may be read as a gesture of invalidating the efforts to find a 'good' theory and combat the 'wrong' ones, as if *any* theory could do the rhetorical job, providing that it is persuasive enough.[10] This would be a fundamentally wrong assumption. The perspective of radical heterogeneity, which I borrow from Laclau, does not mean that 'anything goes'. On the contrary, it clearly points to *radical responsibility* not only for what we 'do' in education, but also for what we 'say' and how we 'talk' about it. This issue relates to the question of exclusion, which is a prerequisite of identity construction in Laclau's theory. For a society striving for identity, the first step is to form an equivalence of heterogeneous demands that can be built only in relation to an excluded element. It is apparently a Hegelian trope (a dialectic of identity and difference), but Laclau is critical of the logical nature of difference in Hegel, which makes it possible to sublate difference to the structure of identity. In the apparent, heterogeneous world, this will never happen. This impossibility of synthesis calls for radical responsibility. In other words, the first normative consequence of this way of seeing identity is a demand that we think, and take responsibility for, who, what and how we exclude in the process of identity construction. Not only in our educational practices (Szkudlarek 2007; 2011), but also in the ways of theorizing education.

There are numerous problems that need further investigation here. In this brief analysis, I have not been able to present a systematic outline of the functions of educational theory that would integrate its diverse operations into a coherent typology. It seems that this task should be undertaken in relation to a kind of processual ontology, where it is possible to account for both 'Hegelian' and 'Laclauan' references; that is, to reflect on how we build theories in conceptual domains of ideas, and how they work as 'contaminated', or over-determined (in Althusser's sense) discursive practices in the apparent world (Althusser 1969). This is not a question of theoretical vs. empirical cognition (I leave this matter aside), but one pertaining to the circulations and displacements of theory itself. Further attention is needed with regard to the ideological functions of theory as well. We are accustomed to seeing them as attached to fairly stabilized political ideologies of modernity (we can identify conservative vs. liberal pedagogies, for instance), but the thing in question – only hinted at in this text – is understanding theory in the light of Žižek's notion of ideology as a constructive phantasmatic force (Žižek 1989). A very important issue that is in fact missing in this analysis is the one of emancipation (the third function of theory in its 'Habermasian' description) and subjectification (in Biesta's terms). If rhetoric has been described here as contributing to the operation of 'police', or power/knowledge regimes, we need to investigate the rhetorics of resistance and emancipation as well. Last but not least, it is of fundamental importance to test the proposed metatheoretical way of seeing theories of education in the analysis of contemporary theoretical projects. I believe that the first question that needs to be asked here, both ethical and ontological in nature, is this: What subjectivities and social ontologies do they imply, and what do they exclude in order to make them conceptually coherent?

Notes

1 The idea of 'finding' the foundational logic to what 'there is' sounds paradoxical, but it is not at odds with Hegel's theory (see e.g. Hegel 1990). A very interesting analysis of the idea of grounding in Hegel, with an application to contemporary theory of identity, can be found in Žižek (1994).

2 One of the differences between Herbart and Foucault concerns understanding the notion of power (Baker 2001: 383-384).

3 The term has been used for some time in a way that is not always coherent. For Kwieciński (1978), it means assigning an excessive role to education, a belief that pedagogy has a great impact on the world and on people's lives. For others (Hejnicka-Bezwińska 2003, Sarnowski 1993), it is synonymous with educational positivism (along with psychologism and sociologism), although Sarnowski points to deeper cultural contexts. In my understanding, it denotes discursive practices and power relations, which operate as dispersed and proliferated pedagogical regimes of political control (Szkudlarek 1995). In contemporary literature this phenomenon is sometimes described within the debate on the educationalization of social problems.

4 This delay does not pertain to the relation of Herbart's educational theory to psychology (which nowadays would be a good example of the 'secondariness' of educational thinking), as the foundations of cognitive psychology are created by him in parallel to his outline of the theory of education (Herbart, 1908 [1806], Baker 2001).

5 In another context, the issue of the 'not-yet' temporality of educational discourse, which makes the recognition of the nature of education impossible, has been addressed by Gert Biesta (in press) and Biesta & Säfström (2011).

6 I have addressed this problem in several other publications. See Szkudlarek 2003, 2007, 2010, 2011, in press.

7 This Hegelian trait of Laclau's theory is a matter of dispute between Laclau and Žižek. See for instance, Laclau 2000, 2005, and Žižek 1994, 2000, 2008.

8 It is not possible to summarise the premises of Laclau's theory within the limits of this paper. See for instance, Laclau and Mouffe 1985, Laclau 1990, 1996, 2005.

9 For the distinction between the ontic and the ontological see Laclau, 2005.

10 This issue is a reflection of the debate on an alleged 'normative deficit' in Laclau's theory (see Critchley 2004, and Szkudlarek, in press).

References

Althusser, L. (1969) *For Marx,* Allen Lane: Penguin Press.

Biesta G. (in press) 'Time out: can education do and be done without time?'

Biesta, G.J.J. (2010) *Good Education in an Age of Measurement,* London: Paradigm Publishers.

Biesta, G.J.J. (2011) 'Disciplines and theory in the academic study of education: a comparative analysis of the Anglo-American and Continental construction of the field', *Pedagogy, Culture and Society,* 19: 175-192.

Biesta, G.J.J. and Säfström, C.A. (2011) 'A manifesto for education', *Policy Futures in Education,* 9: 540-547.

Bridges, D. (2008) 'Educationalization: on the appropriateness of asking educational institutions to solve social and economic problems', *Educational Theory,* 58: 461-474.

Depaepe, M. and Smeyers, P. (2008) 'Educationalization as an ongoing modernization process', *Educational Theory,* 58: 379-389.

Foucault, M. (1979) 'Governmentality', *Ideology and Consciousness,* 6: 5-21

Foucault, M. (1995) *Discipline and Punish. The Birth of the Prison,* New York: Vintage Books.

Giroux, H. (1983) 'Theories of reproduction and resistance in the new sociology of education', *Harvard Educational Review*, 53: 257-93.

Habermas, J. (1972) *Knowledge and Human Interests*, Boston: Beacon Press.

Hegel, G.W.F. (1990) *Encyklopedia nauk filozoficznych*, Warszawa: PWN. (English version: *Encyclopedia of the Philosophical Sciences in Outline*, available at: <http://www.marxists.org/reference/archive/hegel/works/sl/slappear.htm>. (Accessed 2 Sept. 2012)

Hejnicka-Bezwińska, T. (2003) 'Pedagogika pozytywistyczna' ('Positivist Theory of Education'), in Z. Kwieciński and L. Witkowski (eds.) *Pedagogika. Podręcznik akademicki*, Warszawa: PWN

Herbart, J.F. (1908) *The Science of Education. Its general principles deduced from its aim*, and *The Aesthetic Revelation of the World*, trans. Henry M. and Emmie Felkin, Boston: D.C. Heath & Co.

Kwieciński. Z. (1978) 'Paradygmaty reform oświatowych' ('The Paradigms of Educational Reform'). *Acta Universitatis Nicolai Copernici, Socjologia Wychowania*, Volume 2, pp. 53-62.

Labaree, D.F. (2008) 'The winning ways of a losing strategy: educationalizing social problems in the United States'. *Educational Theory*, 58: 447-460.

Laclau, E. (1996) *Emancipation(s)*, London: Verso.

Laclau, E. (1997) *New Reflections on the Revolution of Our Time*, London: Verso.

Laclau, E. (2005) *On Populist Reason*, London: Verso.

Mouffe, Ch. (2005) *The Democratic Paradox*, London: Verso.

Paulston, R. (1993) *Mapping Paradigms and Theories in Comparative Education*, ERIC document, ED344531

Rancière, J. (2007) *Dzielenie postrzegalnego. Estetyka i polityka.* Kraków: Ha!art (Polish edition of *Le Partage du Sensible*, La Fabrique-Editions, 2000).

Sarmowski, S. (1993) 'O krytyce rozumu pedagogicznego' (*On Critique of Pedagogical Reason*), in S. Sarnowski, S. (ed.), *Krytyka rozumu pedagogicznego*, Bydgoszcz: Wyższa Szkoła Pedagogiczna.

Simons M., and Masschelein, J. (2008) 'The governmentalization of learning and the assemblae of a learning apparatus', *Educational Theory*, 58: 391-415.

Staniszkis, J. (2006) *Ontologia socjalizmu* (*Ontology of Socialism*), Warszawa: Ośrodek Myśli Politycznej.

Szkudlarek, T. (1990) 'Wyzwania pedagogiki krytycznej' (The Challenge of Critical Pedagogy), in B. Śliwerski and T. Szkudlarek, *Wyzwania pedagogiki krytycznej i antypedagogiki*, Kraków: Impuls.

Szkudlarek, T. (1995) 'Pedagogizm i pedagogika' (Pedagogism and Pedagogy), in T. Hejnicka-Bezwińska (ed.), *Racjonalność pedagogiki*, Bydgoszcz: Wyższa Szkoła Pedagogiczna

Szkudlarek, T. (2003) 'Educational theory, displacement and hegemony', *International Journal of Applied Semiotics*, 4: 109-130.

Szkudlarek, T. (2007) 'Empty signifiers, education and politics', *Studies in Philosophy and Education*, 26: 237-52.

Szkudlarek, T. (2010) 'Meaning and power: education as political semiosis', in I. Semetsky (ed.), *Semiotics, Education, Experience*, Rotterdam, Boston, Taipei: Sense Publishers.

Žižek, S. (1989) *The Sublime Object of Ideology*, London: Verso.

Žižek, S. (1994) 'Identity and its vicissitudes: Hegel's "logic of essence" as a theory of ideology', in E. Laclau (ed.), *The Making of Political Identities*, London: Verso.

Chapter 10

Speaking *educationally* about teacher education

Anne M. Phelan

Researching teacher education

As an organisational term, teacher education is a relatively restrictive concept referring specifically to the programmatic preparation of teachers – initial preparation and professional development – prior to and while in-service. As a concept designating a scholarly field of inquiry with a specific history and related professional identity, teacher education is more expansive. However, a review of the history of concerns in the field suggests a tight connection between initial teacher preparation programmes and teacher education research (Cochran-Smith and Zeichner 2006). Historically, research has played a practical role and is consequence-oriented. Research questions have derived directly from 'the doing' of teacher education and/or have sought to directly improve 'the doing' of teacher education (Condliffe Lagemann 2008). The intent is either to control or constrain the production of certain outcomes through teacher education or to improve the learning of prospective teachers in teacher education programmes.

There is little doubt that research in teacher education has a practical role to play. However, the practical bias of research can lead to various kinds of parochialism – intellectual, moral and institutional – confining the purpose and promise of teacher education research (and ultimately, teacher education) to an educational endeavour.

To speak educationally about teacher education means 'to express an interest in freedom…the freedom of the other' who is the student of teacher education, the soon-to-be educator, as well as the pupils they will teach (Biesta and Säfström 2011: 540). One could argue that educators can teach only if they are free to teach according to their professional intellectual judgments: 'without such academic freedom, there is no freedom or teaching at all' (Pinar 2012: xvii). While freedom is foregrounded in terms of individuality, that is, originality, creativity and capacity for dissent, it is always relational – at once socially structured and historically primed – and as such requires a more complicated conversation than teacher education research currently offers.

An expressed interest in the freedom and the teaching subject poses particular challenges for teacher education research, however. Teacher education has long been a modernist project with an emphasis on producing and sustaining predictable, stable and normative identities (Sumara *et al.* 2008). The very term 'teacher' (and concomitantly, teacher education) seems to suggest a recognisable identity, a presumed body of knowledge and skill and a set of vocational responsibilities. The inclination is to think about teacher education in terms of either *what is* – as a process of teacher socialisation to the norms of present day schooling; or *what is not* – as a process of teacher preparation for a different future for schooling and/or society. By basing freedom on a future promise (e.g. teacher as transformative intellectual – Giroux and McLaren 1986), teacher education becomes tied to the idea of progress, loses its grounding in the present moment and is placed 'beyond reach' (Biesta and Säfström 2011: 540). However, by basing teacher education in the present, it becomes little more than a process of adaptation to what society and its institutions are and/or what we perceive the teacher to be (e.g. teacher as enabler of achievement). Veering toward either one or the other, teacher education is in danger of forfeiting interest in an 'excess' that announces something new and unexpected (Biesta and Säfström 2011). If teacher education could find a footing in the tension between what is and what is not, it might have a better chance of being open and responsible to the present.

> The tension between 'what is' and 'what is not' arises out of the confrontation of 'what is' with 'what is not.' It concerns the way in which 'what is' is interrupted by an element that is radically new rather than a repetition of what already exists…To stay in the tension between 'what is' and 'what is not' thus means to take history seriously and to take education as fundamentally historical, that is, open to events, to the new and the unforeseen, rather than as an endless repetition of what already is or as a march towards a predetermined future that may never arrive.
>
> (Biesta and Säfström 2011: 541)

Speaking educationally about teacher education, therefore, may involve attending to moments of tension when taken-for-granted meanings are interrupted or simply break down. This is when the (teaching) subject appears in all its uniqueness, where speech is neither repetition nor self-affirmation of a pre-existent and recognisable identity. To study teacher education with an expressed interest in freedom of the other may require languages heretofore disavowed in teacher education research (Taubman 2012). Thinking about teacher education educationally may be less a matter of representing some truth in relation to the means and ends of teacher education and more a matter of edification, that is, 'finding new, better, more interesting and more fruitful ways of speaking' (Rorty 1980: 360) that would not only enable us to attend to the tension between what is and what is not, but also to create conditions wherein the new can emerge. A plurality of vocabularies – ethical, political, aesthetic – may be necessary. The ethical invites a focus on transient moments of encounter with others in which subjectivity is performed or achieved (Biesta 2010; Phelan 2011). The political provokes a concern with the power dynamics of such encounters. The aesthetic summons a consideration of how new ideas and theories can rupture well-worn lines of thought, disrupting familiar trajectories and opening up pathways 'to new knowledge, new insights, new modes of being' (Davies 2008: 1). Such a complicated, interdisciplinary conversation (Pinar 2012) will not be easy. The difficulties it presents may take the form of 'awful thoughts' about the illusions that bolster the promise of teacher education and the transformation of itself, teachers, and schooling (Britzman and Dippo 2000).

Speaking educationally in and for teacher education means that the field must recognise a cultural role for research (Biesta 2007). In its cultural role, research nurtures thought and imagination. Such research is non-consequentialist in character; it pursues understanding rather than improvement; it can tolerate interminable questions; it doesn't try to resolve the difficulties that its explorations may surface. When teacher education research takes a cultural role, researchers can emphasise the significance and complexity of becoming a teacher, and by implication, the value of teacher education; they portray and promote a vision of teacher education itself as an educational project. Finally, they can influence the kinds of questions that the profession asks of itself and the depth and scope of its response.

In what follows, I explore further the question of what it might mean to speak educationally about teacher education. I outline a brief history of teacher education research in terms of its preoccupation with the practical. I speculate about curriculum theory as a possible resource for speaking educationally. I conclude with a discussion of the benefits that can be accrued when teacher education research makes a curriculum turn.

Practical preoccupations: a brief history of concern

The field of teacher education research is a relatively mature area of study in North America, having established its relevance and its academic rigour in the past fifty years (Clarke 2001). As an academic area, teacher education emerged as an identifiable field separate from research on teaching only during the last half of the twentieth century with a substantive literature emanating from the United States, Britain, Canada and Australia. Clarke (2001: 606) identified four distinct research trends in the field of teacher education: 'research on individual student learning traits, research "on teachers" (teacher actions), research "with teachers" (teacher thinking), and research "by teachers" (teacher –research)'. These trends have been evident across three time periods – 1950s, 1970s and 1990s – characterised in each era by a central question (Cochran-Smith and Fries 2006; Grimmett 2008, 2009):

1 Teacher Education as a Training Problem: How do we produce effective behaviours in prospective teachers so that programme and policy decisions can be empirically based? (1950s–1980s)
2 Teacher Education as a Learning Problem: What should teachers learn and be able to do? (1980s–2000s)
3 Teacher Education as a Policy Problem: Does teacher education make a difference to student learning in schools? (Mid-to-late 1990s – present)

In the 1950s and 1960s, research seemed pointed at producing a science of teacher education, preoccupied as it was with teacher effectiveness training, competency-based, process-product research within an empirical analytic tradition. Initial efforts were associated with the cognitive psychological effort to isolate elements of student learning into discrete units (e.g. memory, retention, information transfer) for intensive study with the hope of informing teaching and teacher education practices. This led to efforts to research the relationship between student learning and teachers' actions. Experimental and quasi-experimental studies sought to specify the knowledge, skills and competencies of teachers in advance and to apply those insights to the field of teacher education.

The role of teacher education research, in the first phase, was to identify effective interventions so that they could be generalised across a range of programme contexts in order to bring about pre-determined outcomes. A desire to effect particular outcomes re-emerged in the third phase of teacher education research, albeit within a different policy context fixated on professionalization and deregulation. The governance of teacher education has largely shifted from institutional to professional and the delicate balance between professional accreditation and institutional autonomy is a constant source of concern to academics. Higher education institutions want to contest what they view as the unwarranted intrusion into programmes and autonomy. The worst case scenario for North American scholars is the dismantling of teacher preparation, breaking the perceived monopoly that schools of education have long enjoyed, and the consignment of teacher education to schools (Grimmett 2008; Cochran-Smith 2006).

Questions about the appropriateness, effectiveness and efficiency of universities in providing teacher education prevail (Pinar *et al.*1995) and have led to increased attention by researchers to matters of justification (delineation of knowledge base needed for teaching) and legitimation (assertion of the need for university-based teacher education) by researchers. *Preparing Teachers for A Changing World: What Teachers Should Learn and Be Able To Do* (Darling-Hammond and Bransford 2005) and *Teacher Education in Canada: A Baseline Study* (Crocker and Dibbon 2008) provide compilations of research from phase two to make the case for professional relevance of knowledge and skills to be provided in teacher education.

The limitations of research in phases one and three centre on the assumption that the only way in which research can be relevant for the practice of teacher education is through the provision of instrumental or technical knowledge that can inform and transform teacher education as a production process (Biesta 2007; Kemmis 2010).

Questions of programme effectiveness and outcomes suggest a technological model of professional action and completely ignore the moral question. Biesta explains the causal assumption underlying the model:

> It is based on the idea that professionals do something – they administer a treatment, they intervene in a particular situation – in order to bring about certain effects…Effective interventions are those in which there is a secure relation between the intervention (as cause) and its outcomes or results (as effects)…the ends of professional action are given…the only relevant (professional and research) questions to be asked are about the most effective and efficient ways of achieving those ends.
>
> (Biesta 2007: 7)

This view not only neglects that (teacher) education is a process of mutual interpretation by participants (professors, teacher mentors, teacher candidates and their students), it also sidesteps the question of the very desirability of ends. Even if we can produce a certain type of teacher by means of a particular kind of teacher education programme, does not mean that the 'teacher' is *desirable*? Neither can we take recourse to any set of means to produce what might be considered desirable ends because the means are part and parcel of what is produced. This is why teacher education, like education itself, is a *moral* practice rather than a technological project (Biesta 2007; Phelan 1996). As such, it is always necessary to enquire about the values that set the stage for action and to raise controversial and contested questions about the direction of human flourishing in teacher education.

While the impact of research in the third phase is yet to be determined, Clarke (2001) argues that process-product, teacher effectiveness and teacher competency research in phase one had little impact on teacher education, unlike the work that was to follow. There is little doubt that research on teacher learning has dominated the field in the last 30 years. In the 1980s and 1990s, with the growing acceptance of qualitative research and a growing dissatisfaction with technical rational premises of teacher education and teacher education research in its initial phase, a shift in interest from teacher behaviours to teacher thinking occurred (Clarke 2001). Research was interpretive-hermeneutical and it aimed to inform the deliberation of teacher educators involved in teacher education (Kemmis 2010). The assumption was that teachers are knowledgeable, deliberative and rational decision-makers. Teacher education was framed as a 'learning problem' and there was much research interest into teachers' knowledge, cognition, decision-making, attitudes, beliefs, dispositions, development of skills and performance in classrooms (Cochran-Smith and Fries 2006; Phelan 2005).

Research in teacher thinking led to collaborative research between university researchers and teachers, which further evolved to research by teachers and eventually by teacher educators themselves, affording a certain level of autonomy to all concerned and interrupting the theory-practice binary. Research in teacher education was directed toward this new relationship between educational research and teacher education practice. Self-study of teacher education practices was a case in point.

The primary purpose of self-study was to research one's own practice with a view to improving the learning of prospective teachers (Farr-Darling *et al.* 2009; Loughran *et al.* 2004; Cole and Knowles 2000). The promise of self study is the collective and personal growth of teacher educators who conduct studies within their own institutions, potentially enhancing their openness, reflexivity, and moral judgment (Furlong and Oancea 2005). Inspired by the critique of instrumentalism and apparent use-value of Donald Schon's (1983) insights about reflection-in-action, self-study in teacher education became the avenue for naming and reframing problems associated with the practice of teacher education, with a view to new or different action. Research, in this vein, is not limited to deliberation about which means one should use in order to arrive at previously agreed upon ends. Rather, the researcher defines means and ends interactively, in the context of particular relationships, as she frames a problematic situation. She does not separate thinking (e.g. researching) from doing (teaching teachers); the researcher is immersed in action even as she researches. Because the research is a form of experimental action, implementation is already built into the inquiry (Schon 1983). The resulting research literature presents a form of knowledge that is perceived as more valid as a representation of practice and more directly useful to teacher educators as practitioners (Bulterman-Bos 2008).

Adopting self-study as a paradigmatic example of phase two research, one could argue that it embodies a 'freedom of intelligence' – 'the power to frame purposes, judge wisely, to evaluate desires by the consequences which will result from acting upon them; power to select and order means to carry chosen ends into operation' (Dewey 1938: 64). However, Dewey's consequentialist thinking can restrict researchers' interest to matters linked only to their own practice. The threat of institutional parochialism is palpable. The research becomes driven exclusively by the empirical conditions of the researcher's teacher education programme and is often constrained by institutional discourses. For instance, teacher education plays largely a maintenance role in universities, functioning as a major source of institutional income but rarely playing a radicalising role in the cultural/political life of the institution. Teacher candidates and teacher educators remain closeted, as it were, rarely connecting with other faculties or professional schools. The institutional separation reflects an intellectual separation (Harnett and Naish 1990). Theoretical developments in the humanities have been minimally felt in teacher education research, unlike many other areas of educational research. There is little attention paid to the role of language and the manner in which the individual's lived experience and identity are socially located, politically positioned, and discursively formed. The tendency is to adopt what one might term a 'natural' stance to practice, with little critical appreciation of the way in which practice embodies culturally established ways of thinking, speaking and acting. The replacement of the term 'education' with the term 'learning' as a core value of teacher education research might bear some attention, for example, where the term is used to connote professional compliance with the will of governments and accrediting institutions (Kemmis 2010).

An intellectual parochialism is also reflected in the separation of teacher education practices from generative contact with currents of national political, cultural and social developments with which the forms and purposes of teacher education interact in significant ways. Engagement with macro issues of power is minimal and the result is a disconnection between teacher educators (and what becomes rather private, programme-bound concerns) and the more public educational reality. At the heart of the matter are the ethical positionings available to teacher educators; one wonders if teacher education operates as a form of 'cultural imperialism by baptising generations of teachers, (primarily white) in mainstream curricula and pedagogies' (Brennan and Zipin 2008: 110).

In summary, both paradigms of teacher education research show a tendency towards a parochial narrowness of vision that moves the field's attention away from educational concerns. In the case of technologically driven research, teacher education becomes too easily linked 'to the everyday functioning of the institution' rather than the 'everyday flourishing of human life worlds' (Grimmett 2010: 248). While the institution (or system world) should exist in the service of the life world and its interests, it can often enclose the life-world, restricting life within it. When teacher education is cast as a production of pre-determined ends, then research questions no longer emerge from 'the perspective of how best, under changing and sometimes difficult and distorted circumstances, to develop the capacities of every individual [teacher]...for individual and collective self-expression, self-development and self-determination' (Kemmis 2010: 24). In the case of interpretive research, the tendency is to contain the conversation about teacher education to issues of immediate use and apparent relevance resulting in the neglect of teacher education, and concomitantly the teaching subject, as cultural entities with a social history, anchored in ideology and nested in layers of meaning that call for clarification and interpretation (Grumet *et al.* 2008), in the interest of a creative and conceptual artistry of the self.

If teacher education research is to extend its current concerns to questions about freedom and subjectivity (human agency and action), society, and historical moment, then the field of teacher education might well look to curriculum theory for a scholarly foundation (Carson *et al.* 2008).

Teacher education and the curriculum turn

> Curriculum theory is that interdisciplinary field in which teacher education is conceived as the professionalization of intellectual freedom, forefronting teachers' and students' individuality, that is to say their originality, their creativity, protecting their opportunities to dissent, engaged in ongoing if complicated conversation informed by a self-reflexive, interdisciplinary erudition.
>
> (Pinar 2010: 183)

Pinar's conversation is an educational conversation. In the space remaining, I wish to explore a sample of scholarship, located at the interstices of teacher education and curriculum theory, which reflects such a multi-referenced conversation about teacher education, and an expressed interest in the freedom of the other.

An ethics of subjectivity

In her autoethnography, *Silent Moments in Education*, Collette Granger (2011) explores the intellectual, emotional and social relationships teachers and learners make with knowledge, ideas and one another, including those moments in which individuals are rendered silent. She argues that silences are not only personal, context-related, and changeable over time but are also symbolic of breaks in meaning and inherently difficult to think about. To explore those breaks in meaning, Granger returns to her experience of learning to teach, specifically her experience what she terms 'defeat' and 'survival' during her teacher education practicum. Acknowledging that it is tricky to admit that 'one has not been successful in the field in which one has tried to make a home' (Granger 2011: 217), she peels away layer after layer of her experience with the help of very different interlocutors, including Foucault (1997) and Winnicott (1990). Foucault's theorizing of power guides Granger's exploration of the dynamic of authority and conformity, as well as confrontation and resistance during her student teaching practicum. She describes herself as a pre-service teacher 'eager and obliged to gain practical experience' who found herself 'unable to use her new knowledge and skills in a practicum classroom' due to a difficult relationship with her mentoring teacher (Granger 2011: 5). The author's exploration of the nature of that difficulty next takes her to Winnicott's psychoanalytic theorizing. Never far from home, Granger's telling is conscious of its own act of transference as she recalls a question posed, on separate occasions, by both her mother and her mentoring teacher, Ms. K, 'Who do you think you are?' (Granger 2011: 221). While admitting to that transference was only part of the story, she writes: 'I went looking for a mother substitute, and I found Ms. K' (Granger 2011: 226).

Silent Moments in Education illustrates and complicates the play that is learning in/from experience in teacher education. This autobiographical work draws attention to that which teacher education research rarely notices or engages – the excess of becoming in moments when, as Granger (2011: 217) expresses it, 'education...defeats its own purposes'.

The politics of natality

In an article entitled, 'Violence and subjectivity in teacher education', Phelan *et al.* (2006) illustrate and explore the tensions that result when newcomers to the profession – student teachers – introduce alternative ideas about the meaning of teaching, thereby making the familiar strange. In their turn, aspiring teachers may be subjected to mundane violence as the boundaries of the profession are carefully policed according to established professional norms (Butler 1999). Refusals on the part of experienced professionals to recognise and consider non-standard practices signify interdictory moments where a tension is evident between what is known and permissible within the profession and what is known but must be kept concealed (Bhabha 1994). Drawing on Lyotard's (1988) concept of the différend, the authors examine the narratives of a practicum triad – one student teacher and two mentors – as they each attempt to make sense of their irreconcilable differences. The article concludes by discussing how the profession might fulfill its obligation to judge the adequacy of new teachers, while remaining hospitable to the difference they introduce. This would require, the authors argue, that the value of teacher education programmes lies not in how well student teachers meet requirements of being 'well-prepared' or 'demonstrating initiative', but rather on 'how individuals are responded to, which requires not treating those laws as though the contents of them were transparent' (Todd 2005: 3).

An aesthetics of transformation

Researchers often continue to project old questions and frameworks onto new situations because the way we see the present situation has everything to do with our past experience. In an article entitled, 'What will have been said about gayness in teacher education?', Britzman and Gilbert (2004) illustrate how common sense meanings in and about teacher education may be transformed when juxtaposed with quite different, but equally valid, theories and ideas. The authors explore the anxieties and pleasures that the concept of AIDS evokes when juxtaposed with 'teacher' and 'education'. Thinking with AIDS, they suggest, can serve such occasions for noticing other realities, provided that our educational narratives have the audacity to enjoy their own margins. Moving from a time of difficulty (fighting homophobia), to relationality (asking what queer theory means for teacher education), and finally to hospitality (when inquiry into difference, Eros, and pleasure creates the conditions for new communities to participate in their becoming), these authors argue for the value of queer theory to our thinking about teacher education. Queer theory raises the problem of 'learning to be normal' as a place of legitimate inquiry.

Michael Singh and Jinghe Han (2008) bring the critical momentum of postcolonial theories to their research and invite readers to appreciate teacher education as a transnational and translational project. The authors engage in a reassessment of self-other and centre-periphery relations as they are produced in teacher education. They question the abiding assumption that the canon of academic knowledge, practice, and pedagogy are culturally neutral (Tastsoglou 2000). They document how the arrival of World English students in teacher education in Australia underscored just how much teacher education embodies a particular educational culture. Students hailing from South East Asia found that the progressive student-centred pedagogies espoused by faculty were not necessarily evident in the teacher education programme and that their own experience of test-driven, text-based pedagogy was largely ignored. The opportunity to move towards a broader framework within which to educate teachers about alternative approaches to teaching, learning, schooling and education was lost (Phelan and Sumsion 2008).

The foregoing examples of scholarship do not provide prescriptions on what to think or what truths to believe. The concern is solely to move in the tension-filled gap between what has been and what might be. They offer us spaces of conflict and confrontation that can provoke new questions and imaginings. Theorizing enables them to raise questions without providing neat answers or feeling duty-bound to resolve the difficulties their thinking creates (Kohn 2006). As such, the work invites us to remain alert to questions of purpose, content and relationship – the legitimacy – of what we do in the name of education. While critics may argue that such work constitutes an unwelcome retreat from practice, I suggest that it constitutes a necessary, if temporary, retreat from the consequence-oriented thinking in teacher education research. I use the term 'temporary' in the sense that the contribution of curriculum theorizing may enable teacher educators to return to practical preoccupations about knowledge, learning, and outcomes with fresh eyes, prepared to complicate, critique, and converse in more educational ways.

Conclusion: returning to the subject of (teacher) education

When considering the potential contribution of curriculum theorizing, David Smith, renowned Canadian theorist, suggested that a conversation of this kind will not '"get us" anywhere' (in Pinar *et al.* 1995: 420). It may, however, return us to what is quintessentially educational – a concern with the freedom associated with the self-formation of the other (entangled in the social and historical) through knowledge and experience. Education so understood provokes profound questions including: what knowledge is of most worth, to what purposes, and in whose interest? Who decides and on what basis? To engage in this conversation about what matters requires teachers and teacher educators to be fully responsible to and courageous in the present, and not succumb to mandates or idealisations, all the while realising that a profession supposes 'beyond and in addition to knowledge, know-how, and competence, a testimonial commitment, a freedom' that obligates each one of us to give an account of ourselves 'to some tribunal yet to be defined' (Derrida 2002: 222).

References

Bhabha, H. (1994) *The Location of Culture,* London: Routledge.

Biesta, G. (2007) 'Why "what works" won't work: Evidence-based practice and the democratic deficit in educational research', *Educational Theory*, 57, 1: 1-22.

Biesta, G. and Säfström, C. A. (2011) 'A manifesto for education', *Policy Futures in Education,* 9, 5: 540-547.

Brennan, M. and Zipin, L. (2008) 'Neo-colonization of cultural struggles for justice in Australian education and teacher education', in A. Phelan and J. Sumsion, (eds) *Critical Readings in Teacher Education: Provoking Absences,* Rotterdam: SENSE Publishers, pp. 99-114,

Britzman, D.P. and Dippo, D. (2000) 'On the future of awful thoughts in teacher education' *Teaching Education,* 11, 1: 31-37.

Britzman, D. and Gilbert, J. (2004) 'What will have been said about gayness in teacher education?' *Teaching Education,* 15, 1: 81-96.

Bulterman-Bos, J.A. (2008) 'Will a clinical approach make education research more relevant for practice?' *Educational Researcher,* 37, 7: 412-420.

Butler, J. (1999) *Gender Trouble: Feminism and the Subversion of Identity.* New York: Routledge.

Carson, T., Chapman, O., Chinnery, A., Kanu, Y., Lupart, J. and Mazurek, K. (2008) 'Working group report for Theme #3: Understanding of practices in teacher education related to diversity, identity and inclusion, and demographic change' in T. Falkenberg and H. Smits, (eds) *Mapping Research in Teacher Education in Canada: Proceedings of the Working Conference on Research in Teacher Education in Canada,* Winnipeg: University of Manitoba Faculty of Education, pp. 73-75.

Clarke, A. (2001) 'The recent landscape of teacher education: Critical points and possible conjecture', *Teaching and Teacher Education,* 17: 599-611.

Cochran-Smith, M. and Fries, S. (2006) 'Researching teacher education in changing times: Politics and paradigms' in M. Cochran-Smith and K. Zeichner (eds) *Studying Teacher Education: the Report of the AERA Panel on Research and Teacher Education,* pp. 69-109, Washington: American Educational Research Association and Lawrence Erlbaum Associates.

Cochran-Smith, M. and Zeichner, K. (2006) *Studying Teacher Education: the Report of the AERA Panel on Research and Teacher Education,* Washington: American Educational Research Association and Lawrence Erlbaum Associates.

Cole, A. and Knowles, J. G.(2000) *Researching Teaching: Exploring Teacher Development through Reflexive Inquiry,* Toronto: Allyn and Bacon.

Condliffe Lagemann, E. (2008) 'Education research as a distributed activity across universities', *Educational Researcher,* 37, 7: 424-429.

Crocker, R. and Dibbon, D. (2008) *Teacher Education in Canada: a Baseline Study*, Kelowna. Available BC: SAEE at <http://www.saee.ca/pdfs/Teacher_Education_in_Canada.pdf>.

Darling-Hammond, L. and Bransford, J. (2005) *Preparing Teachers for a Changing World: What Teachers Should Learn and Be Able to Do*, New York: Jossey-Bass.

Davies, B. (2004) 'Introduction: Poststructuralist lines of flight in Australia', *International Journal of Qualitative Studies in Education*, 17, 1: 1-9.

Derrida, J. (2002) *Without Alibi*, trans. P. Kamuf (ed.) Stanford, California: Stanford University Press.

Farr-Darling, L., Erickson, G. and Clarke, A. (2009) *Collective Improvisation: A Case of Self-Study in Teacher Education*, Dordrecht: Springer.

Foucault, M. (1997) 'The ethics of the concern for self as a practice of freedom' (R. Hurley *et al.*, Trans.) in P. Rabinow (ed.) *Michel Foucault: Ethics, Subjectivity and Truth, the Essential Works of Michel Foucault 1954-1984* (vol. 1), 281-301, London: Penguin Press.

Furlong, J. and Oancea, A. (2005) *Assessing Quality in Applied and Practice-based Educational Research: a Framework for Discussion*, Oxford: Oxford University Press.

Giroux, H. and McLaren, P. (1986) 'Teacher education and the politics of engagement: The case for democratic schooling' *Harvard Educational Review*, 56, 3: 213-238.

Granger, C. (2011) *Silent Moments in Education: An Autoethnography of Learning, Teaching, and Learning to Teach*, Toronto: University of Toronto Press.

Greene, M. (1977) 'The matter of mystification: Teacher education and unquiet times', in *Landscapes of Learning*, New York: Teachers College Press, pp. 53-73.

Grimmett, P. and Halvorson, M. (2010) 'From understanding to creating curriculum: The case for the co-evolution reconceptualised design with reconceptualised curriculum', *Curriculum Inquiry*, 40, 2: 241-262.

Grimmett, P. (2008) 'Teacher education governance, policy, and the role of the university', in T. Falkenberg and H. Smits, (eds) *Mapping Research in Teacher Education in Canada: Proceedings of the Working Conference on Research in Teacher Education in Canada*, Winnipeg: University of Manitoba Faculty of Education, pp. 41-58.

Grimmett, P. (2009) 'The best lack all conviction, while the worst are full of passionate intensity' in A. Pitt (ed) *Key Notes in Teacher Education: CATE Invited Addresses 2004-2008*, 55-77, Canadian Association for Teacher Education: Canadian Research in Teacher Education: A Polygraph Series. Available at <http://www.csse.ca/CATE/CATE/PBS.htm>.

Grumet, M., Anderson, A, and Osmond, C. (2008) 'Finding form for curriculum research' in K. Gallagher (ed.) *The Methodological Dilemma: Creative, Critical and Collaborative Approaches to Qualitative Research*, London: Routledge, pp. 136-156.

Hillis, V. (1999) *The Lure of the Transcendent: Collected Essays by Dwayne E. Huebner*, London: Lawrence Erlbaum Associates.

Kemmis, S. (2010) 'Research for praxis: knowing doing', *Pedagogy, Culture and Society*, 18, 1: 9-27.

Kohn, J. (2006) 'Introduction' in H Arendt *Between Past and Future: Eight Exercises in Political Thought*, New York: Penguin, pp. vii-xxii,

Loughran, J. J., Hamilton, M.L., LaBoskey, V. K. and Russell, T.L. (2004) *International Handbook of Self-Study of Teaching and Teacher Education Practice*, Dordrecht: Springer.

Lovelie, L. (2008) 'Deliberative democracy and civic education' in D. Coulter and J. Wiens (eds) *Why Do We Educate? Renewing the Conversation*, The National Society for the Study of Education (NSSE) Yearbook, 1. Malden: Blackwell, pp. 112-124,

Lyotard, J.-F. (1988) *The Différend: Phrases in Dispute,* Minneapolis: University of Minnesota Press.

Markell, P. (2003) *Bound by Recognition,* Princeton: Princeton University Press.

Phelan, A. (1996) 'Strange pilgrims: nostalgia and disillusionment in teacher education reform', *Interchange,* 27, 3-4: 331-348.

Phelan, A. (2001) 'Power and place in teaching and teacher education', *Journal of Teaching and Teacher Education: An International Journal of Research and Studies,* 17, 5: 583-597.

Phelan, A. (2005) 'A fall from (someone else's) certainty: Recovering practical wisdom in teacher education', *Canadian Journal of Education,* 28, 3: 339-358.

Phelan, A. (2010) '"Bound by recognition:" Some thoughts on professional designation for teachers', *Asia-Pacific Journal of Teacher Education,* 38, 4: 317-329.

Phelan, A. and Sumsion, J. (2008) 'Introduction: Lines of flight and lines of articulation in teacher education' in A. Phelan and J. Sumsion (eds) *Critical Readings in Teacher Education: Provoking Absences,* Rotterdam: SENSE Publishers, pp. 5-22.

Phelan, A., Sawa, R., Barlow, C., Hurlock, D., Myrick, F., Rogers, G. and Irvine, K. (2006) 'Violence and subjectivity in teacher education', *Asia-Pacific Journal of Teacher Education,* 34, 2:161-179.

Pinar, W. F. (1988) *Contemporary Curriculum Discourse,* Scottsdale, AZ: Gorsuch Scarisbrick Publishers.

Pinar, W. (2004) *What is Curriculum Theory?* Mahwah: Lawrence Erlbaum Associates.

Pinar, W. F. (2012) *What is Curriculum Theory?* Second edition, Mahwah: Lawrence Erlbaum Associates.

Pinar, W. F., Reynolds, W. M., Slattery, P. and Taubman, P. (1995) *Understanding Curriculum,* New York: Peter Lang Publishing, Inc.

Popkewitz, T. (1993) *Changing Patterns of Power: Social Regulation and Teacher Education Reform,* New York: SUNY Press.

Rorty, R. (1980) *Philosophy and the mirror of nature.* Princeton, N. J.: Princeton University Press.

Schon, D. A. (1983) *The Reflective Practitioner: How Professionals Think in Action,* New York: Basic Books.

Singh, M. and Han, J. (2008) 'Trans-national mobility, world Englishes and student-teachers: Bologna's interruption of absences in teacher education' in A. Phelan and J. Sumsion (eds) *Critical Readings in Teacher Education: Provoking Absences,* , Rotterdam: Sense Publishers, pp. 115-137

Sumara, D., Davis, B. and Iftody, T. (2008) '101 ways to say "normal": Revealing normative structures of teacher education', in A. Phelan and J. Sumsion (eds) *Critical Readings in Teacher Education: Provoking Absences,* Rotterdam: Sense Publishers, pp. 155-172.

Tastsoglou, E. (2000) 'Mapping the unknowable: the challenges and rewards of cultural, political and pedagogical border crossings', in G. J. S. Dei and A. Calliste (eds) *Power, Knowledge and Anti-racism Education,* Halifax, NS: Fernwood, pp. 98-121.

Taubman, P. (2012) *Disavowed Knowledge: Psychoanalysis, Education and Teaching,* New York: Routledge Press.

Todd, S. (2005) 'Promoting a just education: dilemmas of rights, freedom, and justice'. Available at: <http://k1.ioe.ac.uk/pesgb/x/Todd.pdf>. (Accessed November 10, 2005).

Willinsky, J. (1991) 'Postmodern literacy: a primer' *Interchange,* 22, 4: 56-76.

Winnicott, D.W. (1990) *Home is Where We Start From: Essays by a Psychoanalyst,* New York: Norton.

Chapter 11

Teaching theories

Lynn Fendler

I am intrigued by what teaching *does* mean and what teaching *might* mean. To investigate the question of teaching theories in the context of this book, I acknowledge three possible relationships between teaching and theory:

- Theorizing about teaching, in which teaching is the object of inquiry, and theories are the lenses (Most educational theory assumes this configuration).
- Assessing the pedagogical value of a theory, in which the theory is the object of inquiry, and pedagogy is the lens (see e.g. Fendler, 2004).
- Generating new objects of inquiry and new lenses through creative interplay and blurring of boundaries between teaching and theories.

In an attempt to engage with teaching theories, the title of this paper is intentionally ambiguous; it is meant to signal any of those three possible relationships between teaching and theory, all of which are relevant to some degree in this paper. I do not intend for teaching theories to stand in as a proxy for all of education; various teaching theories might imply different perspectives within any educational endeavor, and there are many other dimensions of education that could be theorized outside of teaching.

I focus on teaching theories primarily in order to put tacit assumptions about teaching into explicit language that is accessible to critique by a wider range of people. I see the effort of making assumptions explicit as one of the most important purposes of teaching theories. I am more interested in providing language that connects teaching to fundamental questions about the quality of life. I am less interested in trying to define 'good teaching' or 'effective teaching' except insofar as teaching can be classified as good or effective to the degree it supports quality and equality.

What is the issue?

Teaching and teacher education are under attack on several fronts, challenged by governmental, corporate, community, religious, and public sectors. Some detractors assert that teaching is ineffectual, and teacher education is a waste of time (see Walsh 2006). Some critics tend to assume that schooling can be most successful without teacher-education credentials, as long as the class is conducted by people who are knowledgeable about subject matter, who follow scripted curriculum guidelines, and institute 'logical consequences' to manage student behavior (see e.g. Will 2006). Other stakeholders believe that teacher education is crucially important, but they disagree about what education is for, and *pari pasu* what teaching is for (Cochran-Smith and Fries 2001). There has been little productive debate between warring factions because proponents and opponents of teaching and teacher education tend to argue using claims that the other side regards as irrelevant.

Both defenders and detractors of teaching and teacher education tend to conceptualize teaching in a relatively narrow way, namely as the professional activities of a person leading a class. For the most part, teaching is defined in relation to the narrow topic of schooling, rather than in relation to the broader topic of education. The term *teacher* almost always refers to a professional position in a position of institutional authority, and the term *teaching* usually implies a beneficent and hierarchical relationship relative to students or learners.

Such a narrow conceptualization of teaching is problematic in a couple of ways. Historically, assumptions of teaching have remained relatively stable even though the world has changed, educational institutions have diversified, and modes of social communication have been transformed by computer technologies. The definition of *teacher* as a professional person leading a class also constrains the range of political possibilities that are available for teaching theories. Politically, when teaching is limited to the activities of a professional person of authority leading a class, then teaching theories remain stuck in the modern dichotomy of individual versus society. Moreover, these narrow definitions of teaching are then in danger of being stuck reproducing institutional power hierarchies. This essay attempts to help teaching theories become unstuck.

Even in the most ordinary senses of the term, teaching is problematic. In traditional or mainstream discourses, there are at least three distinct frameworks that can be used for thinking about teachers' qualifications:

- What credentials does the teacher have?
- What does the teacher do in the classroom?
- How do the teacher's pupils perform on standardized tests? (see e.g. Ravitch 2012).

Even within mainstream thinking about schooling, there is disagreement about which of those frameworks should be used as the basis for evaluating teaching, and some educational theorists challenge all of those conventional frameworks (see e.g. Biesta 2010a). The competing purposes of education have been debated by educational historians and curriculum theorists (see e.g. Kliebard 1986; Labaree 1997), and evaluations of teaching are dependent on assumed purposes of education. Terms like 'best practices' unfortunately tend to muddy the waters because when the purposes of education are not explicit, we do not know what teaching practices are best *for*.

To make matters worse, we don't really know what teaching can or cannot do because there is no satisfactory way to distinguish the effects of a student's studying from the effects of a teacher's teaching. The relationship of teaching to studying or learning is bewildering and convoluted; cause and effect are indeterminate. It may be possible to draw correlations between teaching practices and test scores, but most educators recognize that test scores are a poor proxy for student achievement. Test scores have even less value as evidence for making ethical judgments about good education. So, in spite of educational policy prescriptions that assume causality, it is simply impossible to determine the degree to which teaching is related to learning or good education.

One argument that expands previous definitions of teaching is the role of computers in education, particularly Web 2.0 and social media. Sugatra Mitra's 'Hole in the Wall' experiment is now held as compelling evidence that 'Kids Teach Themselves' (Mitra, 2012). Flipping has famously inverted classroom and homework activities, which has been simultaneously welcomed as effective teaching reform and criticized as a move to replace teachers with computers (see e.g. Flipped Learning Network; Bergman and Sams 2012; Parry 2012). Addressing the influences of computers in education, Jakes (2007) summarized how collaborative authorship, hyperlinking, and graphics/video embedding, non-synchronic dialogue, and online publishing have changed what texts are, and in that way, have altered what teaching can mean. Research on teaching has expanded beyond school settings because a great deal of so-called 'informal' education now happens through social media sites like Facebook, YouTube, and Second Life. Current events, vocabulary and memes get circulated; opinions and arguments get formulated, and resources get shared. For example:

> [E]ducators must recognize that much of young people's learning with information and communication technologies happens outside of school… This recognition requires us to acknowledge a wider 'ecology' of education where schools, homes, playtime, and library and the museum all play their part.
>
> (Ito *et al.* 2010, p. 12)

In these ways, computer technologies have reframed possibilities for what teaching might mean both inside and outside school settings. In current historical circumstances it is difficult to justify maintaining the old narrow definition of teaching (a professional person leading a class in an institutional setting), and it is irresponsible to underestimate the effects of computers, for better or worse, in current educational practices.

What is important about teaching theories?

Educational institutions are at least as ubiquitous as governments, religions, cultural practices, health care, public safety, basic utilities, transportation, communication, and military institutions. Education is one of the most widely accepted mechanisms for socializing and governing, and whole societies regard education as a means for social advancement, sometimes even for basic survival. Virtually every educational institution has teaching at its core; it is almost impossible to imagine education without teachers. Every person in the world has been influenced by teaching in one way or another.

Teaching theories must account for an astounding array of factors including interdisciplinary epistemologies, pedagogical principles, communication skills, the full complement of dispositions, competing demands from multiple stakeholders, vacillating laws and standards, limited resources, several levels of unpredictability, and ethical relationships that include taking responsibility for other people's children who are compelled by law to attend schools. A child can be irrevocably damaged or miraculously transformed by a teacher. On the basis of a teacher's actions, a child may establish foundational assumptions about who they are and how they can expect to be treated in the world. The stakes could not be higher. So, teaching theories *are* like rocket science.

However, for the most part teaching has not been recognized as being complicated or powerful. For the most part, teaching theories have focused on relatively technical questions like research on 'best practices' for raising test scores, building community, or inclusion and diversity. These are important questions, but technical questions do not even begin to address what is really important about teaching. When teaching is defined in a narrow way as the professional activities of a person leading a class, then teaching theories tend to limit themselves to instrumental questions, which construe teaching as a relatively unimportant phenomenon – more like tinkering than rocket science.

The traditional image of the teacher, though, is firmly established and enduring. Even when we accept a high degree of uncertainty in the potential efficacy of teaching, and even when we are committed to radical critiques of teaching, most of us who have devoted our lives to teaching and teacher education cannot bear to give up hope that teachers might be able to do good in the world. Many of us are also ambivalent in the face of educational theories that would minimize the importance of teaching or demote the teacher from the center to the margins of educational activity.

Given our commitments to teaching, and the profession's history of low status, it can be easy to become defensive of teaching. It may be difficult to accept the possibility that some devastating challenges to teaching are actually constructive acts of appreciation. Profound critiques that take teaching seriously help establish higher expectations for what teaching might mean. If we limit our vision of teaching to the role of a professional person leading a class in an institutional setting, then theories may be constrained to questions about efficacy or best practices in a classroom, which are tinkering questions (Tyack and Cuban 1997). I believe that teaching is far more important than that; teaching theories should be confronting *really* important issues like threats to fundamental human dignity, and realizing equality and quality of life.

Governance is just one aspect. Beyond the technical questions of whether teacher preparation should take place in schools, universities, or private corporations, there are more important questions. Who gets to make the rules and set the terms of debate about teaching and teacher education in the first place? What are the mechanisms and power relations that produce knowledge for teaching and whom do they serve? How do we draw the line between parents' and teachers' responsibilities for the child? When you and I disagree not only about the purposes of education, but also about the procedures for decision-making, where do your rights end and my responsibilities begin? What should we teach for?

In practice, governance issues include questions of money and distribution of resources. When teaching is conceptualized in narrow institutional terms, then research funding tends to support instrumental investigations such as research on best practices to raise test scores. Even if a huge amount of money is spent on efficacy questions, such funding policies still trivialize teaching because the research questions themselves are relatively inconsequential in comparison to issues of human dignity and equality of life.

Ethics are related to governance, and there are contradictory ethical views even among educators who consider themselves critical educators for social justice. Ethical teaching theories might address acts of everyday violence inadvertently perpetrated by commonplace classroom practices like sitting in chairs, asking permission to drink water, or speaking in someone else's language (see Socol 2012). Unfortunately, however, teaching ethics rarely engage this level of significance. Teaching ethics have too often been reduced to instrumental issues of legality (in which ethical means lawful) or effectiveness (in which ethical means principled or dutiful). Issues of legality and effectiveness are necessary, but relatively unimportant for teaching theories in the grand scheme of things. More important than legality or effectiveness are issues of the purposes of education, the activities and sensibilities we regard as educational, and fundamental questions about how to avoid harm in our relationships with other people.

Some critiques of teaching and teacher education are relatively trivial, and they are insulting to the teaching profession (see e.g. Walsh 2008; Will 2006). Other critiques raise the stakes and recognize teaching's ultimate importance (see e.g. Biesta 2010b). By daring to make profound criticisms and shifting the terms of debate to questions of life and death or good and evil, teaching theories are poised to overcome limitations and expand possibilities for teaching, which is the opposite of teacher bashing, even while traditional definitions and images of teaching may be overturned in the process.

For example, the recent theories of Jacques Rancière have posed devastating challenges against traditional versions of teaching because Rancière's *The*

Ignorant Schoolmaster portrays a favorable image of a teacher who does not know the subject and cannot explain anything. Rancière's challenges to conventional assumptions about teaching have been welcomed by some teachers and deplored by others. Most threatening to earlier versions of critical pedagogy is Rancière's stance that it is not ethical for teachers to presume to emancipate or empower students. Instead, Rancière argues, to be ethical means to begin with the assumption of equality, a stance that constructs a radically different image of teaching, and may even be regarded as threatening or reactionary for some critical pedagogues (see e.g. Galloway 2012).

I am particularly interested in teaching theories that: 1) expand possibilities for teaching beyond the image of the professional person at the head of a class; 2) take into account the historical context of twenty-first century computer technologies; and 3) incorporate the political challenges leveled by Rancière's theories of ethics.

Some contextual dimensions of teaching theories

I could have framed the contextual dimensions of teaching theories in terms of the history of educational policy (e.g. Nation At Risk; PISA; No Child Left Behind; Race to the Top; ET2020). Alternatively, I could have contextualized teaching theories in an historical narrative that accounted for continuities and discontinuities of pedagogical practices over time. A third possible approach to contextualization would have been to analyze and synthesize, or compare and contrast, debates on teaching and curriculum in current research literature.

Rather than using any of these approaches, I instead contextualize teaching theories by mapping the field analytically. By mapping the terrain of existing conceptualizations, I can then identify boundaries and limitations around those conceptualizations, which allows me to perceive patterns and similarities (i.e. systems of reason) that define what teaching can mean (what is on the map) and what teaching cannot mean (what is off the map). Mapping the conceptual terrain and specifying current meanings for teaching helps me identify 'the distribution of the sensible' [*le partage du sensible*] (Rancière 2004). To identify the distribution of the sensible is to apprehend the limits of what is conceivable as teaching, and to imagine what else teaching might mean.

As the launching point for my analytical map I use *Models of Teaching*, a widely used textbook originally published in 1972 and now in its eighth edition (Joyce and Weil 1972; 1980; 1986; 1992; 1996; Joyce, Weil and Calhoun 2000; 2003; 2008). Because *Models of Teaching* has been influencing US teacher education for 40 years, and because its purpose is to theorize teaching, its analytical framework is durable enough to generate a comprehensive map.

Models of Teaching is a US-based educational psychology textbook, and therefore limited. Its examples are drawn primarily from North American psychological theories, rarely from elsewhere in the world, and rarely from philosophy, sociology, or pedagogy. Each of the eight editions explicates 13 to

16 different models of teaching that range from direct instruction and memorization to jurisprudence and non-directive teaching. More interesting than the specific models of teaching, however, are the four *families* of models, the classifications of purposes into which those models of teaching have been sorted. According to Joyce and Weil (1972: 8), the four families 'represent different orientations toward man and his universe'. The specific models of teaching are revised in every new edition; however, the four *families* have remained constant from the first edition in 1972 through to the eighth edition in 2008.

In this section I map the conceptual boundaries around teaching theories made available through *Models of Teaching*. The four families of teaching are Social Interaction, Information Processing, Personal, and Behavior Modification.

Social Interaction

Social Interaction approaches to teaching are those in which the primary purpose of education is to prepare citizens for a functional democratic society:

> The social models, as the name implies, emphasize our social nature, how we learn social behavior, and how social interaction can enhance academic learning....a central role of education is to prepare citizens to generate integrative democratic behavior, both to enhance personal and social life and to ensure a productive democratic social order.
>
> (Joyce, Weil and Calhoun 2000: 29)

John Dewey's philosophy is listed as exemplary of a Social Interaction approach to teaching, as are the approaches of Donald Oliver, James Shaver, Herbert Thelen, and Bruce Joyce (one of the authors of *Models of Teaching*).

Models of Teaching does not explicitly mention critical theories, but we could include Paulo Freire's *Pedagogy of the Oppressed* and other critical pedagogies as exemplary of Social Interaction because their approaches are based on the commitment to a central role of education as preparing citizens to generate integrative democratic behavior. A.S. Neill's Summerhill schooling could also be classified as Social Interaction insofar as a major focus of Summerhill is the cultivation of capacities for democratic interaction. Second Life pedagogies are also Social Interaction models because fluency in social communication is the primary focus (Vickers online).

Table 11.1 Models of teaching: models classified as social interaction

1972	*2000*	*2008*
Group Investigation	Partners in Learning	Partners in Learning
Jurisprudential	Role-Playing	Study of Values: Role-Playing
Social Inquiry	Jurisprudential	
Laboratory Method		

Information Processing

Social Interaction models of teaching share epistemological commitments with political science, economics, and sociology; in contrast, Information Processing models derive from cognitive psychology. Information Processing models are those most readily and intuitively associated with teaching:

> Information-processing models emphasize the ways of enhancing the human being's innate drive to make sense of the world by acquiring and organizing data, sensing problems and generating solutions to them, and developing concepts and language for conveying them.
>
> (Joyce, Weil and Calhoun 2000: 17)

Information Processing models are those that are reflected in most standardized testing instruments, which measure concept attainment rather than capacities for social interaction, personal relationships, or behavioral competencies. As exemplars of Information Processing theorists, *Models of Teaching* lists Jean Piaget, Joseph Schwab, and Jerome Bruner.

Joyce and Weil do not mention them, but some approaches to religious education could also be classified as Information Processing. Buddhist chanting practices that aim toward enlightenment, and litanies or recitations of religious texts (Catechism, Talmud, Qur'an) could also be regarded as examples of Information Processing, even though those models are not typically regarded as informational or cognitive. Most online materials for flipped classrooms are designed for Information Processing (see, e.g. Khan Academy, www.khanacademy.org/)

The most interesting of the Information Processing models is what Joyce and Weil call 'synectics', which is a model for teaching creativity. Synectics are based on three assumptions: 1) creativity can be taught by bringing the creative process to consciousness and explicit practices; 2) emotion is more important than intellect, and the irrational is more important than the rational; 3) creativity can be increased by understanding and controlling emotion and irrationality

Table 11.2 Models of teaching: models classified as information processing

1972	*2000*	*2008*
Concept Attainment	Inductive	Inductive
Inductive	Attaining Concepts	Attaining Concepts
Inquiry Training	Scientific Inquiry and Inquiry Training	Picture-Word Inductive
Biological Science Inquiry	Memorization	Scientific Inquiry and Inquiry Training
Advance Organizers	Synectics	Memorization
Developmental	Advance Organizers	Synectics
		Advance Organizers

(Joyce, Weil and Calhoun 2000: 222-223). Synectic teaching is a semi-structured method that asks students to use metaphor, association, and problem-solving as 'stretching exercises' (p. 225) designed to awaken fresh perspectives and empathy for the unfamiliar.

Personal

The third family in *Models of Teaching* prioritizes the development of the individual as the most important purpose of education; these models are called Personal. The Personal family resembles what some educators have called child-centered approaches: 'The Personal family of teaching places high value on self awareness...from the perspective of the selfhood of the individual' (Joyce, Weil and Calhoun 2000: 21).

Personal models of teaching include the approaches of Carl Rogers, William Glasser, and Abraham Maslow in which teaching follows the child. The Personal models of teaching tend to share a romantic view of human nature; they assume that the development of selfhood will be altruistic rather than nasty and brutish.

Table 11.3 Models of teaching: models classified as personal

1972	*2000*	*2008*
Non-directive Classroom Meeting Synectics Awareness Training	Non-directive Concepts of Self	Non-directive Developing Positive Self-Concepts

The pedagogical theories of Pestalozzi could also be classified in the Personal family, as could most theories of *Bildung*, which focus on the cultivation of admirable human character. Montessori's teaching theories might also be classified as Personal because of the emphasis on following the child's interests (Montessori 1912). Personal teaching models are also represented online in hundreds of self-help or life-coaching sites (see, e.g. Costello-Dougherty 2009).

Behavioral

The Behavioral family of teaching models is the least theoretically developed classification in *Models of Teaching*. Behavioral seems to refer primarily to the work of B.F. Skinner, although later editions also include Bloom's Mastery Learning. Models in the Behavioral Systems family rest on the assumption that human beings are self-correcting communication systems that modify behavior in response to information about how successfully tasks are navigated. In addition, all physical activity and skill development are classified within the Behavioral family.

Table 11.4 Models of teaching: models classified as behavioral

1972	*2000*	*2008*
Operant Conditioning	Mastery Learning Direct Instruction Simulations	Mastery Learning Direct Instruction Simulations

Off the grid: Not in any family

The four families of *Models of Teaching* encompass a wide range of what teaching does mean; however, the framework is very much limited to US psychology. As a way of suggesting how Joyce and Weil's framework might be extended, the following section outlines four other models of teaching currently available in educational literature, which do not fit into any of Joyce and Weil's families.

Teaching Perspicuity and Propriety

Adam Smith's (1762) theories construe an unfamiliar model of teaching. The most interesting insight offered by Smith is that the purpose of teaching is perspicuity about how *authors must have felt while writing their texts*. In other words, if I am trying to teach *The Ignorant Schoolmaster* then my teaching task is to evoke in readers a feeling of empathy for how Jacques Rancière – born in Algiers, and 41 years old at the time – must have felt while writing. How many drafts of opening paragraphs did Rancière reject before he came up with the idea to start the article with the anecdote of Jacotot's teaching? Did he feel frustrated? Who did Rancière imagine his readers were? Was he afraid of them? Did Rancière feel competitive, angry, or discouraged? Perspicuity implies an ethical relation of subjectivity between the reader and the writer. The aim of teaching is not to objectify meaning in the text, but to sympathize with the author.

Adam Smith's rhetorical theories also construe an unfamiliar definition of professionalism. For Smith, *propriety* means that teaching is highly individualized and 'proper to' the particular character of the teacher. In other words, teachers are not supposed to convey what is most true about a text; we are supposed to convey what is most authentic about ourselves:

> a gay man should not endeavour to be grave nor the grave man to be gay, but each should regulate that character and manner that is natural to him and hinder it from running into that vicious extreme to which he is most inclined.
>
> (Smith, *Lecture 8*, v. 99 1983: 40)

> These [great] authors did not attempt what they thought was the greatest perfection of stile but that perfection which they thought most suitable to their genius and temper.
>
> (Smith, *Lecture 11*, 1762/1983: 56)

Smith's propriety aligns with Rancière's uniqueness as an ethical stance. For both Smith and Rancière, teachers are not interchangeable; teachers are unique human beings, and the quality of teaching is – at least in part – evaluated on the degree to which teaching expresses unique subjectivity of the teacher. For propriety's sake, it would not be good for two different people to teach the same way. Good proprietary teaching is an utterly subjective expression of a unique person. Propriety also does not fit within *Models of Teaching,* and I am not aware of educational policies or evaluation systems that take the teacher's unique personality as the standard against which good teaching is assessed.

Teaching relations

Not included in *Models of Teaching* is teaching as a personal relationship, rather than a role. Teaching relations are often explicitly implicated in coaching: 'The saying "Relationships are the container everything else fits into" certainly applies to a coach and coachee relationship' (Performance Coaching 2012). This does not imply that a relationship is a prerequisite to effective teaching; rather, this model implies that the relationship itself teaches.

In educational philosophy and curriculum theory, teaching relations have frequently been cast in terms of eros (see, e.g. Burch 1999; Deresiewciz 2007; Garrison 1997; Schwab 1954): 'Teaching, finally, is about relationships. It is mentorship, not instruction' (Deresiewciz 2007, online version). "I'm inclined to think that Deresiewciz (and Plato) are correct that great teaching has an erotic element, a kind of fevered grip on the mind" (In Socrates' Wake 2008 March 28). Ethical teaching relations are not limited to eros, but educational philosophers seem to prefer the erotic to other kinds of relationships.

Teaching relations does not imply that teachers and students should form relationships first as a means of facilitating more effective communication later. Rather, in teaching relations, the relationship itself is the teaching. One way to understand teaching relations would be to imagine how, without speaking, an animal or child teaches cognitive awareness, emotional sensitivity, and physical skills to adults in relation. Teaching relation theories are conducive to asking the Big Questions about quality and equality of life.

Co-teaching 2.0

Web 2.0 communications, now called *social scholarship* in most educational literature, blur the lines between reading and writing, so social scholarship blurs the lines between teaching and learning, which constitutes a different model of teaching. Latour (2010) calls this Web 2.0 communication modality 'compositionism', which exemplifies co-teaching because social scholarship does not distinguish between teachers and students. Social-scholarship spaces have the compositionist capacity to create and support co-teaching using mechanisms that have not been available in pre-computer spaces. Co-teaching in social-scholarship spaces is not governed by the same regulatory mechanisms or conventions as other teaching models because all participants are both teaching and studying. Co-teaching occurs because readers are also writers, and students are also teachers. Web 2.0 capacities of shared documents make co-teaching feasible in ways that were previously unavailable, which introduces new configurations of ethical relationships. Co-teaching 2.0 theories invite investigations into power relations that are constituted in compositionist spaces.

Language teaching

How do children learn their first language? For many theorists, first language acquisition serves as a unique exception to teaching theories. Rancière (1991) used the example of first-language acquisition when analyzing Jacotot's teaching in *The Ignorant Schoolmaster.* Literary theorist David Bleich (2001: 117-118) argued that using language is the same thing as teaching and learning language: "To use the language means to teach and to learn it…language use as a formal subject matter necessarily includes its pedagogy'. Bleich highlights power relations in the pedagogy of language use:

> [S]tudents are rewarded by teachers, sometimes consciously, sometimes not consciously, for using the teacher's language, usually without citation, on examinations and essays. This is understood as "learning". Yet the identical phenomenon of learning takes place when students overtake from one another, but…this process is called *cheating*.
>
> (Bleich 2008: 132; emphasis in original)

The point here is not that we learn language for purposes of acquiring knowledge; rather, using language is itself teaching. The multiple regression of using language to teach language to use language to teach language is a little bit like teaching teacher educators how to teach teacher candidates how to teach. The performative cannot be separated from the pedagogical, and all conceivable teaching relationships are implicated in the ethics of language use.

My views on teaching theories

> O body swayed to music, O brightening glance.
> How can we know the dancer from the dance?
>
> (W.B. Yeats, *Among Schoolchildren*)

I started teaching in 1974, before there were personal computers, and so I have lived through – and taught through – the major changes that computers have brought to our educational lives. Since 1974, I have also taught through a few generations of critical pedagogy and critical theories from Freire's *Pedagogy of the Oppressed*, through Elizabeth Ellsworth's *Why Doesn't This Feel Empowering?* to Michel Foucault's *Discipline and Punish* and Rancière's *Ignorant Schoolmaster.* I think it is still possible to imagine teaching in new ways, and I believe teaching theories generate possibilities for thinking differently about teaching and about theory. It has been helpful for me to study the history of teaching theories both for inspiration and to spare me from struggling to reinvent the wheel. In this section, I draw from places other than history or educational literature to help conjure possibilities for teaching theories that do not exist yet.

Teaching unrepeatability

Some of the most memorable moments in life are one of a kind. We remember unique occurrences, and sometimes we remember them *because* they are unique. Making something memorable might be called teaching. The problem is that modern teaching tends not to value uniqueness; it tends to value repeatability and generalizability, as we can see in current prescriptions for educational research methods. In modern epistemologies, the unique can be dismissed, ignored, excluded, or pushed off the radar screen, especially when the unique is called an "outlier" or a "deviation" (see also Fendler and Muzaffar, 2008). Within most modern teaching theories, unique is seen as a kind of mistake. However, when we generalize people as if they were interchangeable or replaceable, then we have objectified them or stereotyped them, which is not respectful. In that way, uniqueness is an ethical issue for teaching theories.

Linking theories

In documents and webpages, hyperlinks are pedagogical. It matters which terms are linked, and whether the links connect to Wikipedia, the Urban Dictionary, or the Online Encyclopedia of Philosophy. Linking constructs knowledge; links teach. Links enact conceptual relationships, and exercise power. They make some information more accessible than other, and establish hierarchies of knowledge. Linking invites some paths of discovery and discourages others. Links enact teaching by imposing particular kinds of connections between concepts, and by selecting particular referents for words and phrases. Linking is teaching. Theorizing linking in terms of teaching would be an approach to critical literacy and a model of teaching that departs from that of a professional person leading a class. Linking practices could be theorized in terms of how they teach power, censorship, and privilege.

Teaching receptivity

In 1986, a four-year-old girl called 'CF' taught me an unforgettable lesson about teaching. By the time she was four, CF had been attending a Montessori Children's House for a year, which had been her only previous experience in school. One day CF was upstairs playing very quietly. As most parents know, quiet is a very suspicious state of affairs, so I walked upstairs to see what was going on. CF neither spoke nor gestured; she was simply walking around slowly, looking at a collection of Cabbage Patch Kids, Care Bears, and Strawberry Shortcakes that were arranged all over the floor. I watched her for several minutes before asking, "What are you doing?" She responded, "This is my school and I am the teacher." "Oh," I said, "and what are the children doing?" "The children are singing," explained CF. "Hmm," I said, "That's nice. And what are you doing?" "It is my job to listen to the children sing." Stunned, I walked back downstairs knowing I had just witnessed something extraordinary. In CF's example, the teacher was still a person leading a class. But for her, teaching was an entirely receptive capacity: listening not speaking; inwardly appreciating, not instructing, motivating, or inspiring. In her experience, how did she see that?

Those of us who have been language teachers are aware of the pedagogical differences between the productive skills (speaking and writing) and the receptive skills (listening and reading). Receptive skills are problematic because they cannot be assessed directly; if both speaking and writing skills are weak, we have no way of knowing if reading or listening skills are strong. The high premium placed on assessment in education tends to push receptivity off the grid (in terms of distribution of the sensible). In teacher education, how would we teach receptivity? How would we know whether someone had acquired receptivity? How does receptivity alter possibilities for quality and equality?

Stopping teaching

> FLANDERS KITTREDGE: Why are all your students geniuses?
> Look at the first grade – blotches of green and black.
> The third grade – camouflage.
> But your grade, the second grade...Matisses, every one.
> You've made my child a Matisse...What is your secret?
> TEACHER: I don't have any secret.
> I just know when to take their drawings away from them.
>
> Guare 1993, *Six Degrees of Separation*

A friend recently asked me what I thought were the most important skills for academic advising. I replied, 'Stopping and waiting'. By that I meant as an advisor I always try to answer questions by outlining possibilities and tradeoffs, but then I think it's important to stop before issuing directives or recommendations. I think the stopping is as important as, and maybe more important than, providing information and analyzing possibilities. At the same time, it is mostly up to me to decide when to take their writing away from them, which is a profoundly ethical issue. The problem is that I don't know how I know that, or how to teach someone else to know that. Except for the play *Six Degrees of Separation*, I don't know of any teaching model or literature that addresses good teaching as knowing when to take their drawings away from them.

If we theorized teaching in terms of linking, receptivity, uniqueness, or stopping, then the entire modern epistemological basis for teaching theories would be scrambled. The idea of assessment would be overhauled. Questions of generalizability and scale would become moot. Research methodologies would have to be utterly reconceived. How would we teach receptivity? How would we know whether someone had acquired the pedagogical capacity to link effectively? On what basis could we assess whether one kind of stopping had more value than another? And would we ever use the same test for two different people, or assess the same way twice? What impact might uniqueness have on democracy?

Issues for further inquiry

In addition to inspiring and imagining off-the-grid possibilities for teaching theories, there are some recent contributions from poetics and geography that promise exciting new prospects for further inquiry on teaching theories.

Poetics refers to both the conventional notion of poetry and the Greek *poiesis* [to create] (Parsons 2012; Feigenbaum 2012). We are taught by *poiesis*, perhaps also through *autopoiesis*. The idea is that creation is pedagogical. Poetics theorists have suggested that we are taught through poetry. Distinguishing poetry from explanation, Macaluso (n.d.) writes, 'Poets recognize and embrace the incompatibility of language and truth, while explanation aims to convince us of their inseparability'. Poetic teaching theories render the quality-equality debate moot because there is no dualism, no imposition, and no agonism to negotiate. Intentional ambiguity might serve as an example of teaching poetic theories; ambiguity raises different ethical questions.

Finally, geographers in the United Kingdom have offered some breakthroughs for theorizing teaching by positing 'non-representational theory' as an alternative to both logical empiricism and social constructionism. Non-representational theory is:

> a manifesto for changing the direction and methods of social science…an umbrella term for diverse work that seeks to better cope with our self-evidently more-than-human, more-than-textual, multisensual worlds.
>
> (Lorimer 2005: 83)

Non-representational theories aim to construct a more generative conceptualization of the relationship between subject and object that neither replaces the material with the discursive, nor represents the material with the discursive. If we imagine that teaching could be non-representational, then we have access to a different order for teaching theories.

Non-representational theories deal with the problem of the subject-object split by putting everything on the same qualitative plane. Borrowing heavily from Deleuze and Guattari, Anderson and Harrison (2010: 14) explain that non-representational theories deal with things as if everything existed on the same 'plane of immanence'. To illustrate this claim of radical equality (and reminiscent of Borges' Chinese encyclopedia entry) Anderson and Harrison provide a list of things that are all regarded as equal in non-representational theory:

> beliefs, atmospheres, sensations, ideas, toys, music, ghosts, dance therapies, footpaths, pained bodies, trance music, reindeer, plants, boredom, fat, anxieties, vampires, cars, enchantment, nanotechnologies, water voles, GM Foods, landscapes, drugs, money, racialised bodies, political demonstrations.
>
> (Anderson and Harrison 2010: 14)

In this way, non-representational theories recast the problem of teaching ethics by appealing to a kind of nominalism in which all things that can be named have a right to be treated equitably in research as both recipients of and providers to each other as constituents of worldly activities. In non-representational theories, watermelons can also be teachers.[1]

Notes

1 I am deeply grateful for several teachers who contributed generously to this essay: Julie Allan, CF, Heejoo Suh, Lucia Elden, Adam Greteman, Hà Thanh Nguyen, Thanh Hà Phung, Nai-Cheng Kuo, Karenanna Creps, Hsuan-Yi Huang, Anders Aamot, and Cường Nguyen.

References

Anderson, B. and Harrison, P. (eds) (2010) *Taking-Place: Non-representational Theories and Geography*, Farnham: Ashgate.

Bergmann, J. and Sams, A. (2012) 'How the flipped classroom is radically transforming learning'. Available at: <http://www.thedailyriff.com/articles/how-the-flipped-classroom-is-radically-transforming-learning-536.php>.

Biesta, G. (2010a) *Good Education in an Age of Measurement: Ethics, Politics, Democracy*, New York: Paradigm Press.

Biesta, G. (2010b) 'Learner, student, speaker. Why it matters how we call those we teach', *Educational Philosophy and Theory 42*(4), 540-552.

Bleich, D. (2001) 'The materiality of language and the pedagogy of exchange', *Pedagogy,* 1: 117-141.

Burch, K. (1999) 'Eros as the educational principle of democracy', *Studies in Philosophy and Education,*18: 123-142.

Cochran-Smith, M. and Fries, M.K. (2001) 'Sticks, stones, and ideology: The discourse of reform in teacher education', *Educational Researcher,* 3: 3-15.

Costello-Dougherty, M. (2009). Teach yourself how to be happier. Available at: <http://www.edutopia.org/job-satisfaction-happiness-project-tips>.

Deresiewciz, W. (2007) 'Love on campus'. *The American Scholar.* Available at: <http://theamericanscholar.org/love-on-campus/>.

Feigenbaum, A. (2012) 'Carving compassion, camouflaging antagonism and building cooperative alternatives: An interview with Anna Feigenbaum', *Class War University* Avaliable at: <http://classwaru.org/2012/08/27/carving-compassion-camouflaging-antagonism-building-cooperative-alternatives-an-interview-with-anna-feigenbaum/?CMP=>.

Fendler, L. (2004) 'Praxis and agency in Foucault's historiography', *Studies in Philosophy and Education,* 23: 445-466.

Fendler, L. and Muzaffar, I. (2008) 'The history of the bell curve: Sorting and the idea of normal', *Educational Theory,* 58: 63-82.

Flipped Learning Network Available at: <http://flippedclassroom.org/>.

Galloway, S. (2012) 'Reconsidering emancipatory education: Staging a conversation between Paulo Freire and Jacques Rancière', *Educational Theory,* 62(2), 163-184.

Garrison, J.A., (1997) *Dewey and Eros: Wisdom and Desire in the Art of Teaching,* New York: Teachers College Press.

Guare, J. (Writer), Schepisi, F. (Director) (1993). *Six Degrees of Separation,* Metro-Goldwyn-Mayer Studios Inc.

In Socrates' Wake: 'A blog about teaching philosophy', (2008 March 28). *The eros of teaching.* Available at <http://insocrateswake.blogspot.com/2008/03/eros-of-teaching.html>.

Ito, M. *et al.* (2010). *Hanging Out, Messing Around, and Geeking Out: Kids Living and Learning with New Media.* Cambridge, MA: MIT Press.

Jakes, D. (2007) 'Web 2.0 and the New Visual Literacy', *Technology and Learning,* 27(9), 21.

Joyce, B. and Weil, M. (1972) *Models of Teaching,* First edition. Englewood Cliffs: Prentice-Hall.

Joyce, B., Weil, M. and Calhoun, E. (2000) *Models of Teaching,* Sixth edition. New York: Allyn and Bacon.

Joyce, B., Weil, M. and Calhoun, E. (2008) *Models of Teaching.* Eighth edition. New York: Pearson.

Kliebard, H.M. (1986) *Struggle for the American Curriculum,* London: Routledge and Kegan Paul.

Labaree, D. F. (1997) 'Public goods, private goods: the American struggle over educational goals', *American Educational Research Journal,* 34: 39-81.

Latour, B. (2010) 'An attempt at a "Compositionist Manifesto"', *New Literary History,* 41: 471-490.

Lorimer, H. (2005) 'Cultural geography: the busyness of being 'more-than-representational"', *Progress in Human Geography,* 29: 83-94.

Macaluso, K. (n.d.) Jacques Rancière and the call for the poetic: An ethical defense of poetic literacy in K-12 education. Unpublished paper.

Mitra, S. (2012) Hole-in-the-Wall: Lighting the spark of learning. Available at: <http://www.hole-in-the-wall.com/>.

Montessori, M. (1912) *The Montessori Method*. Available at: <http://digital.library.upenn.edu/women/montessori/method/method.html>.

Parry, M. (2012) Debating the 'Flipped Classroom' at Stanford. Available at: <http://chronicle.com/blogs/wiredcampus/debating-the-flipped-classroom-at-stanford/34811>.

Parsons, A. (2012) Poiesis and prolepsis. Available at: <http://prolepsis-ap.blogspot.com/>.

Performance Coaching International (2012) Coaching and relationships: trust is the foundation. Available at: <http://www.performancecoachinginternational.com/resources/articles/relationships.php>.

Rancière, J. (1991) *The Ignorant Schoolmaster: Five Lessons in Intellectual Emancipation*. Stanford, CA: Stanford University Press.

Rancière, J. (2004) *The Politics of Aesthetics: The Distribution of the Sensible,* Gabriel Rockhill (Trans.). London and New York: Continuum.

Ravitch, D. (2012 March 28) Arne Duncan is imposing NCLB on teacher education. Available at: <http://dianeravitch.net/2012/08/01/arne-duncan-is-imposing-nclb-on-teacher-education/>.

Schwab, J.J. (1954) 'Eros and education', *Journal of General Education,* 8: 54-71.

Smith, A. (1983 [1762]) *Lectures on Rhetoric and Belles Lettres,* J.C. Bryce (ed.) New York: Oxford.

Socol, I. (2012) School restart: change on day one. Available at: <http://speedchange.blogspot.com/2012/08/school-restart-change-on-day-one.html>.

Thrift, N. (2008) *Non-Representational Theory: Space, Politics, Affect,* New York: Routledge.

Tyack, D. and Cuban, L. (1997) *Tinkering Toward Utopia: A Century of Public School Reform,* Cambridge, MA: Harvard University Press.

Vickers, H. (n.d.). Language teaching gains Second Life: Virtual worlds offer new methods to teach languages. Available at: <http://www.omniglot.com/language/articles/secondlife.php>.

Walsh, K. (2006) 'Teacher education: coming up empty', *Fwd,* 3 Online. Available at: <www.nctq.org/p/.../docs/Teacher_Education_fwd_20080316034429.pdf>.

Will, G. (2006) 'Ed schools vs. education; Prospective teachers are expected to have the correct "disposition", proof of which is espousing "progressive" political beliefs', *Newsweek*. Available at: <http://www.highbeam.com/doc/1G1-140720600.html>.

Chapter 12

Towards an agenda for theoretical interventions in education

Julie Allan, Richard Edwards and Gert Biesta

In this final chapter we provide some reflections on the insights offered by the contributors to this book and consider an agenda for theorizing in education and what this might constitute. We are deliberately presenting this as 'an' rather than 'the' agenda: in the gathering of ways of enacting theory we recognise that a path is made by travelling. We have also framed this as theoretical interventions to mark the practical and material aspects of theory work, and to counter the often common sense view that theory sits simply in the realism of ideas. Such interventions can take many forms, including explanation, understanding and possibility. So we seek to avoid totalising theory into one form or one form of work. This itself points to the importance of a theory of theory in educational work and, as we indicated in the introduction, there is theoretical work in education and educational theory at work that are both for consideration.

The contributors to this volume have concerned themselves with *educational* questions, and questions generated from the disciplines of philosophy, sociology, history and psychology. Most have attempted, in Sidorkin's words 'to squarely face the issue of the nature of education' and, in so doing, they have undertaken three types of theoretical work:

1 Critical: offering analysis of educational issues and problems and critiques of the emergence of particular forms of educational theorizing.
2 Political: considering intentions and effects in educational policies and practices and the appropriation of certain theories for political purposes.
3 Generative: envisioning new forms of theorizing and new forms of practice that are derived from theoretical work.

These are considered in detail below.

Critical

The critical theoretical work undertaken by many of the contributors provide both commentary on the emergence and function of educational theory and theoretical analysis of aspects of and issues within education. The picture of educational theory that emerges from these impressive analyses is one that is both complex and subject to various interpretations. Tröhler dismantles what he calls a 'delusion' of a universal educational theory, while Usher and Anderson observe the valiant efforts to claim such a status. The impossibility of educational theory as a universal entity, according to Tröhler, relates to its dependence on different ideologies, according to which education is either technical, ethical or aesthetical; the absence of agreement on the function of education; and the historical specificity of educational theory. Usher and Anderson note that efforts to claim universality through theorizing conflate universality and generalisation and fail to apprehend the importance of attending to particularities.

Yet, Popkewitz, pointing out the inevitability of theory and its empirical presence, asserts that 'theories don't just stand there' but 'are actors' which 'inscribe differences, divisions and exclusions.' Szudlarek makes a similar point, arguing that although educational theories are conceived in the world of ideas and are concerned with conceptual clarity and coherence, they 'live' in the apparent, the heterogeneous and the incomprehensible; their incomplete structures and lame incarnations play complex roles in this world. In this sense, theories are interventions in the world rather than simply being about it.

Historical analysis has had an important function in the criticality of several contributors. Tröhler, for example, traced a need for education to be explained – through theory – as a distinct educational practice, but notes that this led to a merger of idealism and practice, in which the real had to be ideal, a perception which he notes mirrored the dawn of German idealism. Central concepts were needed that would form a particular theoretical frame of education in which the soul of the child was at the centre, yet different perceptions of the soul led to different theories being legitimized. Writing of the German-speaking part of Europe, Tröhler notes that psychology was the universalising force as the science of the soul and came to dominate education. This point is made by several authors who also comment on how knowledge about education, frequently produced outside the discipline of education but particularly from psychology, has contributed to its diminution. We would also comment on the way education became focused on the child as the site for both practice and theory at the expense of wider concerns with the education of the person as part of ongoing life practices.

Tröhler, Fendler, Bellman, Phelan and Popkewitz all note how the subject of the teacher, and his or her soul, as Tröhler emphasised, was standardized and moulded through educational theory. We might argue, however, that standardization has emerged from certain practices which themselves contain theoretical assumptions. For Bellman, the standardized subject is part of the framework of a modernist philosophy of the subject which has dominated educational theory and which inhibited the development of forms of theory that took account of social phenomenon. In other words, there has been a centring of the subject and the educated subject through the theory and practices of modern education; this outcome has become the starting point for much theorizing. The ideal character of the effective teacher that emerged in educational theory, which continued to be shaped by 'the individualist premises of its formative period' (Bellman) was to be found through forms of 'best practice'. Furthermore, as Tröhler points out, professionalisation took the form of 'organised moralisation, most of all nationalistic moralisation'. Contemporary notions of 'value added' knowledge about the effective teacher, 'learning' mathematics education function, according to Popkewitz, as 'cultural theses' about the particular kind of child to be developed and also other others (e.g. ethnic minorities) who might endanger an idealised future of a knowledge and innovative society. These cultural theses, in turn, enter social life as actors fashioning what to do, how to administer the lives of children and setting out how the children are to act upon themselves. Here we see that making children the object of educational study in some ways opens a space for the education of others, e.g. adults, to find alternative theoretical enactments that are not focused on the administration of lives. Popkewitz also argues that the abstract notion of the 'effective teacher' was served by research which set about finding out the 'empirical fact' of that particular kind of teacher in reform and which fostered a 'belief in the truth telling of numbers.'

Fendler underlines the narrow conceptualisation of teaching, promoted within theories of teaching as 'leading' and notes how the recent influx of computer technologies have changed what teaching can mean, in some cases potentially for the better. However, as Friesen observes, Skinner saw the machine as placing the teacher 'out of date'. Fendler notes that teaching theories have largely focused on 'relatively trivial technical questions.' While Gallagher also bears witness to the marshalling of theories which still hold in education today. Gallagher suggests that prediction and control over education has failed but has also succeeded in corrupting our understanding of educational theory and education as a whole, most particularly because it has distorted the very act of teaching itself. Children have been turned into 'eunuchs of analysis'.

The aspirational actions within educational theory have provoked interested critique from both Bellman and Phelan and a suggestion that this has not helped matters. Bellman's analysis of the expansion of educational science, in Germany as elsewhere, notes the consequence of a shift from Erziehungswissenschaft as a discipline of education (singular) to *Bildung*swissenschaften (pluralist and multidisciplinary). He argues that this orientation towards *Bildung*swissenschaften is an indication of the 'adjustment' of the German field to 'international' conventions (that is, conventions emerging in the English-speaking world). Bellman also suggests that the rise of evidence-based research negates the need for a specific educational theory. Phelan, observing the effort in the US and elsewhere to produce a science of teacher education, notes similar dissipating effects on educational theory as well as the framing of teacher education as a 'learning problem'.

Friesen and Lundahl both draw attention to the crucial role language has had in both enabling and constraining possibilities for educational theorizing.

According to Lundahl, some of the difficulties with educational theory relate to language and the way in which it fails to articulate contemporary phenomena. She notes how language in the social sciences quickly becomes redundant, making it unable to describe current phenomena. Furthermore, as Bernstein (1999: 163) points out, both the language itself and its speakers become 'specialised and excluding', because of the hierarchical knowledge structures they inhabit. Friesen notes how the 'vocabulary bequeathed by behaviourism and subsequent paradigms of educational psychology' has forced education into 'trading on terms that are supposed to carry the everyday weight of intention, interest, morality and value.' These terms, he points out, are unable to sustain the multiple meanings and associations demanded of them. Sidorkin also comments on the limitations of language, observing that educational theory remains imprecise and ineffective because we are dealing with 'a partial and contaminated set of phenomena brought together by convention rather than understanding'. In engaging in educational theorizing therefore we are already implicated within particular discursive regimes and both the possibilities and constraints they offer, subject as they are to endless processes of difference and the deferral of meaning.

Bellman highlights the significance of the counter movements of pragmatism and critical theory, and later critical pedagogy, in asserting the importance of intersubjectivity over subjectivity. Interaction rather than simply the centred subject becomes the theoretical enactment of education. Yet, as Tröhler points out, pragmatism itself came in for much criticism within German-speaking contexts, with *Bildung* considered necessary to counter the 'despicable kitchen and handyman utilitarianism' that was pragmatism. Friesen highlights the significance of the version of *Bildung*, developed by Fröbel, which encompassed a self that had matured in the wider social and cultural context. As Friesen notes, this Hegelian-inspired version of *Bildung* offered a way out of the individualistic impasse and offered great potential for educational theorizing. *Bildung*, however, also was not immune from either difficulty or from criticism and according to Bellman is said to have gone out of favour for several years. It has, however, seen a resurrection since the 1990s with key players – neuroscientists – who have turned up to rescue *Bildung* from its self-inflicted crisis. They have done this by seeking to exploit *Bildung*'s humanistic element whilst also emphasising the importance of evidence-based research, critiquing existing educational research and claiming to be looking at the 'big picture' in which the country's future is at stake. Bellman suggests that the counter-movements of critical theory and critical pedagogy failed to succeed in abandoning the modernist framework of the subject since, for example, critical pedagogy remained firmly focused on interactions rather than transactions and largely ignored the wider social configurations of education. In this sense, to be critical is not always sufficient if one also wants theory that is powerful and capable of creating emancipation.

The normative orientation of critical theory and critical pedagogy, with close ties of communication and interaction being drawn to emancipation and autonomy, has also, for Bellman, and for Usher and Anderson, been an intractable barrier to educational theorizing. Furthermore, as Usher and Anderson observe, critical theory, through its own 'power-knowledge nexus' has aspired to become a masterful and universalising discourse itself, which means it fails its own emancipatory ambitions (see also Biesta 1998).

The 'self' is alive and well, at least within educational psychology and Friesen notes the prolific nature of 'self phenomena': 'self-control', 'self-regulation' and 'self-efficacy', which have become particularly prominent in the so-called 'learning sciences'. The fact that this self is usually a child-self is a critical point of engagement for educational theorizing.

Political

The theoretical work undertaken by several of the contributors has a strong political orientation and, indeed, these individuals are active proponents of the political purpose and function of educational theorizing. While most of the contributors herein took the political to be an integral aspect of being critical, it is important to remember that theory itself also plays a role in ordering in ways that are political but not necessarily critical.

Concerns about the obfuscatory role of educational theorizing were raised by several contributors who noted some negative consequences for both understanding and practice. Szkudlarek argues that educational theory contributes to the economy of power by making structures invisible, 'disguised in pedagogical rather than political attire'. Szkudlarek's 'epistemology of evasion' is a powerful notion of how educational theory serves to render the status of reality and its ontological fault – its incompleteness – invisible. Education, in this regard, merely becomes 'a device making educationists domesticated in an 'absurd' political system.' This is an uncritical theory in support of the established political order.

The diversion of educationists' attention to matters of school improvement or teacher improvement and away from educational theory is denounced by Sidorkin, Fendler, Popkewitz and others. For Sidorkin this is partly a problem of the failure to understand the limits of education or of educational theory: 'When the agency is ignorant of limits, we start destroying something in order to improve it'. Sidorkin observes that the debates about whether it is teacher quality or other factors that are key to school improvement detracts from considerations of the importance of understanding the theoretical limits of educational improvement. He also argues that the limits of improving mass schooling are theoretical limits of education, which we would also suggest precisely entail a collapsing of education into schooling. These limits are exercised through compensation, enforcement mechanisms, support and methods, all of which demonstrate how elite and mass schools are 'very different social institutions', based on very different labour arrangements. Sidorkin is critical of 'putting resources into one particular system of canned curriculum' and of systems that 'emphasise fidelity of implementation over independent thinking of teachers, and often degrade teacher skills.' Phelan suggests the complicity of professionals in these processes and argues that refusals on the part of experienced professionals to recognise and consider non-standard practices signify 'interdictory moments where a tension is evident between what is known and permissible within the profession and what is known but must be kept concealed'.

Language again drew the intensive attention of our contributors, but this time in relation to its political effects. Szkudlarek describes how the language of much of educational theory is 'persuasive, saturated with terms of obligation, and filled with postulates and condemnations.' He notes the excessive use of 'postulational language', for example, enjoinders such as 'You should work hard'; or 'Teachers should respect cultural diversity in the classroom', which represent a call for action but which are grounded in denial. These, he argues, help to 'maintain a world that has no conceptual form and cannot be grasped in logical terms. The theories that sustain and flourish, notes Szkudlarek, are those that appeal in the normative sense, almost regardless of their empirical possibility, despite the discourses of evidence-informed practice and the like.

Lundahl, Popkewitz and Bellman write with some indignation about the political attacks on educational researchers and the favouring of the 'white coat' science and scientistic 'what works' approaches. Phelan, on the other hand, denounces the 'parochialism' arising from the practical bias in educational research, confining teacher education to an educational endeavour and rarely having a radicalizing role in the cultural or institutional life of the university or beyond. It therefore seems that in the realm of the political, educational theorizing finds itself in a problematic space with both supporters and detractors positioning it as lacking in either being able to contribute to practices or being too firmly located within existing practices. Educational theory therefore would appear to be stuck within certain limits, despite the desire by some to be politically trangressive or powerful.

Demonstrating the potency of a political dimension of theoretical work, Popkewitz and Lundahl outline the bleak consequences of reforms emanating from the market transformation of education. Continuing his notion of cultural theses, Popkewitz helpfully alerts us to the 'empirical fact' that markets are actors – 'Market is theory that generates cultural theses about modes of living' – while Lundahl's analysis of the political context behind the development of the free school idea created uneducational consequences that might not have been envisaged by the original proponents (Spicer, no date). The idea of the free school, which has now travelled and taken route within England, appears again to be producing some very particular consequences. Both Lundahl and Popkewitz suggest that the absence of political educational theorizing is one of the factors that allows disadvantage and difference to become entrenched and institutionalized. We would suggest that there have been efforts at political educational theorizing but these have tended to be polemical and lacking in analytical depth and in criticality. The attempts to turn such matters of concern into matters of fact itself signifies the political work of theory, if of a different order to those who want theory to keep such matters open.

Generative: theory work to be done

The task of determining the theory work to be done is undertaken with some caution and has been generated from the insights from the contributors and from our own concerns. Our suggestions are not meant to be exhaustive and will no doubt be subject to change through the ongoing dialogues in and about educational theory.

A different orientation to doing theory

Several of the contributors suggest that much of the educational theorizing that is required involves a different orientation to thinking. Gallagher posits theory as a working out of possibilities, suggesting pragmatism as a 'way of thinking' (Bernstein, drawing on Putnam) and Bernstein's fallibilism; practical science (Carr) and practical philosophy (Schwandt) as possible theoretical resources, while Popkewitz emphasizes theoretical work as 'styles of thought'. Fendler proposes that even the psychology-based 'Models of teaching' map by Joyce and Weil and the teaching theories contained therein 'generate possibilities for thinking differently about teaching and about theory'.

For Sidorkin understanding the theoretical limits of education and the educational limits of theory is a crucial part of a different orientation to thinking. This means saying 'enough' and acknowledging that 'the contemporary institution of mass schooling is nearing its theoretical limit.' Improvement, he asserts, 'belongs to the world of fiction, not to the world of educational policy'. Focusing on limits does not equal pessimism or passivity, according to Sidorkin, rather, it opens up new possibilities for imagining alternatives. However, one of those limits may be to consider theory as being about thinking situated with a representationalist view of knowledge and the world, where one is an imperfect mirror of the other. In considering the work of theory, we would suggest the need to reconsider theorizing as practices within the world rather than being simply thinking about the world (Edwards, 2011).

Undoing theory as school/child thinking

For Popkewitz, Tröhler and Usher and Anderson, a major task is in dismantling or undoing existing regimes of thought. Popkewitz posits 'styles of thought' as a strategy for unthinking the common sense of schooling, to denaturalize what is taken-for-granted, to turn 'matters of fact' into 'matters of concern' and to make fragile the causalities of the present'. For Tröhler, there is much work to be done in breaking down what we currently know: 'rather than continuing to multiply discourses of salvation in the clothing of theory, we might be better advised to historicize and contextualize educational theories and to compare them across the different religions and nations.' Tröhler argues that theory needs to emancipate itself from the Protestant ideas of educationalizing social problems and the theories derived from the Protestant interpretations of the soul. He enjoins researchers to collect:

> cultural data in order to understand how education has been envisaged as a technology to solve alleged problems and to plan an envisaged future and to see how obstacles and systems of professional or public feedback have modified theory (less likely) or organization (more likely). Maybe by extracting and gathering modes of resistance in practices across time and space and their effect on organization and curriculum, we might find something like a grammar not of schooling but of education, which then might serve as the basis of an educational theory.

This task of undoing theory is a project, according to several contributors, of making the certain uncertain, the familiar unfamiliar. However, it also, as we suggested in the introduction, entails making the unfamiliar familiar, one aspect of which is precisely to be able to engage with theory. Undoing theory entails reconsidering the theory of theory informing our enactments of education as well as the limits of those enactments focused on schools and children alone as the subjects of discourse. As we also argue in the introduction, it involves recognising that theory is not about thinking as a simple cognitive activity alone.

Recovering history

Friesen advocates going back to education's past, as a linguistic project of recovery and to find the *elementaria* of its theory and practice, suggesting that this will enable educationists to find more integrative ways of speaking of the self, and to radicalize and extend these 'in responsiveness to present cultural and historical circumstances'. Friesen recovers from *Bildung* a language of the self (assuming we want one), a way of speaking about the self and about developing a notion of the self as a 'centre of awareness, set off contrastively against its social and natural background'. This is more in keeping with continental philosophy, but as he notes, has been strangely absent from educational theorizing and is a notion of self 'that is worthy of its remit and responsibility'. The human subject is contextualized but remains at centre of theoretical concern.

Usher and Anderson suggest a particular kind of history in the form of Foucauldian genealogy as a positive and productive method with reflexivity as an explicit feature. Genealogy, they argue, is not just a method but a particular way of conceptualizing and approaching the practice of critique. It is characterised by scepticism and by paying attention to the positive effects of modern power, privileging historical investigation and destabilising rather than relativizing the present. They argue that genealogy opens up a politicised space that make challenge possible and this kind of 'eventalization', through case-histories or case-studies, which we mentioned in the introduction, could transform ways of life, power relations and identities. Genealogy then is a practice of resistance working not in the service of the big emancipatory project but at a local, regional level. Critique through genealogy does not need to be grounded in truth or in a theory of the subject and, as Usher and Anderson point out, it is freed from the expectation that theory can only be good if it is universal. At the same time, however, genealogy reminds us of the subjectifying and normalizing effects of theorizing through the reflexivity it demands. The critical remains within the realm of power even as it resists certain powerful manifestations.

Finding a new language

Szkudlarek calls for a language that helps us grasp what there is as well as what is not, making it comprehensible in its own ontological terms. This would involve uncovering the 'hidden epistemologies functional to the ontology of heterogeneity', which are educational theories, conceived within the world of ideas and concerned with control within its own rationality. However, Szkudlarek warns that this would not lead to a world free of ambiguities. Rhetorical work is needed, according to Szkudlarek, to replace the failed concepts, alongside ethical considerations and a radical responsibility on the part of the educationists. This is particularly important in relation to addressing inequalities, concerns about which were raised emphatically by Popkewitz and Lundahl. This involves taking responsibility for 'who, what and how we exclude in the process of identity construction'. Phelan suggests that studying teacher education with an interest in freedom may require new languages that have hitherto been disavowed but could amount to a productive educational project, 'finding new, better, more interesting and more fruitful ways of speaking'. Phelan advises that there may be a need for a plurality of new vocabularies – for example ethical, political and aesthetic. New vocabulary often entails making the familiar strange, or using analogy and metaphor to open up different possibilities for meanings and actions. Thus, for instance, the recent attempts to draw into educational theory work from areas such as complexity theory, actor-network theory and quantam physics to open different discursive enactments of education.

Simons and Masschelein (2006) offer a framework for producing new language in the form of a creative ontology. This involves finding new words or phrases that do theoretical work or at least reminds policy and policymakers of the '*impossible* domain' (p. 302) of educational policy because it seeks to govern that which is to come. As Hacking (2002, p. 8) suggests, 'With new names, new objects come into being. Not quickly. Only with usage, only with layer after layer of usage'.

Advocating different forms of practice – with theory

Fendler explicitly advocates teaching practices that are informed by theory and these include teaching unrepeatability; linking theorizing; teaching receptivity; stopping teaching; and poetic teaching. Sidorkin also outlines practical imperatives to counter the impossible dream of educational improvement without limits. He suggests resolving the problem of a lack of interest in education either by paying students to go to school or to find ways of providing students with what they want. As Sidorkin suggests, and as he has written much about this (2002; 2009), neither suggestion is so difficult to implement, but we might speculate that what students want may not include schools. Phelan advocates re-envisioning teacher education as a moral practice rather than a technological project and for her, this involves 'thinking with' difficult concepts such as homosexuality, something also advocated by Britzman and Gilbert (2004). This would make it possible to 'move in the tension-filled gap between what has been and what might be' and to engage in 'spaces of conflict and confrontation that can provoke new questionings and imaginings.

Looking forward to theory

This book is a provocation to theorize education. It is not the first attempt to do such a thing. Educational theory has also been mapped in many different ways and the traces of those mappings remain. An agenda, then, has to look to the history of educational theorizing, at the multiple possibilities for theorizing, and must aspire to be not simply cumulative or parasitical, but also to imagine. In the introduction we made reference to the roles of theory in empirical research that aim at explanation, understanding, and as contributing to emancipation. We have repeated the need to embrace the doubleness of theory in making the familiar strange and the strange familiar. We have also argued that educational theory needs to engage with education as more than children and schools, and with the theoretical 'work' done in the construction of the very objects of what counts as education. And we have raised the question whether the theoretical 'resources' for educational research and practice necessarily have to come from 'other' disciplines or whether a case can and ought to be made for forms of theorizing that are in some way 'educational'.

There were many roads to this text and there are many from it. We encourage further theoretical experimentation and interventions. Not all of them will be good, and here we are left with a critical question for all in education; what constitutes 'good theory?' We can only respond that, given the impossibility of education as a mandatable practice, fallibility, conditionality and responsibility would be good grounds for theorizing.

References

Bernstein, B. (1999) Vertical and horizontal discourse: An essay. *British Journal of Sociology of Education*, 20, 265-279.

Biesta, G.J.J. (1998) '"Say you want a revolution..." Suggestions for the impossible future of critical pedagogy', *Educational Theory*, 48, 499-510.

Biesta, G.J.J. (2010) 'Why "what works" still won't work: from evidence-based education to value-based education', *Studies in Philosophy and Education*, 29, 491-503.

Britzman, D. and Gilbert, J. (2004) 'What will have been said about gayness in teacher education?' *Teaching Education*, 15, 81-96.

Edwards, R. (2011) 'Theory matters: Representation and experimentation in education', *Educational Philosophy and Theory*, 44, 522-534.

Fischer, J. (2010) 'Tertiarität/Der Dritte: soziologie als Schlüsseldisziplin', in T. Bedorf, J. Fischer and G. Lindemann (eds) *Theorien des Dritten. Innovationen in Soziologie und Sozialphilosophie*, Munich: Fink.

Hacking, I. (2002) Inaugural Lecture: Chair of Philosophy and History of Scientific Concepts at the Collège de France, 16 January 2001, *Economy and Society*, 31, 1-14. Available at: <http://dx.doi.org/10.1080/03085140120109222>. (Accessed 1 May 2007).

Sidorkin, A.M. (2002) *Learning relations: Impure Education, deschooled schools, and dialogue with evil*, New York: Peter Lang.

Sidorkin, A.M. (2009) *Labor of learning: Market and the next generation of educational reform*, Rotterdam: Sense Publishers.

Simons, M and Masschelein, J. (2006) The permanent quality tribunal in education and the limits of educational policy, *Policy Futures in Education*, 4, 292-305.

Spicer, A (no date) 'Free schools are not the magic bullet', Warwick Knowledge Centre. Available at: <http://www2.warwick.ac.uk/knowledge/culture/education/>. (Accessed 15 January 2013).

Index

References in **bold** indicate tables and followed by a letter n indicate end of chapter notes.